To

_____

From

_____

Date

_____

A 365 MORNING LIGHT
DEVOTIONAL

THE BEST-SELLING CLASSIC

JOY &
STRENGTH

COMPILED BY

Mary Wilder Tileston

UPDATED EDITION

Ellie Claire®
gift & paper expressions
...*inspired by life*

Ellie Claire® Gift & Paper Corp.
Brentwood, TN 37027
EllieClaire.com
A Worthy Publishing Company

Joy and Strength: A 365 Morning Light Devotional
A Compilation by Mary Wilder Tileston
© 2013 by Ellie Claire Gift & Paper Corp.

ISBN 978-1-60936-824-1

Edited by Marilyn Jansen
Cover and interior design by Jeff Jansen | aestheticsoup.net

Printed in China.

1 2 3 4 5 6 7 8 9 – 18 17 16 15 14 13

MARY WILDER TILESTON'S much-loved devotional is as relevant today as it was when she compiled it more than one hundred years ago. Pursuing a relationship with God, finding joy in the midst of busyness, and balancing rest with responsibility are issues that transcend time. Men and women were discussing these concerns in the early 1900s just as we are e-mailing and texting about them today.

Bringing a timeless perspective, *Joy & Strength* is surprisingly fresh—as if it were written specifically for this time, addressing our contemporary anxieties with amazing insight. With lines for your own thoughts, this heart-touching devotional journal will encourage and challenge you to hold on to the joy and strength in your own life.

Although selections are taken from the original 1901 edition, we have carefully updated wording and punctuation that may distract modern readers. Except in Scripture and some poetry, pronouns such as *thee* and *thy* have been changed to *you* and *your*; verbs such as *cometh* and *shalt* have been changed to more modern forms; the generic terms *man, men,* and *he* have been changed to *person, people,* or *they* when referring to both men and women. The original Scripture quotations were from the King James Version of the Bible; some have been changed to other versions for readability. In all cases, the timeless meaning remains unchanged.

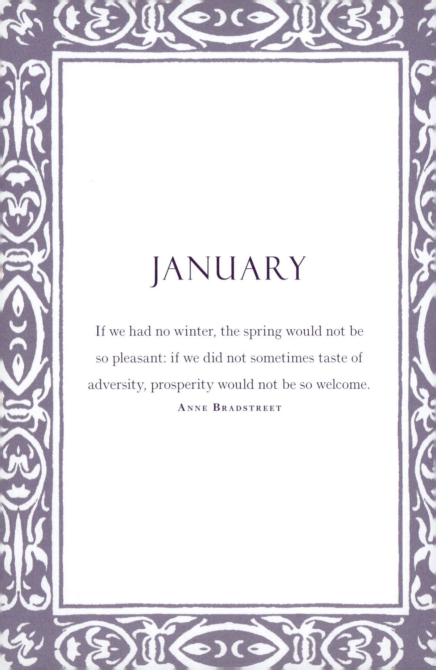

JANUARY

If we had no winter, the spring would not be
so pleasant: if we did not sometimes taste of
adversity, prosperity would not be so welcome.

ANNE BRADSTREET

January 1

Be strong and courageous.... Do not be afraid or discouraged, for the LORD God, my God, is with you. He will not fail you or forsake you.

I CHRONICLES 28:20 NIV

We should serve in newness of spirit.

ROMANS 7:6 KJV

Help us, O Lord! Behold we enter
    Upon another year today;
In You our hopes and thoughts now center,
    Renew our courage for the way;
New life, new strength, new happiness,
    We ask of You; oh, hear, and bless!

JOHANN RIST

The year begins; and all its pages are as blank as the silent years of the life of Jesus Christ. Let us begin it with high resolution; then let us take all its limitations, all its hindrances, its disappointments, its narrow and common-place conditions, and meet them as the Master did in Nazareth, with patience, with obedience, putting ourselves in cheerful subjection, serving our apprenticeship. Who knows what opportunity may come to us this year? Let us live in a great spirit, then we shall be ready for a great occasion.

GEORGE HODGES

January 2

As the mountains surround Jerusalem,
so the LORD surrounds his people
both now and forevermore.

PSALM 125:2 NIV

I hope it may be the happiest year of your life, as I think each succeeding year of everybody's life should be.... It is certain that there really exists, laid up and ready...for those who will just lay hands upon it, enough for every one and enough forever.... How could I be anything but quite happy if I believed always that all the past is forgiven, and all the present furnished with power, and all the future bright with hope?

JAMES SMETHAM

Walk cheerfully and freely in God's service.

TERESA OF AVILA

The belief that youth is the happiest time of life is founded on fallacy. The happiest person is the person who thinks the most interesting thoughts, and we grow happier as we grow older.

WILLIAM LYON PHELPS

January 3

May all who search for you be filled with joy and gladness in you. May those who love your salvation repeatedly shout, "The LORD is great!"

PSALM 40:16 NLT

We doubt the word that tells us: Ask,
    And you shall have your prayer;
We turn our thoughts as to a task,
    With will constrained and rare.
And yet we have; these scanty prayers
    Yield gold without alloy;
O God, but he who trusts and dares
    Must have a boundless joy!

GEORGE MACDONALD

From a weary laborer, worn with slavish and ineffectual toil, I had become as a little child receiving from God the free gift of eternal life and of daily sustenance; and prayer, from a weary spiritual exercise, had become the simple asking from the heavenly Father of daily bread, and thanking Him.

ELIZABETH RUNDLE CHARLES

January 4

How gracious he will be when you cry for help! As soon as he hears, he will answer you.

ISAIAH 30:19 NIV

That was the Shepherd of the flock; He knew
 The distant voice of one poor sheep astray;
It had forsaken Him, but He was true,
 And listened for its bleating night and day.

And thou, fallen soul, afraid to live or die
 In the deep pit that will not set thee free,
Lift up to Him the helpless homeward cry,
 For all that tender love is seeking thee.

ANNA L. WARING

Our Divine Shepherd followed after His lost sheep for thirty-three years, in a way so painful and so thorny that He spilt His heart's blood and left His life there. The poor sheep now follows Him...calling upon Him and beseeching Him earnestly for help; is it possible that He should now refuse to turn upon it His life-giving look? Will He not give ear to it, and lay it upon His divine shoulders, rejoicing over it with all His friends and with the angels of heaven? For if our Lord ceased not to search most diligently and lovingly for the blind and dear sinner, the lost coin of the gospel, till He found it, how is it possible that He should abandon him who, as a lost sheep, cries and calls upon his Shepherd?

LORENZO SCUPOLI

January 5

Be imitators of God, therefore, as dearly loved children and live a life of love, just as Christ loved us and gave himself up for us as a fragrant offering and sacrifice to God.

EPHESIANS 5:1–2 NIV

O Joy supreme! I know the Voice,
    Like none beside on earth or sea;
Yea, more, O soul of mine, rejoice,
    By all that He requires of me,
    I know what God Himself must be.

JOHN GREENLEAF WHITTIER

Either there is a God supremely good, One whom His children may love and trust to the very uttermost point without the slightest fear of the reality falling short of the heart's desire, or else there is no God, no love, no forgiveness, no redress. God is wholly good, if good at all, and those who hope in Him will be wiser if they hope with all their hearts than if they hope with only half their hearts.

WILLIAM R. HUNTINGTON

We know what God is like because we know the character of Jesus Christ.

GEORGE HODGES

January 6

When they had opened their treasures, they presented unto him gifts; gold, and frankincense and myrrh.

MATTHEW 2:11 KJV

Give yourselves anew to God and to God's service, and He will give you the desire and the power to open your treasures; to give to Him, it may be wealth, it may be time, it may be personal service, it may be life itself. In His store there is a place for all, for the tears of the penitent, the barley loaves of the child, the two mites of the widow, the savings of the Philippians' "deep poverty," as well as for Mary's ointment, for the land of Barnabas, for the gold and incense and myrrh of these Eastern sages. And if the vision of Christ be before his eyes, and the love of Christ be in his heart, the man of wealth will give his large offering, the man of learning his dear-bought knowledge, the man of business his hard-earned leisure, for the glory of God, for the benefit of his fellow-men, for the church or for the poor; to feed the hungry, or to teach the ignorant, to help the struggling, or to guide the erring. And each gift will be welcomed by Him who gave Himself for us all, and who asks in return for ourselves as a living sacrifice to Him.

JOHN ELLERTON

January 7

We should help others do what is right and build them up in the Lord.

ROMANS 15:2 NLT

Let us consider one another in order to stir up love and good works.

HEBREWS 10:24 NKJV

Look around you, first in your own family, then among your friends and neighbors, and see whether there be not someone whose little burden you can lighten, whose little cares you may lessen, whose little pleasures you can promote, whose little wants and wishes you can gratify. Giving up cheerfully our own occupations to attend to others is one of the little kindnesses and self-denials. Doing little things that nobody likes to do, but which must be done by someone, is another. It may seem to many that if they avoid little unkindnesses, they must necessarily be doing all that is right to their family and friends; but it is not enough to abstain from sharp words, sneering tones, petty contradiction, or daily little selfish cares; we must be active and earnest in kindness, not merely passive and inoffensive.

HENRIETTA WILSON

The labor of the baking was the hardest part of the sacrifice of her hospitality. To many it is easy to give what they have, but the offering of weariness and pain is never easy. They are indeed a true salt-to-salt sacrifice.

GEORGE MACDONALD

January 8

He stilled the storm to a whisper;
the waves of the sea were hushed.
They were glad when it grew calm,
and he guided them to their desired haven.

PSALM 107:29–30 NIV

As you learn this lesson, to carry all your sorrows to God, and lie
at your Savior's feet, and spread your grief before Him, you will
find a calm come over you, you know not from where; you will see
through the clouds a bright opening, small perhaps and quickly
closed, but telling of eternal rest, and everlasting day, and of the
depth of the love of God. Your heart will still rise and sink, but it
will rise and sink not restlessly, nor waywardly, not in violent gusts
of passion, but resting in stillness on the bosom of the ocean of the
love of God. Then shall you learn, not to endure only patiently, but,
in everything against your will, humbly and quickly to see and to
love the loving will of God. Your faith and your love and your hope
will grow, the more you see the work of God with you; you will
have joy in your sorrow, and your sorrow will be turned into joy.

EDWARD B. PUSEY

January 9

Be anxious for nothing, but in everything by prayer and supplication, with thanksgiving, let your requests be made known to God; and the peace of God, which surpasses all understanding, will guard your hearts and minds through Christ Jesus.

PHILIPPIANS 4:6–7 NKJV

Just think of having His wonderful peace guarding one's heart and one's thoughts all day long. But it is only on condition that we fulfill the sixth verse, "In nothing be anxious"—this is a distinct command, and, if we fail to fulfill it, we shall not get the blessing. Sorrow even is anxiety, and should be laid upon our blessed Lord. Then in prayer and supplication we must not forget that thanksgiving is also distinctly commanded; we must praise God for His dealings with us, even though we cannot make them out at times. Pray God to make you cease from anxiety about yourself and your plans; just be willing to do the work our dear Father gives you at the time.

JOHN KENNETH MACKENZIE

Oh, what great peace and quietness would he possess who should cut off all vain anxiety and place all his confidence in God.

THOMAS À KEMPIS

January 10

I am the LORD, and there is no other; apart from me there is no God. I will strengthen you, though you have not acknowledged me.

ISAIAH 45:5 NIV

"For I know the plans I have for you," says the LORD. "They are plans for good and not for disaster, to give you a future and a hope."

JEREMIAH 29:11 NLT

You know—oh, the precious truth / That bids my soul be strong!
The care, the never-weary care / That cannot lead me wrong!
There is a blessed end for me, / Where on your eyes are set;
You have a comfort in Your love, / Too great to show me yet.

ANNA L. WARING

No room for a discouraged or depressed feeling is left you. If your sphere is outwardly humble, if it even appears to be quite insignificant, God understands it better than you do, and it is a part of His wisdom to bring out great sentiments in humble conditions, great principles in works that are outwardly trivial, great characters under great adversities and heavy loads of encumbrance. Let it fill you with cheerfulness and exalted feeling, however deep in obscurity your lot may be, that God is leading you on, girding you for a work, preparing you for a good that is worthy of His divine magnificence. If God is really preparing us all to become that which is the very highest and best thing possible, there ought never to be a discouraged or uncheerful being in the world.

HORACE BUSHNELL

January 11

The secret of the LORD is with those who fear Him,
And He will show them His covenant.

PSALM 25:14 NKJV

Then shall my days be Thine,
    And all my heart be love;
And joy and peace be mine,
    Such as are known above.
Come, Holy Spirit, quickly come,
    And make my heart Thy lasting home.

ANDREW REED

It is a sign that the soul is living in God if it maintain calmness within through the consciousness of His presence, while working for Him in active ministrations. Such restfulness will show itself in the commonest ways, in doing common duties at the right time, in preserving a sweetness and evenness of temper in the midst of ordinary interruptions and disturbances, in walking to and fro quietly on the day's varied errands, in speaking gentle words, in sweetly meeting unexpected calls. A calm, restful temper grows as self is learning to lose itself in God. Such grace tells gradually on the daily life; even the minutest detail may be brought under the power of God, and carried out in union with Him.

T. T. CARTER

January 12

Do not delay!

2 Chronicles 24:5 NLT

> And grant me, Lord, to do,
> With ready heart and willing,
>   Whatever You shall command,
> My calling here fulfilling;
>   And do it when I ought,
>   With all my strength, and bless
>   The work I thus have wrought,
>   For You must give success.

Johann Heermann

No unwelcome tasks become any the less unwelcome by putting them off till tomorrow. It is only when they are behind us and done that we begin to find that there is a sweetness to be tasted afterwards, and that the remembrance of unwelcome duties unhesitatingly done is welcome and pleasant. Accomplished, they are full of blessing, and there is a smile on their faces as they leave us. Undone, they stand threatening and disturbing our tranquility, and hindering our communication with God. If there be lying before you any bit of work from which you shrink, go straight up to it, and do it at once. The only way to get rid of it is to do it.

Alexander MacLaren

January 13

"Tell not abroad another's faults
    Till thou hast cured thine own;
Nor whisper of thy neighbor's sin
    Till thou art perfect grown:
Then, when thy soul is pure enough
    To bear My searching eye
Unshrinking, then may come the time
    Thy brother to decry."
        "Jesu, Savior, pitying be;
    Parce mihi, Domine!"

LYRA MYSTICA

The habit of judging is so nearly incurable, and its cure is such an almost interminable process, that we must concentrate ourselves for a long while on keeping it in check, and this check is to be found in kind interpretations. We must come to esteem very lightly our sharp eye for evil, on which perhaps we once prided ourselves as cleverness. We must look at our talent for analysis of character as a dreadful possibility of huge uncharitableness. We are sure to continue to say clever things, so long as we continue to indulge in this analysis; and clever things are equally sure to be sharp and acid. We must grow to something higher, and something truer, than a quickness in detecting evil.

FREDERICK W. FABER

January 14

I listen carefully to what God the LORD is saying, for he speaks peace to his faithful people.

PSALM 85:8 NLT

Now, O my God,
My comfort, portion, rest!
You, none but You, shall reign within my breast.
Call me to You! Call me Yourself—oh, speak,
And bind my heart to You, whom most I seek!

GERHARD TERSTEEGEN

Just as in prayer it is not we who momentarily catch His attention, but He ours, so when we fail to hear His voice, it is not because He is not speaking so much as that we are not listening. We must recognize that all things are in God and that God is in all things, and we must learn to be very attentive, in order to hear God speaking in His ordinary tone without any special accent. A man must not stop listening any more than praying when he rises from his knees. No one questions the need of times of formal address to God, but few admit in any practical way the need of quiet waiting upon God, gazing into His face, feeling for His hand, listening for His voice. "I will hearken to what the Lord God will say concerning me." God has special confidences for each soul. Indeed, it would seem as though the deepest truths came only in moments of profound devotional silence and contemplation.

CHARLES H. BRENT

January 15

Wait for the LORD; be strong and take heart and wait for the LORD.

PSALM 27:14 NIV

With smile of trust and folded hands,
The passive soul in waiting stands
To feel, as flowers the sun and dew,
The One true Life its own renew.

JOHN GREENLEAF WHITTIER

The whole duty and blessedness of waiting on God has its root
in this, that He is such a blessed Being, full, to overflowing, of
goodness and power and life and joy, that we, however wretched,
cannot for any time come into contact with Him, without that life
and power secretly, silently, beginning to enter into us and blessing
us. God is Love! God's love is just *His delight to impart Himself and
His blessedness* to His children. Come, and however feeble you feel,
just wait in His presence. As a feeble invalid is brought out into
the sunshine to let its warmth go through him, come with all that
is dark and cold in you *into the sunshine of God's holy, omnipotent
love*, and sit and wait there, with the one thought: Here I am, in the
sunshine of His love. As the sun does its work in the weak one who
seeks its rays, *God will do His work in you.*

ANDREW MURRAY

January 16

Even the very hairs of your head are all numbered.

MATTHEW 10:30 NIV

I will go in the strength of the Lord GOD.

PSALM 71:16 KJV

No trouble is too small to see the will of God for you in it. Great troubles come but seldom. Daily worry may often, when put into God's hands, conform you more to His gracious will. There are daily touches where He traces on you the likeness of His divine will. There is nothing too small to practice the oneness with the will of God. By daily practice...we learn the lesson our Lord taught, "Not as I will, but as You." All the things men daily complain about may perfect you to the will of God. The changes of the seasons, bodily discomforts or ailments, rude words, petty slights, little jealousies, deviations of temper in those with whom you live, misunderstandings, censures of your faith...ingratitude, interruptions, distraction of your work—whatever you can think of where others worry themselves, and even more, worry you; in that you see how to be of one will with God.

EDWARD B. PUSEY

You will know that I have done nothing in it without cause, declares the Sovereign LORD.

EZEKIEL 14:23 NIV

Joy is the lesson set for some,
    For others pain best teacher is;
We know not which for us shall come,
    But both are heaven's high ministries.

SUSAN COOLIDGE

The outward features of our life may not be all that we should choose them to be; there may be things we wish for that never come to us; there may be much we wish away that we cannot part from. The persons with whom we live, the circumstances by which we are surrounded, the duties we have to perform, the burdens we have to bear, may not only be other than what we should have selected for ourselves, but may even seem inconsistent with that formation and discipline of character which we honestly wish to promote. Knowing us better than we know ourselves, fully understanding how greatly we are affected by the outward events and conditions of life, He has ordered them with a view to our entire and final, not only our immediate, happiness; and whenever we can be safely trusted with pastures that are green, and waters that are still, in the way of earthly blessing, the Good Shepherd leads us there.

ANTHONY W. THOROLD

January 18

I delight to do Your will, O my God, and Your law is within my heart.

PSALM 40:8 NKJV

Crown us with love, and so with peace;
 Transfigure duty to delight;
Our lips inspire, our faith increase,
 Brighten with hope our darkest night.
Bring us from earthly bondage free
To find our heaven in serving Thee.

HENRY WILDER FOOTE

We often make our duties harder by thinking them hard. We dwell on the things we do not like till they grow before our eyes, and, at last, perhaps shut out heaven itself. But this is not following our Master, and He, we may be sure, will value little the obedience of a discontented heart. The moment we see that anything to be done is a plain duty, we must resolutely trample out every rising impulse of discontent. We must not merely prevent our discontent from interfering with the duty itself; we must not merely prevent it from breaking out into murmuring; we must get rid of the discontent itself. Cheerfulness in the service of Christ is one of the first requisites to make that service Christian.

FREDERICK TEMPLE

January 19

Do to others whatever you would like them to do to you. This is the essence of all that is taught in the law and the prophets.

MATTHEW 7:12 NLT

Take the trouble to spend only one single day according to God's commandments, and you will see yourself, you will feel by your own heart, how good it is to fulfill God's will (and God's will in relation to us is our life, our eternal blessedness). Love God with all your heart; value with all your strength His love and His benefits to you; enumerate His mercies, which are endlessly great and diverse. Furthermore, love every man as yourself—that is, do not wish him anything that you would not wish for yourself; do not let your memory keep in it any evil caused to you by others, even as you would wish that the evil done by yourself should be forgotten by others; do unto them as you would do unto yourself, or even do not do unto them as you would not do unto yourself. Then you will see what you will obtain in your heart—what peace, what blessedness! You will be in paradise before reaching it—that is, before the paradise in heaven, you will be in the paradise on earth.

JOHN ILYICH SERGIEFF

January 20

Though I walk in the midst of trouble, You will revive me;
You will stretch out Your hand
Against the wrath of my enemies,
And Your right hand will save me.

PSALM 138:7 NKJV

Holy Spirit, Joy divine, / Cheer this saddened heart of mine;
Bid my troubled thoughts be still; / With Your peace my spirit fill.

ANDREW REED

Nothing else but seeing God in everything will make us loving
and patient with those who annoy and trouble us. They will
be to us then only instruments for accomplishing His tender
and wise purposes toward us, and we will even find ourselves
at last inwardly thanking them for the blessings they bring us.
Nothing else will completely put an end to all murmuring or
rebelling thoughts.

HANNAH WHITALL SMITH

Oh, that we could reason less about our troubles and sing and
praise more! There are thousands of things that we wear as
shackles which we might use as instruments with music in them if
we only knew how.

L. B. COWMAN

January 21

Be strong and take heart, all you who hope in the Lord.

Psalm 31:24 NIV

Think not again the wells of Life to fill,
By any conscious act of your own will;
Retire within the silence of your soul,
And let God's Spirit enter, and control.
The springs of feeling which you thought were stilled,
Shall so be deepened, sweetened, and refilled.

Anna J. Granniss

When you find that weariness depresses or amusement distracts you, you will calmly turn with an untroubled spirit to your heavenly Father, who is always holding out His arms to you. You will look to Him for gladness and refreshment when depressed, for moderation and recollection when in good spirits, and you will find that He will never leave you to want. A trustful glance, a silent movement of the heart towards Him will renew your strength; and though you may often feel as if your soul were downcast and numb, whatever God calls you to do, He will give you power and courage to perform. Our heavenly Father, so far from ever overlooking us, is only waiting to find our hearts open, to pour into them the torrents of His grace.

François de Fénelon

January 22

Look, I have come to do your will, O God—
as is written about me in the Scriptures.

HEBREWS 10:7 NLT

Oh, let Your wisdom be my guide,
Nor take Your light from me away;
Your grace be ever at my side,
That from Your path I may not stray;
But, feeling that Your hand is o'er me,
    In steadfast faith my course fulfill,
    And keep Your word, and do Your will,
Your love within, Your heaven before me!

WOLFGANG C. DESSLER

"I come to do Your will, O God."
That is what we are here for—to do God's will. That is the object
of your life and mine—to do God's will. Any of us can tell in a
moment whether our lives are right or not. Are we doing God's
will? We do not mean, Are we doing God's work?—preaching, or
teaching, or collecting money—but God's *will*. A man may think
he is doing God's work when he is not even doing God's will. And
man may be doing God's work and God's will quite as much by
hewing stones, or sweeping streets, as by preaching or praying.
So the question means just this, Are we working out our common
every-day life on the great lines of God's will?

HENRY DRUMMOND

January 23

So shall we ever be with the Lord.

1 THESSALONIANS 4:17 KJV

They will walk with me, dressed in white, for they are worthy.

REVELATION 3:4 NIV

We are taught to believe of the Blessed, that they "serve Him day and night in His temple," that "His servants shall serve Him." And this must be with powers and endowments developed in harmony with higher worlds, so that all the tastes, the desires, the affections, the artistic powers, the intellectual gifts, which belong to each individual, each with his own special capacities, trained and developed and exercised in spiritual modes of life, will be suited to that higher world, where they dwell in the presence of the almighty God, and the "Lamb who is in the midst of them." The activities of a condition of life such as we cannot yet conceive, we shall enter upon, if fitted for it, trained for it, by the exercise of our gifts during our life in this world; we shall be like weapons in the Hand of God, ready for what service He may will.

THOMAS THELLUSON CARTER

For those who live, as she did, with their whole talents dedicated to God's service, death is only the gate of life—the path from joyous work in this world to greater capacities and opportunities for it in the other.

HORATIA K. F. EDEN

January 24

No longer will there be a curse upon anything. For the throne of God and of the Lamb will be there, and his servants will worship him. And they will see his face, and his name will be written on their foreheads.

REVELATION 22:3–4 NLT

And doubtless unto you is given
    A life that bears immortal fruit
    In such great offices as suit
The full-grown energies of heaven.

ALFRED, LORD TENNYSON

If we are to be disciplined and trained, as workmen in various occupations, instruments formed for God's service, what may we look to become in the hereafter?... When this passing life is over, and we appear in God's presence, cleansed and disciplined, with the true workman's hand, will we be set to work in higher spheres, in grander ministries, in a world of nobler service? We speak of heaven as a sort of rest, of sweet consolation, of communion with God, such as we cannot know on earth; but consistently with perfect sweetness, heaven is full of activity, of infinite busyness. For God is active, and out of His activity He formed all creatures. As in the deep seas with its endless movements there is calm beneath, so in God are depths of peace as infinite as the activity of His creation.... His creatures partake of infinite peace and intensely active service.

T. T. CARTER

January 25

I can do all things through Christ who strengthens me.

PHILIPPIANS 4:13 NKJV

Let him take hold of my strength, that he may make peace with me.

ISAIAH 27:5 KJV

Thou canst o'ercome this heart of mine,
    Thou wilt victorious prove;
For everlasting strength is Thine,
    And everlasting love.

CHARLES WESLEY

We are conscious of our own weakness and of the strength of evil;
but not of the third force, stronger than either ourselves or the
power of evil, which is at our disposal if we will draw upon it.
What is needed is a deliberate and whole-hearted realization that
we are *in Christ*, and Christ is *in us* by His Spirit; an unconditional
surrender of faith to Him; a practice, which grows more natural by
exercise, of remembering and deliberately drawing by faith upon
His strength in the moments of temptation and not merely upon
our own resources. "In the name of Jesus Christ of Nazareth I will
do thus and thus." So we too may form, like St. Paul, the habit
of victory.

CHARLES GORE

January 26

So we have not stopped praying for you since we first heard about you. We ask God to give you complete knowledge of his will and to give you spiritual wisdom and understanding. Then the way you live will always honor and please the Lord.

COLOSSIANS 1:9–10 NLT

Something for Thee! Lord, let this be
    Thy choice for me from day to day;
The life I live it is not mine,
Thy will, my will, have made it Thine!
    Oh, let me do in Thine own way
        Something for Thee!

ELIZABETH PRENTISS

Act faithfully according to your degree of light, and what God gives you to see; and you shall see more clearly. Listen to the low whispers of His voice within you, and you shall hear more distinctly. Above all, do not stifle any stirring of conscience. Meditate daily on the things of eternity; and, by the grace of God, do something daily which you would wish to have done when that day comes. Above all things, in all things, "look unto Jesus, the Author and Finisher of your faith." If you fail, look to Him to uphold you; if you stumble, hold His hand to help you; if you fall, lie not hopelessly there, but look to Him to raise you; if, by His grace, you do well, look to Him in thanksgiving, that He has helped you, and pray that you may do better.

EDWARD B. PUSEY

January 27

Sing and make music in your heart to the Lord.

EPHESIANS 5:19 NIV

Lord, make my heart a place where angels sing!
    For surely thoughts low-breathed by Thee
Are angels gliding near on noiseless wings;
    And where a home they see
Swept clean, and garnished with adoring joy,
    They enter in and dwell,
    And teach that heart to swell
With heavenly melody, their own untired employ.

JOHN KEBLE

Let your heart and desires continually hold a conversation with God, in heartfelt simplicity. Reflect on Him with feelings of love and reverence, and often offer up your heart, with all that you have and are, to Him, in spirit and in truth, as cordially and sincerely as possible. If through weakness or unfaithfulness you abandon this exercise, which is so incredibly helpful and beautiful, all you have to do is, meekly and heartily, begin again; and do not be weary of it, although in the beginning you may not find any great advantage from it, or make any rapid progress in it. It is not true that such a mode of life is hard; it is easy and pleasant to the spirit, and becomes in due time like a heaven upon earth. A little patience and courage alone are needed.

GERHARD TERSTEEGEN

January 28

In Your hand is power and might; in Your hand it is to make great and to give strength to all.

1 CHRONICLES 29:12 NKJV

When I have nothing in my hand
    Wherewith to serve my King,
When Thy commandment finds me weak
    And wanting everything,
My soul, upon Thy greatness cast,
    Shall rise divinely free;
Then will I serve with what Thou hast,
    And gird myself with Thee.

ANNA L. WARING

How are we to approach such blessed strength? First of all, through a steadfast will to refuse nothing that God requires of us, and to do nothing deliberately which can displease Him. Next, we must learn to take our faults humbly, as proofs of our weakness, and use them to increase our trust in God, and our mistrust of self. Neither must we be discouraged at our own wretchedness, or give way to the thought that we cannot do or bear any special thing; our duty is, while confessing that of ourselves it is impossible, to remember that God is all-powerful, and that through Him we can do whatever He may require of us. We must learn to say with St. Augustine, "Give me what You command, and command what You will."

JEAN NICOLAS GROU

January 29

The LORD is good to those who wait for Him,
To the soul who seeks Him.

LAMENTATIONS 3:25 NKJV

Be patient till your wings are grown. I fear very much that you are
too vehement and headlong in your wishes and attempts to fly. You
see the beauty of spiritual light and good resolutions; you fancy
that you have almost attained, and your ardor is redoubled; you
rush forward, but in vain, for your Master has chained you to your
perch, or else it is that your wings are not grown and this constant
excitement exhausts your strength. You must indeed strive to fly,
but gently, without growing eager or restless. You resign yourself,
but it is always with a BUT; you want this and that and you
struggle to get it. A simple wish is no hindrance to resignation;
but a palpitating heart, a flapping of wings, an agitated will, and
endless, quick, restless movements are unquestionably caused by
deficient resignation. Do you know what you must do? You must
be willing not to fly, since your wings are not yet grown. Do not be
so eager with your vain desires, do not even be eager in avoiding
eagerness; go on quietly in your path—it is a good path.

FRANCIS OF SALES

January 30

I have indeed seen the misery of my people in Egypt. I have heard them crying out because of their slave drivers, and I am concerned about their suffering.

EXODUS 3:7 NIV

You know, Lord, the weariness and sorrow
Of the sad heart that comes to You for rest;
Cares of today, and burdens for tomorrow,
Blessings implored, and sins to be confessed:
I come before You at Your gracious word,
And lay them at Your feet—You know, Lord.

JANE BORTHWICK

That sorrow which can be *seen* is the lightest form really, however apparently heavy; then there is that which is *not* seen, secret sorrows which yet can be put into words, and can be told to near friends as well as be poured out to God. But there are sorrows beyond these, such as are *never* told, and cannot be put into words, and may only be wordlessly laid before God: these are the deepest. Now comes the supply for each: "I have *seen*" that which is patent and external; "I have heard their *cry*," which is the expression of this, and of as much of the external as is expressible. But this would not go deep enough, so God adds, "I *know* their sorrows," down to the very depths of all, those which no eye sees or ear ever heard.

FRANCES RIDLEY HAVERGAL

January 31

I know, O Lord, that Your judgments are right,
And that in faithfulness You have afflicted me.

Psalm 119:75 nkjv

And my soul complain not,
For no pain or fears dismay her;
Still she clings to God in faith,
Trusts Him though He seem to slay her.
'Tis when flesh and blood repine,
Sun of joy, You cannot not shine.

Johann J. Winckler

Impatience and worrying under trial only increases our suffering,
whereas meek submission relieves all suffering, and fills the
tortured heart with peace amid its anguish. Worship Him in every
sorrow; worship Him in deed and word, but still more in humble
and loving acceptance of each pang and heartache. Be sure that
your mere silent willing endurance is a true act of adoration; and
thus, come what may, weariness, pain, desolation, destitution,
loneliness, all will carry on His gracious work in you, and, amid
the sharpest pressure of suffering, you will be sending up to His
eternal throne the precious incense of submission and trust.

Abbé Guilloré

FEBRUARY

Even in the winter, even in the midst
of the storm, the sun is still there. Somewhere,
up above the clouds, it still shines and warms
and pulls at the life buried deep inside
the brown branches and frozen earth.
The sun is there! Spring will come!

GLORIA GAITHER

February 1

Now I commit you to God and to the word of his grace, which can build you up and give you an inheritance among all those who are sanctified.

ACTS 20:32 NIV

Only the rays of God can cure the heart,
Purge it of evil; there's no other way
Except to turn with the whole heart to God.
In heavenly sunlight live no shades of fear;
The soul there, busy or at rest, has peace;
And music flows from the various world.

WILLIAM ALLINGHAM

Break off things which displease God, and, whatever you do,
do it to please Him. Dedicate, morning by morning, the actions
of the day to God; live in His Presence; offer to Him your acts
beforehand; recall yourself, if the case admits, into His Presence,
in the midst of them; give Him the glory with your whole heart, if
they be well done, since nothing good is our own; if they be amiss,
grieve to Him. If we make God our end, He who gave us His love;
He will increase our longing desire for Him; and whom in all we
seek, whom in all we would please, whom in all we would love, Him
shall we find, Him possess, here in grace and veiled, hereafter,
in glory.

EDWARD B. PUSEY

February 2

I...will refine them as silver is refined, and will try them as gold is tried.

ZECHARIAH 13:9 KJV

As the purifying process is carried on, "the refiner watches the operation, with the greatest earnestness, until the metal has the appearance of a highly polished mirror, reflecting every object around it: even the refiner, as he looks upon the mass of metal, may see himself as in a looking-glass, and thus he can form a very correct judgment respecting the purity of the metal. When he is satisfied, the fire is withdrawn, and the metal removed from the furnace." See Jesus, as the Refiner, watching "with the greatest earnestness" the purifying of your soul in the furnace of earth. His hand has lighted the fire which is now separating the pure metal of holiness from the dross of sin in you. His loving eye is ever eagerly watching for the movement when the purifying work is done. Then, without a moment's delay, He withdraws the fire, and the purified soul is removed from the furnace. See, again, when it is that the purification is completed; it is when the Image of Christ is reflected in us, so that He can see Himself in us as in a mirror. Raise your eyes, then, amidst the flames, and see the face of Jesus watching you with the tender pity and intense interest of His love.

GEORGE BODY

February 3

I will be with you. I will not leave you nor forsake you. Be strong and of good courage.

JOSHUA 1:5–6 NKJV

The people...responded with one voice, "Everything the LORD has said we will do."

EXODUS 24:3 NIV

Our Lord teaches us not to shrink from the consequences which we may see to be involved in any course of duty which we have undertaken. He leads us to accept the results of any choice as they open to our mind...to realize in calmness the future, whatever that future may be. If the calling of God is clear, if the sense of duty becomes the pillar of cloud by day and the pillar of fire by night, ever leading onward, the vision of the cross ought not to hinder our going forward. For one who has put his hand to the plough to look back is to become unfit for the kingdom of heaven. And equally so it must be to disobey God, if distrust of His upholding us in the course along which He would guide our steps, whatever trials may meet us in the path, becomes a stumbling block or hindrance to our faith.

T. T. CARTER

Be of good courage, all is before you, and time passed in the difficult is never lost.... What is required of us is that we live the difficult and learn to deal with it. In the difficult are the friendly forces, the hands that work on us.

RAINER MARIA RILKE

February 4

When I am afraid, I will trust in you.

PSALM 56:3 NIV

They commended them to the Lord, on whom they believed.

ACTS 14:23 KJV

A constant anticipation of evils which perhaps never will come, a foreboding which takes away life and energy from the present, will simply hinder and cloud the soul, and make it timid and sad. If troubling thoughts as to the future press, darkening a bright present, or hurrying on-coming clouds, the safest thing is to offer them continually as they arise to God, offering too the future which they represent, and asking for grace to concentrate our energies on the immediate duties surrounding us. Many have dreaded troubles which they thought must come; and while they went on ever expecting to make the turn in their path which was to open fully the evil, they found that they had reached the journey's end, and were at the haven where they should be. Even [when thinking of] others it is not wise to overindulge in looking forward in fear. Come what may to the dearest ones we have on earth, God and His upholding grace will be there, and He cares for them more than even we can. An earnest acknowledgment of His love will help them more than all our worrying.

H. L. SIDNEY LEAR

February 5

Fear not, for I am with you;
Be not dismayed, for I am your God.
I will strengthen you,
Yes, I will help you,
I will uphold you with My righteous right hand.

Isaiah 41:10 NKJV

Do like a child and lean and rest
Upon your father's arm;
Pour out your troubles on His breast,
And you shall know no harm;
Then shall you by His hand be brought,
By way which now you know not,
Up through a well-fought fight,
To heavenly peace and light.

Paul Gerhardt

Do your utmost to attain such a spiritual attitude that you
may become one with Me, and your will may become so entirely
conformed to My all-perfect will, that not only will you never
desire that which is evil, but not even that which is good, if it be
not according to My will. So that whatever happens to you in this
earthly life, from wherever it may come, whether in worldly things
or spiritual things, nothing will ever disturb your peace, or trouble
your quietness of spirit. But you will be established in a firm belief
that I, your omnipotent God, love you with a dearer love and
watch over you more carefully than you can for yourself.

Catherine of Siena

February 6

Let not your hearts faint, fear not, and do not tremble.

DEUTERONOMY 20:3 KJV

You must begin small, and be glad of a little light to travel with, and be faithful to it; and in faithfulness expect additions of light, and as much power as needed to continue on. And though you may be weak and insignificant for a while, and ready to perish, yet the Father will help you and cause His life to shoot up in you. Thankfully receive the smallest visit that comes from Him to your soul; for there is life and peace in it, and death and confusion in turning from it.

ISAAC PENINGTON

All the evil we do not commit, all the temptations to which we do not consent or which never visit us; all our holy thought and good intentions, all our longings after that which is right, are so many witnesses of His loving kindness towards us. How could He help you in this way unless He cared for you?

CHARLES DE CONDREN

February 7

You are not controlled by your sinful nature. You are controlled by the Spirit if you have the Spirit of God living in you.

ROMANS 8:9 NLT

Secular business is spiritual if it is ruled by the divine Spirit according to the law of righteousness. Politics are spiritual, commercial and municipal life are spiritual, art and science are spiritual, and everything that develops our faculties is spiritual, if we will allow the divine Spirit to rule in all according to the law of righteousness, truth, and beauty. For the whole of our being, with all its sum of faculties, is made by God and meant for God.

CHARLES GORE

It is the very business of your life to cultivate every faculty you have, in the belief that He has given them to you so that you may become His instruments for usefulness; and that He asks this of you, because, if you grant it, you enable Him to give you more of His own happiness than you can otherwise receive, and far more than you can imagine.

THEOPHILUS PARSONS

February 8

The LORD...made my words of judgment as sharp as a sword.
He has hidden me in the shadow of his hand.
I am like a sharp arrow in his quiver.
He said to me, "You are my servant, Israel,
and you will bring me glory."

ISAIAH 49:1–3 NLT

The glory is not in the task, but in
The doing it for Him.

JEAN INGELOW

It is wholly impossible to live according to divine order and to
live out heavenly principles, as long as the necessary daily duties
seem only like a burden to be borne. Every day that dawns brings
something to do, which can never be done as well again. We should,
therefore, try to do it ungrudgingly and cheerfully. It is the Lord's
own work, which He has given us as surely as He gives us daily
bread. We should thank Him for it with all our hearts, as much
as for any other gift. It was designed to be our life, our happiness.
Instead of shirking it or hurrying over it, we should put our whole
heart and soul into it.

JAMES REED

February 9

Pray without ceasing. In every thing give thanks: for this is the will of God in Christ Jesus concerning you.

1 THESSALONIANS 5:17–18 KJV

As thou, Lord, an immortal soul
 Hast breathed into me,
So let my soul be breathing forth
 Immortal thanks to Thee.

JOHN MASON

Let us not be content to pray morning and evening, but let us live in prayer all day long. Let this prayer, this life of love, which means death to self, spread out from our seasons of prayer, as from a center, over all that we have to do. All should become prayer, that is, a loving consciousness of God's presence, whether it be social interaction or business. Such a course as this will ensure you a profound peace.

FRANÇOIS DE FÉNELON

How are we to fulfill our Lord's injunction, "that man ought always to pray and not to faint"? By the heart's prayer, which consists in a constant habitual love of God, trusting Him, submitting in all things to His will; and by giving a never failing heed to His voice, as heard within the conscience.

JEAN NICOLAS GROU

February 10

It is good that a man should both hope and quietly wait for the salvation of the LORD.

LAMENTATIONS 3:26 KJV

Into Thy silent place of prayer
The anxious, wandering mind recall—
Dwell 'mid Thy own creation there,
Restoring, claiming, hallowing all.
Then the calm spirit, won from sin,
Thy perfect sacrifice shall be,
And all the ransomed powers therein
Shall go forth, glorifying Thee.

ANNA L. WARING

Take time to be separate from all friends and all duties, all cares and all joys; time to be still and quiet before God. Take time not only to secure stillness from man and the world, but from self and its energy. Let the Word and prayer be very precious; but remember, even these may hinder the quiet waiting. The activity of the mind in studying the Word, or giving expressions to its thoughts in prayer, the activities of the heart, with its desires and hopes and fears, may so engage us that we do not come to the still waiting on the all-glorious One. Though at first it may appear difficult to know how thus quietly to wait, with the activities of mind and heart for a time subdued, every effort after it will be rewarded; we shall find that it grows upon us, and the little season of silent worship will bring a peace and a rest that give a blessing not only in prayer, but all the day.

ANDREW MURRAY

February 11

Be ye kind one to another.

Ephesians 4:32 kjv

The remedy for sadness is prayer. But as sadness broods in selfishness, and is inclined to rest rather in our own unhappy thoughts than on God, the soul turns to prayer with reluctance. Hence the saddened one must first turn to God by vocal prayer, persevering in which that reluctance will be overcome; and as the sadness subsides, the spirit will enter anew into the heart of prayer. The second remedy against sadness is to break out of it by some external act of kindness or generosity. For the malady consists in a morbid concentration upon one's self, and a brooding within one's self that repels sympathy and kindness, as being adverse to this melancholy mood, a mood that can only be cherished in isolation of spirit. But let the will make a little effort to be kind and considerate towards another, and it is amazing how soon that malignant charm is broken that held the soul spell-bound to her saddened thought and imaginary grievances. A smile, a kind look, a few gentle words, a considerate action, though begun with effort, will suffice to open the soul, and set the spirit free from its delusion.

William Bernard Ullathorne

To cultivate kindness is a great part of the business of life.

Samuel Johnson

February 12

Search me, O God, and know my heart: try me, and know my thoughts: and see if there be any wicked way in me, and lead me in the way everlasting.

PSALM 139:23–24 KJV

"Am I really what I ought to be? Am I what, in the bottom of my heart, I honestly wish to be? Am I living a life at all like what I myself approve? My secret nature, the true complexion of my character, is hidden from all men, and only I know it. Is it such as I should be willing to show? Is my soul at all like what my kindest and most intimate friends believe? Is my heart at all such as I should wish the Searcher of Hearts to judge me by? Is every year adding to my devotion, to my unselfishness, to my conscientiousness, to my freedom from the hypocrisy of seeming so much better than I am? When I compare myself with last year, am I more ready to surrender myself at the call of duty? Am I more alive to the commands of conscience? Have I shaken off my besetting sins?" These are the questions which this season...ought to find us putting fairly and honestly to our hearts.

FREDERICK TEMPLE

February 13

Now that you have purified yourselves by obeying the truth so that you have sincere love for your brothers, love one another deeply, from the heart.

1 PETER 1:22 NIV

Thy wonderful grand will, my God!
Triumphantly I make it mine;
And faith shall breathe her glad "Amen"
To every dear command of Thine.

JEAN SOPHIA PIGOTT

You little think how much the life of all your graces depends upon your ready and cordial obedience to the Spirit. When the Spirit urges you to secret prayer, and you refuse obedience; when He forbids you a known transgression, and yet you will go on; when He tells you which is the way, and which not, and you will not pay attention—no wonder if heaven and your soul be estranged.

RICHARD BAXTER

Whatever the particular call is, the particular sacrifice God asks you to make, the particular cross He wishes you to embrace, whatever the particular path He wants you to tread, will you rise up, and say in your heart: Yes, Lord, I accept it; I submit, I yield, I pledge myself to walk in that path, and to follow that Voice and to trust You with the consequences? Oh! But you say, "I don't know what He will want next." No, we none of us know that, but we know we shall be safe in His hands.

CATHERINE BOOTH

February 14

Walk worthy of God, who hath called you unto his kingdom and glory.

1 Thessalonians 2:12 kjv

Amid our most trivial duties, on days which are passing in the usual round of uneventful routine, He may speak to us as never before. A quiet word may be dropped by a friend—a sentence read in a book—a thought lodged, we know not how or why, in the mind. We are laid under obligations to a new and more dynamic view of life and duty. There is, of course, room for self-delusion of many kinds in the supposed visit of the heavenly call. But we are tolerably safe if two conditions are observed: if, first, the duty is unwelcome to our natural inclinations; and if, secondly, it does not contradict what we know God has taught us so far. To listen for the footsteps of the divine Redeemer passing by us in the ordinary providences of life is a most important part of the trial of every man. How much is contingent on following when He beckons us to some higher duty, to some more perfect service, we shall only know when we see all things as they really are in the light of His eternity.

H. P. Liddon

I will charge my soul to believe and wait for Him, and will follow His providence, and not go before it, nor stay behind it.

Samuel Rutherford

February 15

*I run with purpose in every step. I am not just shadowboxing.
I discipline my body like an athlete, training it to do what
it should.*

1 Corinthians 9:26–27 NLT

The slack, lazy temperament, given to self-indulgence and delay,
will find very practical and helpful practice in strict punctuality, a
fixed habit of rising to the minute, when once a time is settled on;
in being always ready for meals, or the various daily matters in
which our lateness makes others uncomfortable. People have found
their whole spiritual life helped and strengthened by steadfastly
conquering a habit of dawdling, or of reading newspapers and
random bits of books when they ought to be settling about
some work.

H. L. Sidney Lear

Let us "redeem the time." Random working, fitful planning,
irregular reading, ill-assorted hours, careless or delayed execution
of business, hurry and bustle, loitering and unpreparedness—
these, and the like, are the things which take out the whole
purpose and power from life, which hinder holiness, and which eat
like a canker into our moral being.

Horatius Bonar

February 16

I, therefore, the prisoner of the Lord, beseech you to walk worthy of the calling with which you were called.

EPHESIANS 4:1 NKJV

Knowing You need this form, as I Your divine inspiration,
Knowing You shape the clay with a vision and purpose divine,
So would I answer each touch of Your hand in its loving creation,
That in my conscious life Your beauty and power may shine.

CHRISTOPHER P. CRANCH

Let us examine our capacities and gifts, and then put them to the best use we may. As our own view of life is of necessity partial, I do not find that we can do better than to put them absolutely in God's hand, and look to Him for the direction of our life-energy. God can do great things with our lives, if we but give them to Him in sincerity. He can make them useful, uplifting, heroic. God never wastes anything. God never forgets anything. God never loses anything. As long as we live we have a work to do; we shall never be too old for it, nor too feeble. Illness, weakness, fatigue, grief— none of these things can excuse us from this work of ours. That we are alive today is proof positive that God has something for us to do today.

ANNA R. B. LINDSAY

February 17

I, the LORD, have called you in righteousness;
I will take hold of your hand.
I will keep you and will make you
to be a covenant for the people
and a light for the Gentiles.

ISAIAH 42:6 NIV

Don't be content with spending all your time on your faults, but try to get a step nearer to God. It is not He who is far away from us, but we from Him. If you ask me the best means to persevere, I would say, if you have succeeded in getting hold of almighty God's hand, *don't let it go.* Keep hold of Him by constantly renewing prayers to Him...and the seeking to please Him in little things.

FRANCIS RAPHAEL

Strive to be as a little child who, while her mother holds her hand, goes on fearlessly, and is not disturbed because she stumbles and trips in her weakness. So long as God holds you up by the will and determination to serve Him with which He inspires you, go on boldly and do not be frightened at your little pauses and fails, so long as you can throw yourself into His arms in trusting love. Go there with an open, joyful heart as often as possible; if not always joyful, at least go with a brave and faithful heart.

FRANCIS DE SALES

February 18

Submit to God, and you will have peace; then things will go well for you.

JOB 22:21 NLT

Don't be unwise enough to think that we are serving God best by constant activity at the cost of headaches and broken rest. I am getting to be of the opinion that we may be doing too much. We want—at least this is my own want—a higher quality of work. Our labor should be to maintain unbroken communion with our blessed Lord; then we shall have entire rest, and God abiding in us; that which we do will not be ours, but His.

JOHN KENNETH MACKENZIE

Our object in life should not be so much to get through a great deal of work, as to give perfect satisfaction to Him for whom we are doing the work.

W. HAY M. H. AITKEN

Lift up my soul above the weary round of harassing thoughts to Your eternal Presence. Lift up my soul to the pure, bright, clear, serene, radiant atmosphere of Your Presence, that there I may breathe freely, there repose in Your love, there be at rest from myself and from all things that weary me; then return, arrayed with Your peace, to do and bear what shall please You.

EDWARD B. PUSEY

February 19

God is able to make all grace abound to you, so that in all things at all times, having all that you need, you will abound in every good work.

2 Corinthians 9:8 NIV

O Love, Your sovereign aid impart
　　To save me from low-thoughted care;
Chase this self-will through all my heart,
　　Through all its latent mazes there;
Make me Your duteous child, that I
　　Ceaseless may "Abba, Father" cry.

Gerhard Tersteegen

The grace which keeps me from falling one inch further, irrecoverable, and is not worn out by my provocations in this wilderness, is…more prompt, more steady, than I have any experience of among material things and persons. Everything material is simply feeble, and everything personal is shadowy, as compared with this personality under whose shadow I am allowed to dwell…. The want of time to read and think, the shortness and distractions of prayer, seem to threaten one's very existence as a conscious child of God. And yet He is on my right hand and I know it.

Edward White Benson

February 20

Count it all joy when you fall into various trials, knowing that the testing of your faith produces patience.

JAMES 1:2–3 NKJV

Temptation is surely an assault to be withstood, but at the same time it is an opportunity to be seized. Viewed in this light, life becomes inspiring, not in spite of but because of its struggles, and we are able to greet the unseen with a cheer, counting it unmixed joy when we fall into the many temptations which, varied in form, dog our steps from the cradle to the grave. The soldier who is called to the front is stimulated, not depressed; the officer who is bidden by his general to a post of great responsibility, and so of hardship and peril, is thrilled with the joy of his task. An opportunity has been given him to prove himself worthy of great trust, which can be done only at the cost of great trouble.

This is a true picture of temptation. And the result of it all is a nature invigorated and refined, a character made capable of close friendship with God.

CHARLES H. BRENT

Every trial that we pass through is capable of being the seed of noble character. Every temptation that we meet in the path of life is another chance of filling our souls with the power of heaven.

FREDERICK TEMPLE

February 21

I delight in your commands because I love them.

PSALM 119:47 NIV

This everlasting and disappointing study of duty—duty to everybody, everywhere, everyday—it keeps you questioning all the while, grating in a torment of debates and regrets, till you almost groan aloud for weariness. It is as if your life itself were slavery. And then you say, with a sigh, "Oh, if I had nothing to do but just to be with Christ personally, and have my obligation solely with Him, how sweet and blessed and secret and free would it be." Well, you may have it so; exactly this and nothing more! Sad mistake that you should ever have thought otherwise!... Come back then to Christ, retire into the secret place of His love, and pledge your whole duty personally to Him. Only then you will make this very welcome discovery, that as you are personally given up to Christ's authority, you are going where He goes, helping what He does, keeping ever dear, close company with Him, in all His motions of good and sympathy, refusing even to let Him suffer without suffering with Him. And so you will do a great many more duties than you even think of now; only they will all be sweet and easy and free, even as your love is.

HORACE BUSHNELL

February 22

Glory in His holy name;
*Let the hearts of those rejoice who seek the L*ORD*!*

PSALM **105:3** NKJV

Fear not, little flock; for it is your Father's good pleasure to give
you the kingdom.

LUKE **12:32** KJV

This way of seeing our Father in everything makes life one long
thanksgiving, and gives a rest of heart, and, more than that, a
happiness of spirit that is unspeakable. Someone says, "God's will
on earth is always joy, always tranquility." And since He must have
His own way concerning His children, into what wonderful green
pastures of inward rest, and beside what blessedly still waters
of inward refreshment, is the soul led that learns this secret. If
the will of God is our will, and if He always has His way, then we
always have our way also, and we reign in a perpetual kingdom.
He who sides with God cannot fail to win in every encounter;
and, whether the result shall be joy or sorrow, failure or success,
death or life, we may, under all circumstances, join in the apostle's
shout of victory, "Thanks be unto God which always causes us to
triumph in Christ!"

HANNAH **W**HITALL **S**MITH

February 23

For this is the love of God, that we keep his commandments:
and his commandments are not grievous.

1 John 5:3 kjv

His commandments grievous are not,
    Longer than men think them so;
Though He send me forth, I care not,
    While He gives me strength to go.

Francis Quarles

Nothing is grievous or burdensome to him who loves. They are not grievous, because love makes them light; they are not grievous, because Christ gives strength to bear them. Wings are no weight to the bird, which they lift up in the air until it is lost in the sky above us, and we see it no more, and hear only its note of thanks. God's commands are no weight to the soul which, through His Spirit, He uplifts to Himself; no, rather, the soul, through them, all the more soars upward and loses itself in the love of God. "The commandments of God are not grievous," because we have a power implanted in us mightier than all which would dispute the sway of God's commandments and God's love, a power which would lift us above all obstructions, carry us over all temptations...the almighty power of the grace of God.

Edward B. Pusey

February 24

The cornerstone is Christ Jesus himself. We are carefully joined together in him, becoming a holy temple for the Lord. Through him you Gentiles are also being made part of this dwelling where God lives by his Spirit.

EPHESIANS 2:20–22 NLT

When God afflicts you, think He hews a rugged stone,
Which must be shaped, or else aside as useless thrown.

RICHARD CHENEVIX TRENCH

What comforts me is the thought that we are being shaped here below into stones for the heavenly temple—that to be made like Him is the object of our earthly existence. He is the shaper and carpenter of the heavenly temple. *He* must *work* us into shape, our part is to be still in His hands; every annoyance is a little chip. Also we must not be in a hurry to go out of the quarry, for there is a certain place for each stone, and we must wait till the building is ready for that stone; it would mess up the building if we were taken at random.

CHARLES GEORGE GORDON

Oh, three times fools are we, who like newborn princes weeping in the cradle, know not that there is a kingdom before them. Then, let our Lord's sweet hand square us, and hammer us, and strike off the knots of pride, self-love, world-worship, and infidelity, that He may make us stones and pillars in His Father's house.

SAMUEL RUTHERFORD

February 25

Grow in the grace, and in the knowledge of our Lord and Savior Jesus Christ. To him be glory both now and for ever. Amen.

2 PETER 3:18 KJV

Did not our heart burn within us, while he talked with us by the way, and while he opened to us the scriptures?

LUKE 24:32 KJV

The history in the Gospels is so well worn that it often slips through the head without affecting the heart. But if, retiring into solitude for a portion of the day, we should select one scene or trait or incident in the life of Jesus, and with all the helps we can get, seek to understand it fully. Tracing it in the other evangelists, comparing it with other passages of Scripture, etc., we should find ourselves insensibly interested, and might hope that, in this effort of our soul to understand Him, Jesus Himself would draw near as He did of old to the disciples on the way to Emmaus. This looking unto Jesus and thinking about Him is a better way to meet and overcome sin than any physical strictness to spiritual self-reproaches. It is by looking at Him, the apostle says, "as in a glass," that we are "changed into the same image, as from glory to glory."

HARRIET BEECHER STOWE

February 26

*"Can anyone hide in secret places so that I cannot see him?"
declares the Lord. "Do not I fill heaven and earth?" declares
the Lord.*

Jeremiah 23:24 niv

Let me not dwell so much within
    My bounded heart, with anxious heed—
Where all my searches meet with sin,
    And nothing satisfies my need—
It shuts me from the sound and sight
Of that pure world of life and light.

Anna L. Waring

Do you think that the infinite God cannot fill and satisfy
your heart?

François de Fénelon

Let not cares, riches, nor pleasures of this world choke the heart,
which was formed to contain the love of God. Pray, and all is
yours. Yours in God Himself, who teaches you to pray for Himself.
To pray is to go forth from earth, and to live in heaven.

Edward B. Pusey

February 27

Therefore take up the whole armor of God, that you may be able to withstand in the evil day, and having done all, to stand.

EPHESIANS 6:13 NKJV

Soldiers don't get tied up in the affairs of civilian life, for then they cannot please the officer who enlisted them.

2 TIMOTHY 2:4 NLT

Soldiers of Christ, arise,
    And put your armor on,
Strong in the strength which God supplies
    Through His eternal Son.

CHARLES WESLEY

Where are you going? Where is your soul? Is it in peace? If troubled, why? How are you fulfilling the duties of the position? What are they? What effort have you made to amend your disposition, and conquer your sins? Have you been faithful to the light God has given you? What means should you use, especially with regard to your most besetting sin or temptation? Have you fought against it? Have you thought about it at all?

PERE RAVIGNAN

February 28

Whoever does not love does not know God, because God is love.

1 JOHN 4:8 NIV

He rests in God and He in him,
    Who still abides in love;
In love the saints and seraphim
    Obey and praise above;
For God is love; the loveless heart
Has in His life and joy no part.

C. F. GELLERT

Divine love is perfect peace and joy, it is a freedom from all
anxiety, it is all content and happiness; and makes everything
to rejoice in itself. Love is the Christ of God; wherever it comes,
it comes as the blessing and happiness of every natural life, a
redeemer from all evil, a fulfiller of all righteousness, and a peace
of God, which passes all understanding. Through all the universe
of things, nothing is uneasy, unsatisfied, or restless, unless it is not
governed by love, or because its nature has not reached or attained
the full birth of the spirit of love. For when that is done, every
hunger is satisfied, and all complaining, murmuring, accusing,
resenting, revenging, and striving are as totally suppressed and
overcome, as the coldness, thickness, and horror of darkness are
suppressed and overcome by the breaking forth of the light.

WILLIAM LAW

February 29

*From everyone who has been given much, much will be required;
and to whom they entrusted much, of him they will ask all
the more.*

LUKE 12:48 NASB

God is ever seeking an entrance, and the avenue to the heart is
closed against Him; He enters in, and is rudely crowded, or jostled,
or civilly put off, or promised an audience at a more convenient
season, if He is not, by deadly sin, cast out. How many calls by
God's providence...might have been a lasting conversion to God,
and where have they left us? Above the common gifts to all: our
creation, preservation, and all the blessings of this life; besides that
universal gift of "the redemption of the world by our Lord Jesus
Christ," we thank Him for that which is varied to each, "the means
of grace." What we have had might have made glorious saints of
those who have had less.

EDWARD B. PUSEY

Little is much if God is in it.

KITTIE L. SUFFIELD

Don't be afraid to give your best to what seemingly are small jobs.
Every time you conquer one it makes you that much stronger.
If you do the little jobs well, the big ones will tend to take care
of themselves.

DALE CARNEGIE

MARCH

It is the first mild day of March.

Each minute sweeter than before...

There is a blessing in the air.

WILLIAM WORDSWORTH

March 1

For to me to live is Christ and to die is gain…having a desire to depart and to be with Christ; which is far better.

PHILIPPIANS 1:21, 23 KJV

If I were annihilated this moment, I should bless God for having been allowed to live. Far more, if I were to have to toil and suffer in this sorrowful but glorious earth-life through unnumbered ages, and the sorrow and suffering continued to bring the living life with it that it has brought, I would gladly accept sorrow and suffering here on earth. How much more would I accept, then…that a very few years more will place me with these precious life-powers in a world fitted for highest life, with life intensified, and all the pure great life of ages gathered there, besides those whom I have dearly loved.

EDWARD THRING

Our present life in Christ may be compared to that of the seed: a hidden life, contending underground against cold and darkness and obstructions, yet bearing within its breast the indestructible germ of vitality. Death lifts the soul into the sunshine for which a hidden, invisible work has prepared it. Heaven is the life of the flower.

DORA GREENWELL

March 2

And thou, child, shalt be called the prophet of the Highest:
for thou shalt go before the face of the Lord to prepare his ways;
to give knowledge of salvation unto his people by the remission
of their sins, through the tender mercy of our God; whereby the
dayspring from on high hath visited us, to give light to them that
sit in darkness and in the shadow of death, to guide our feet into
the way of peace.

LUKE 1:76–79 KJV

I believe that love reigns, and that love will prevail. I believe that
He says to me every morning, "Begin again your journey and your
life; your sins, which are many, are not only forgiven, but they
shall be made, by the wisdom of God, the basis on which He will
build blessings."

THOMAS ERSKINE

There is no thirst of the soul so consuming as the desire for pardon.
The sense of its attainment is the starting-point of all goodness.
It comes bringing with it, if not the freshness of innocence, then a
glow of inspiration.... To be able to look into God's face, and know
with the knowledge of faith that there is nothing between the soul
and Him, is to experience the fullest peace the soul can know.
Whatever else pardon may be, it is above all things admission into
full fellowship with God.

CHARLES H. BRENT

March 3

Hungry and thirsty, their soul fainted in them. Then they cried out to the LORD in their trouble, and He delivered them out of their distresses.

PSALM 107:5–6 NKJV

Blessed are they which do hunger and thirst after righteousness: for they shall be filled.

MATTHEW 5:6 KJV

If God had not said, Blessed are those that hunger, I know not what could keep weak Christians from sinking in despair. Many times all I can do is to find and complain that I want Him, and wish to recover Him. Now this is my anchor, that He in mercy honors us not only by having, but by desiring also; and…accounts us to have that which we want and desire to have.

JOSEPH HALL

Honest sighing is faith breathing and whispering in the ear. The life is not out of faith where there is sighing, looking up with the eyes, and breathing toward God.

SAMUEL RUTHERFORD

He never yet rejected the feeble soul which clings to Him in love.

H. L. SIDNEY LEAR

March 4

For God, who said, "Let light shine out of darkness," made his light shine in our hearts to give us the light of the knowledge of the glory of God in the face of Christ.

2 CORINTHIANS 4:6 NIV

It was our weaknesses he carried; it was our sorrows that weighed him down.

ISAIAH 53:4 NLT

The way to think of God so as to know Him is to think of Christ. Then we see Him and can understand how tender and merciful and good He is. We see that if He sends us sorrow and difficulties, He only sends them because they are the true blessings, the things that are truly good. He would have us like Himself, with a happiness like His own, and nothing below it. And so as His own happiness is in taking sorrow and infirmity, and ever assisting, and giving and sacrificing Himself, He gives us sorrows too, and weaknesses, which are not the evils that we think them, but are what we should be most happy in, if we were perfect and had knowledge like Him. So there is a use and a service in all we bear, in all we do, which we do not know, but which He knows, and which in Christ He shows to us. It is a use *for others*, a hidden use, but one which makes all our life rich, and that richest which is most like Christ's.

JAMES HINTON

March 5

Fear not, nor be dismayed, be strong and of good courage.

JOSHUA **10:25** KJV

Then combat well, of nothing afraid,
For thus His follower you are made;
Each battle teaches you to fight,
Each foe to be a braver knight,
Armed with His might.

J. H. BOHMER

From now on my soul should fight with the prestige of victory,
with the courage that comes of having tried and won, trusted and
not been confounded.

JULIANA H. EWING

They have had their victories; and when the stress is hardest, it
is wise to look back on these for encouragement, as songs of joy
and triumph bring strength and support along a way beset with
pain and sorrow and disappointments; which, when seen in their
true proportions, are only as faint specks showing in a universe of
infinite light.

LAURENCE OLIPHANT

March 6

According to your faith let it be to you.

MATTHEW 9:29 NKJV

Jesus said to her, "Did I not say to you that if you believe, you will see the glory of God?"

JOHN 11:40 NASB

I find that while faith is steady nothing can upset me, and when faith totters nothing can stabilize me. If I ramble out among countryside and creatures, I am presently lost, and can come to no end. But if I focus myself on God, and leave Him to work in His own way and time, I am at rest, and can lie down and sleep in a promise, though a thousand rise up against me. Therefore my way is not to be planned ahead, but to walk with God by the day. Keep close to God, and then you need fear nothing. Maintain secret and intimate acquaintance with Him.... Do not crowd religion into a corner of the day. If men would spend those hours they wear out in plots and devices in communion with God, and give all to Him in daring belief, they would have more peace and comfort.

JOSEPH ELIOT

Faith is improved with the free air, and of the sharp winter storm in its face.

SAMUEL RUTHERFORD

March 7

Fear not, neither be discouraged.

DEUTERONOMY 1:21 KJV

Happy are they that learn, in Thee,
    Though patient suffering teach,
The secret of enduring strength,
    And praise too deep for speech,
Peace that no pressure from without,
    No strife within, can reach.

ANNA L. WARING

One of the greatest trials and miseries of this life seems to me to be the absence of a grand spirit to keep the body under control; illnesses, distress, and pain, though they are a trial, I think nothing of, if the soul is strong, for it praises God, and sees that everything comes from His hand.

TERESA OF AVILA

Many say they have no peace nor rest, but so many crosses and trials, pains and sorrows, that they know not how they shall ever get through them. Now he who is truth will perceive and take note, understand clearly that true peace and rest lie not in outward things. There lives no man on earth who may always have rest and peace without troubles and crosses. If you yield yourself willingly to them, and seek only that true peace of the heart, which none can take away from you, you may overcome all assaults.

THEOLOGIA GERMANICA

March 8

In all these things we are more than conquerors through him that loved us.

ROMANS 8:37 KJV

Lord, in this awful fight with sin
    I would not just prevail;
Against each lust so strong within
    I would not almost fail.
Full, gladsome, glorious victory
    Should crown the Holy War;
Lord! I would triumph well—would be
    A more than conqueror.

THOMAS H. GILL

Do not try only to abstain from sin, but strive, by God's grace, to gain the opposite grace. If you would not slip back into sin, you must stretch forward to Christ and His holiness. It is a dull, heavy, dreary, toilsome way, just to avoid sin. You would not simply *not* be impatient; you would long to be like the Lord, who was meek and humble of heart.

EDWARD B. PUSEY

The only real relief is in the absolute conquest; and the earlier the battle begins, the easier and the shorter it will be. If one can keep irritability under control, one may escape a struggle to the death with passion.

JULIANA H. EWING

March 9

The LORD is my light and my salvation; whom shall I fear? The LORD is the strength of my life; of whom shall I be afraid?

PSALM 27:1 KJV

God is my strong salvation, / What foe have I to fear?
In darkness and temptation, / My light, my help, is near.
Though hosts encamp around me, / Firm to the fight I stand,
What terror can confound me / With God at my right hand?

JAMES MONTGOMERY

All the spiritual enemies, all the enemies of a man's own house, are to be destroyed by the power of the Lord Jesus Christ, working by His grace in the heart. And when salvation is brought home to the heart, and worked out there by the Lord, it is to be enjoyed and lived in, and the soul is not to return back again into captivity; but, being delivered out of the hands of its inward and spiritual enemies, is to serve God in the authority of His Son's life, in holiness and righteousness all its days here upon the earth.

ISAAC PENINGTON

Who does not know what it is to rise up from a fault—perceived, confessed, and forgiven—with an almost joyous sense of new energy, strength, and will to persevere?

H. L. SIDNEY LEAR

March 10

For you are my hiding place; you protect me from trouble.
You surround me with songs of victory.

PSALM 32:7 NLT

Afraid sometimes that your Father has forgot?
When the clouds around you gather, doubt Him not.
Always has the daylight broken—
Always has He comfort spoken—
Better has He been for years than your fears.

KARL RUDOLPH HAGENBACH

It is the indwelling presence of God, believed in, trusted, reverenced, recollected, which ought to become the support to meet every case of trouble. The soul finds rest from its perplexities, as it turns from what perplexes and disturbs it, to fix its gaze and hope and purpose on Him. If there is a pressure of distress, or anxiety, or care, or perplexity of any kind, a heavy burden weighing down the spirit, then let the soul look off for a moment from itself, and from the trying object, to God. The recollection of His presence within, ever abiding, continually renewed by perpetual closeness, would secure the soul, if duly and constantly cherished, a habitual life of rest.

T. T. CARTER

March 11

You therefore, my son, be strong in the grace that is in Christ Jesus.

2 TIMOTHY 2:1 NKJV

I would arise in all Your strength
    My place on earth to fill,
To work out all my time of war
    With love's unflinching will.
Firm against every doubt of You
    For all my future way—
To walk in heaven's eternal light
    Throughout the changing day.

ANNA L. WARING

Every trouble is an opportunity to win the grace of strength. Whatever else trouble is in the world for, it is here for this good purpose: to develop strength. For a trouble is a moral and spiritual task. It is something which is hard to do. And it is in the spiritual world as in the physical, strength is increased by an encounter with the difficult. A world without any trouble in it would be, to people of our kind, a place of spiritual weakness and moral laziness. Fortunately, every day is crowded with cares. Every day to every one of us brings its questions, its worries, and its tasks, brings its sufficiency of trouble. Thus we get our daily spiritual exercise. Every day we are blessed with new opportunities for the development of strength of soul.

GEORGE HODGES

March 12

For their sakes I consecrate myself.

JOHN 17:19 KJV

It may help us to do battle with our despondency and sadness, with our restlessness and resentment, with the perverting and corrupting misery of ambition. We must be watchful and uncompromising, if the self-consecration is to do its work. One sin alone indulged, condoned, domesticated, may spoil it all; may cripple all our hope of helpfulness; may baffle the willingness of God to use us in His work for others. "For their sakes I consecrate myself." This, then, is our constant hope, that God will so cleanse and purify our hearts that they may not hinder the transmission to others of that light and truth which issue from His presence. For that hope we would cast out all that defiles and darkens us; we would freely give ourselves to Christ, that He may enter in and rule and animate us; so that, through all our unworthiness, something of His brightness and peace may be made known to men.

FRANCIS PAGET

Did I but live nearer to God, I could be of so much more help.

GEORGE HODGES

March 13

God so loved the world, that he gave his only begotten Son,
that whosoever believeth in him should not perish, but have
everlasting life.

JOHN 3:16 KJV

Let your love be wide as His;
With the whole world round His knees;
Gather into your warm heart
All His creatures—not a part;
So your love shall be like His.

KATHARINE TYNAN HINKSON

Your God is love; love Him and in Him all people, as His children
in Christ. Your Lord is a fire; do not let your heart be cold, but
burn with faith and love. Your Lord is a light; do not walk in
darkness. Your Lord is a God of mercy and bountifulness; be also a
source of mercy and bountifulness to your neighbors.

JOHN ILYICH SERGIEFF

"Love the Lord thy God with all thy heart, and thy neighbor as
thyself" and then go on your way. The way in which God shall lead
you may be over rocks and deserts, over mountains and oceans,
amid things perilous to the sight and the touch; but still go on your
way rejoicing.

THOMAS C. UPHAM

March 14

Let all those who seek You rejoice and be glad in You;
And let those who love Your salvation say continually,
"Let God be magnified!"

PSALM 70:4 NKJV

Lord! Along this earthly way
    You Your pilgrim greetest;
To Your thankful child each day
    You Your love repeatest;
You do bid me weep no more,
You do teach this song to soar,
You do all the sweetness pour
    When my life is sweetest.

THOMAS H. GILL

I am thankful that I have learned, not only to understand that I ought to say, but to feel what it is truly to say, "good is the will of the Lord," in little things as well as in great things.... Love to God, that love which receives God Himself as the portion of the soul in every cup, its sweetest ingredient (whatever other sweet ingredients may be in it), is as essential to the right understanding of what God does in providence as the faith that He is love.

JOHN MCLEOD CAMPBELL

March 15

Let all that you do be done in love.

1 Corinthians 16:14 NASB

    If you are blessed,
Then let the sunshine of your gladness rest
On the dark edges of each cloud that lies
Black in your brother's skies.
    If you are sad,
Still be you in your brother's gladness glad.

Anne E. Hamilton

What can be more unkind than to communicate our low spirits to others, to go about the world like demons, poisoning the fountains of joy? Have I more light because I have managed to involve those I love in the same gloom as myself? Is it not pleasant to see the sun shining on the mountains, even though we have none of it down in our valley? Oh, the littleness and the sympathy, which will not let us keep our sorrows to ourselves! Let us hide our pains and sorrows. But, while we hide them, let them also be spurs within us to urge us on to all manner of overflowing kindness and sunny humor to those around us. When the very darkness within us creates a sunshine around us, then has the spirit of Jesus taken possession of our souls.

Frederick W. Faber

March 16

The LORD appeared to us in the past, saying: "I have loved you with an everlasting love; I have drawn you with loving-kindness."

JEREMIAH 31:3 NIV

My song is love unknown;
> My Savior's love to me;
Love to the loveless shown,
> That they might lovely be.

SAMUEL CROSSMAN

He so governs and shapes all the circumstances of life, that if we use them aright we may draw near to Him here, and prepare to be near Him in the forever after. He longs for our love—our love, which is so feeble and faint, and yet so precious in His sight when we give it to Him freely. And why does He so desire it? Ah! I have told you many times before, and yet we cannot too often remember it…if we love Him, He can make us supremely happy. All that belongs to us, or occurs to us, in this life is so ordered that we may find in it the means of putting far from us those obstructions of evil which prevent us from seeing Him as He is, and as He has revealed Himself to us. For if we did but so see Him, how could we fail to love Him with the whole heart and soul?

THEOPHILUS PARSONS

How shall we become lovely? By loving Him who is ever lovely.

AUGUSTINE OF HIPPO

March 17

God has united you with Christ Jesus. For our benefit God made him to be wisdom itself. Christ made us right with God; he made us pure and holy, and he freed us from sin.

1 Corinthians 1:30 nlt

Christ with me, Christ before me,
Christ behind me, Christ within me,
Christ beneath me, Christ above me,
Christ at my right hand, Christ at my left.

Christ in the heart of every man who thinks of me,
Christ in the mouth of every man who speaks to me,
Christ in every eye that sees me,
Christ in every ear that hears me.

Saint Patrick

Christ is in all His redeemed, as the soul of their soul, the life of their life. He is the pitying heart and the helping hand of God with every needy, praying spirit in the world. He is the sweet light of the knowledge of God that breaks in upon every penitent heart. He is not only with those who believe in Him and love Him, but also with those who neither believe in Him nor love Him, that He may be to them also *Jesus their Savior.* The Christ of God is in your heart, waiting and aiming to get the consent of your will, that He may save you.

John Pulsford

March 18

Hate evil, you who love the LORD.

PSALM 97:10 NASB

There is a general fund of evil in the world to which we all contribute, or which, by God's grace, some may diminish; a vast and fertile tract of ungodliness, of low motives, of low aims, of low desires, of low sense of duty or no sense at all. It is the creation of ages, that tradition; but each age does something for it, and each individual in each age does, if he does not advisedly refuse to, his share in the increasing it, just as the chimney of every small house does something to thicken and darken the air.

And this general fund of evil touches us all like the common atmosphere which we breathe. And thus it is that when you or I, even in lesser matters, do or say what our conscience condemns, we do really make a contribution to that general fund of wickedness which, in other circumstances and social conditions than ours, produces flagrant crime. Especially if it should happen that we defend what we do, or make light of it, or most actively and seriously increase this common fund or tradition or wickedness.

HENRY PARRY LIDDON

March 19

The brothers and sisters in Rome had heard we were coming, and they came to meet us at the Forum on the Appian Way. Others joined us.... When Paul saw them, he was encouraged and thanked God.

ACTS 28:15 NLT

Through the night of doubt and sorrow
  Onward goes the pilgrim band,
Singing songs of expectation,
  Marching to the promised land.
Clear before us through the darkness
  Gleams and burns the guiding light;
Brother clasps the hand of brother,
  Stepping fearless through the night.

BERNHARD S. INGEMANN

We fight not for ourselves alone. These—our friends—are the clouds where we walk surrounded; it is for them that we wrestle through the long night; they count on the strength that we might bring them, if we so wrestle that we win. The morning that follows the night of our lonely trial would, if we are faithful, find us new people, with a new name of help, and of promise, and of comfort, in the memory of which others would endure bravely, and fight as we had fought. Oh! Turn to God in fear, lest through hidden disloyalty we have not a cup of cold water to give those who turn to us for assistance in their dire need!

HENRY SCOTT HOLLAND

March 20

Through Christ Jesus the law of the Spirit of life set me free from the law of sin and death.

ROMANS 8:2 NIV

Not yet you know what I do
    Within your own weak breast,
To mold you to My image true,
    And fit you for My rest.
But yield you to My loving skill
    The veiled work of grace,
From day to day progressing still,
    It is not yours to trace.

FRANCES RIDLEY HAVERGAL

Be content to go on quietly. When you discover somewhat in yourself which is earthly and imperfect, be patient while you strive to cast it out. Your perceptions will grow. At first God will show you very obvious stumbling blocks—be diligent in clearing these away, and do not aim at heights to which you are not yet ready. Leave all to God, and while you earnestly desire that He would purify your intention, and seek to work with Him to that end, be satisfied with the gradual progress He sets before you; and remember that He often works in ways unseen by us.

JEAN NICOLAS GROU

March 21

He will reply, "I tell you the truth, whatever you did not do for one of the least of these, you did not do for me."

MATTHEW 25:45 NIV

If today you turn aside
In your luxury and pride,
Wrapped within yourself, and blind
To the sorrows of your kind,
You a faithless watch do keep,
You are one of those who sleep.

ANNA C. LYNCH BOTTA

I have been sorrowfully convinced that in what I thought necessary attention to home duties, my time and strength have been engrossed to a degree that I fear has interfered with my duty to others. It is a serious consideration, how much good we miss of doing by our want of watchfulness for opportunities, and our engrossment even in our lawful and necessary cares. And there is another way, too, in the influence we might continually exert over all who come in contact with us, and through them over others, to an extent of which we are probably not aware, if we continually keep in a meek and quiet spirit. Ah, it may be with some of us that it is more for what we leave undone than for what we do, that we shall be called to an account.

ELIZABETH TABER KING

March 22

You shall diligently keep the commandments of the LORD your God, His testimonies, and His statutes which He has commanded you. And you shall do what is right and good in the sight of the LORD, that it may be well with you, and that you may go in and possess the good land of which the LORD swore to your fathers.

DEUTERONOMY 6:17–18 NKJV

We ought to become holy in the state in which Providence has placed us, instead of making projects of goodness in the future; we need the greatest faithfulness to God in the smallest things.... Accustom yourself to adore His holy will frequently, by humbly submitting your own [will] to His orders and His Providence. Let us do what we know He requires of us, and, as soon as we know His will, let us not spare ourselves, but be very faithful to Him. Such faithfulness ought not merely to lead us to do great things for His service, but whatever our hands find to do, and which belongs to our state of life. The smallest things become great when God requires them of us; they are small only in themselves; they are always great when they are done for God, and when they serve to unite us with Him eternally.

FRANÇOIS DE FÉNELON

March 23

The sheep listen to his voice. He calls his own sheep by name and leads them out. When he has brought out all his own, he goes on ahead of them, and his sheep follow him because they know his voice.

JOHN 10:3–4 NIV

He only asks you to yield yourself to Him, that He may work in you to will and to do by His own mighty power. Your part is to yield yourself, His part is to work; and never, never will He give you any command which is not accompanied by ample power to obey it. Take no thought for tomorrow in this matter; but abandon yourself with a generous trust to your loving Lord, who has promised never to call His own sheep out into any path without Himself going before them to make the way easy and safe. Take each little step as He makes it plain to you. Bring all your life in each of its details to Him to regulate and guide. Follow gladly and quickly the sweet suggestions of His Spirit in your soul. And day by day you will find Him bringing you more and more into conformity with His will in all things; molding you and fashioning you, as you are able to bear, into a vessel in His honor, sanctified and made for His use, and fitted to every good work.

HANNAH WHITALL SMITH

March 24

Being confident of this very thing, that he which hath begun a good work in you will perform it until the day of Jesus Christ.

PHILIPPIANS 1:6 KJV

You belong to God, my dear children. You have already won a victory over those people, because the Spirit who lives in you is greater than the spirit who lives in the world.

1 JOHN 4:4 NLT

Why is it that we, in the very kingdom of grace, surrounded by angels, and preceded by saints, nevertheless can do so little, and, instead of mounting with wings like eagles, grovel in the dust, and do but sin, and confess sin alternately? Is it that the *power* of God is not with us? Is it literally that we are *not able* to perform God's commandments? God forbid. We are able. We have that given us which makes us able. We do have a power within us to do what we are commanded to do. What is it we lack? The power? No; the will. What we lack is the simple, earnest, sincere inclination and aim to use what God has given us, and what we have in us.

JOHN HENRY NEWMAN

God is on my side. He makes Himself responsible for my being. If I will only entrust myself to Him with the cordial return of trustful love, then all that He has ever breathed into my heart of human possibility He will realize and bring to perfection.

CHARLES GORE

March 25

I am the Lord's servant. May everything you have said about me come true.

LUKE 1:38 NLT

Oh, let my thoughts, my actions, and my will
    Obedient solely to Your impulse move,
My heart and sense keep You blameless still,
    Fixed and absorbed in Your unbounded love.
Your praying, teaching, striving, in my heart,
Let me not quench, nor make You to depart.

GERHARD TERSTEEGEN

Life, if true, should be always the offering up of what we are,
to do our best for Him who has called us. The responsibilities,
the ventures, the conscious obligations which press on the soul,
with all their conditions and unknown possibilities, supply the
question that is to be solved. But the true response is that result of
a habit formed through countless, nameless acts of conscientious
obedience, which by use have become the bright and cheerful
exercise of the one purpose of giving its best and purest to One
most fully loved.

T. T. CARTER

March 26

I have given you an example, that you should do as I have done to you.

JOHN 13:15 NKJV

There are often bound to us, in the closest intimacy of social or family ties, natures hard and unfriendly, with whom sympathy is impossible, and whose daily presence necessitates a constant conflict with an adverse influence. There are, too, enemies—open or secret—whose enmity we may feel yet cannot define. Our Lord, going before us in this hard way, showed us how we should walk. It will be appropriate...to ask ourselves, Is there any false friend or covert enemy whom we must learn to tolerate, to forbear with, to pity and forgive? Can we in silent offices of love wash their feet as our Master washed the feet of Judas?

And, if we have no real enemies, are there any bound to us in the relations of life whose habits and ways are annoying and distasteful to us? Can we tolerate them in love? Can we avoid harsh judgments, and harsh speech, and the making known to others our annoyance? The examination will probably teach us to feel the infinite distance between us and our divine Ideal, and change censorship of others into prayer for ourselves.

HARRIET BEECHER STOWE

March 27

Not as I will, but as You will.

MATTHEW 26:39 NKJV

Your will, not mine, O Lord, / However dark it be!
Lead me by Your own hand, / Choose out the path for me.
I dare not choose my lot; / I would not, if I might;
Choose You for me, my God; / So shall I walk aright.

HORATIUS BONAR

"Lord, not what I will, but what You," not what I in my misery,
and ignorance, and blindness, and sin, but what You, in Your
mercy, and holiness, and wisdom, and love.

EDWARD B. PUSEY

In the beginning, as we are learning to pray, our will is in a
struggle with God's will. In time, however, we begin to enter into
a grace-filled releasing of our will and a flowing into the will of
the Father.

RICHARD J. FOSTER

Pray until prayer makes you forget your own will,
and leave it or merge it in God's will.

F. W. ROBERTSON

March 28

Hereby perceive we the love of God, because he laid down his life for us.

1 JOHN 3:16 KJV

Love which outlives
All sin and wrong, Compassion which forgives
To the uttermost, and Justice whose clear eyes
Through lapse and failure look to the intent,
And judge our frailty by the life we meant.

JOHN GREENLEAF WHITTIER

In return for the love which brought the Son of Man down from heaven, in return for the love which led Him to die for us on the cross, we cannot give Him holy lives, for we are not holy; we cannot give Him pure soul, for our souls are not pure; but this one thing we can give, and this is what He asks, hearts that shall never cease from this day forward, till we reach the grave, to strive to be more like Him; to come nearer to Him; to root out from within us the sin that keeps us from Him. To such a battle I call you in His name. And even if at the last day you shall not be able to show any other service, yet be sure that when thousands of His saints go forth to meet Him, and to show His triumph, He will turn to embrace with arms of tenderness the poor penitent who had nothing to offer but a life spent in one never-ceasing struggle with himself, an unwearied battle with the faults that have taken possession of his soul.

FREDERICK TEMPLE

March 29

*Let the peace of Christ rule in your hearts, to which indeed
you were called in one body; and be thankful.*

COLOSSIANS 3:15 NASB

May faith, deep rooted in the soul,
Subdue our flesh, our minds control;
May guile depart, and discord cease,
And all within be joy and peace.

AURELIUS AMBROSIUS

The repose, the quiet balanced rest which marks our Lord's
perfected life, is intended to grow more and more steadfast in
those who are truly His; not the repose of indolence, not the
calm arising from absence of trial and lack of temptation, a mere
accidental freedom from inward struggle or difficulty, but the
repose which lives in the conquest of passion, in the crucifixion
of self, in a subdued will, in the reconciliation of every thought
with a perfected obedience, as the whole inner being, entrenched
in God, yields itself in delighted harmony with His perfect mind.
Such repose is attained through the continual progress of a life
of grace, as it gradually overcomes the restlessness of nature,
the excitement of self, the disturbance of temper or passion, the
fruitless impatience of the will.

T. T. CARTER

Peace, when "ruling" the heart and "ruling" the mind,
opens in both every avenue of joy.

SARAH W. STEPHEN

March 30

He died for all, that they which live should not henceforth live unto themselves, but unto him which died for them, and rose again.

2 Corinthians 5:15 KJV

Then let your life through all its ways
    One long thanksgiving be,
Its theme of joy, its song of praise,
     "Christ died, and rose for me."

J. S. B. Monsell

If you come to seek His face, not in the empty sepulcher, but in the living power of His presence, as indeed realizing that He has finished His glorious work, and is alive forevermore, then your hearts will be full of true Easter joy, and that joy will shed itself abroad in your homes. And let your joy not end with the hymns and the prayers and the communions in His house.

Take with you the joy of Easter to the home, and make that home bright with more unselfish love, more hearty service; take it into your work, and do all in the name of the Lord Jesus; take it to your heart, and let that heart rise anew on Easter wings to a higher, a gladder, a fuller life; take it to the dear graveside and say there the two words "Jesus lives!" and find in them the secret of calm expectation, the hope of eternal reunion.

John Ellerton

March 31

Behold what manner of love the Father has bestowed on us, that we should be called children of God!

1 JOHN 3:1 NKJV

Do think your prayers He does not heed?
He knows full well what you do need,
    And heaven and earth are His;
My Father and my God, who still
Is with my soul in every ill.

HANS SACHS

Behold and see your Lord your God that is your Maker, and your endless joy.... Behold and see what liking and bliss I have in your salvation...rejoice with me.

JULIAN OF NORWICH

Did not Jesus say, "I am the door of the sheepfold"? What to us is the sheepfold, dear children? It is the heart of the Father, where Christ is the Gate that is called Beautiful. O children, how sweetly and how gladly has He opened that door into the Father's heart, into the treasure-chamber of God! And there He unfolds to us the hidden riches, the nearness and the sweetness of companionship with Himself.

JOHN TAULER

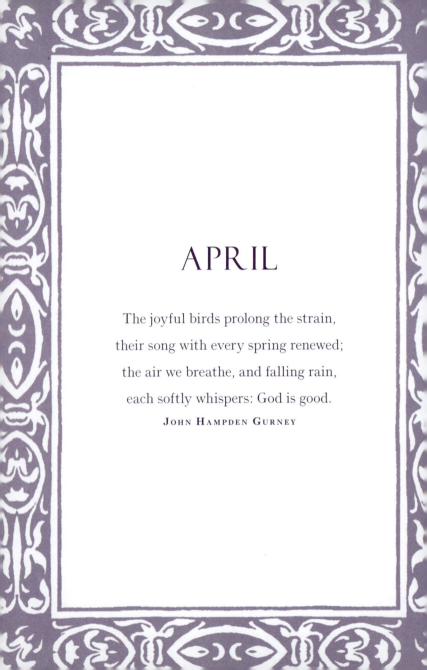

APRIL

The joyful birds prolong the strain,

their song with every spring renewed;

the air we breathe, and falling rain,

each softly whispers: God is good.

JOHN HAMPDEN GURNEY

April 1

If you keep yourself pure, you will be a special utensil for honorable use. Your life will be clean, and you will be ready for the Master to use you for every good work.

2 TIMOTHY 2:21 NLT

I am an instrument for His use; perhaps to bear burdens, as of pain, sorrow, or shame; perhaps to convey messages, writing, speaking, conversing; perhaps simply to reflect light, showing His mind in the commonest of all daily activities. In only one way can I truly do any of these: in the way of inner harmony with Him, and peace and joy in Him.

HANDLEY C. G. MOULE

Mold us, great God, into forms of beauty and usefulness...by the touch of Your hand. Fulfill Your ideal, and conform us to the image of Your Son. In Your great house may we stand as vessels for Your use. We are little better than common earthenware, but we can be cleansed, and offer refreshment to many parched and weary hearts.

F. B. MEYER

The soul which gives itself wholly and without reserve to God is filled with His own peace; and the closer we draw to our God, so much the stronger and more steadfast and tranquil will we become.

JEAN NICOLAS GROU

April 2

He that is faithful in that which is least is faithful also in much; and he that is unjust in the least is unjust also in much.

LUKE 16:10 KJV

You are to be perfect, as your heavenly Father is perfect.

MATTHEW 5:48 NASB

Perfection in outward conduct consists not in extraordinary things, but in doing common things extraordinarily well. Neglect nothing; the most trivial action may be performed to ourselves, or performed to God. If love is in your heart, your whole life may be one continual exercise of it. Oh, if we did but love others! How easily the least thing, the shutting of a door gently, the walking softly, speaking low, not making a noise, or the choice of a seat, so as to leave the most convenient to others, might become occasions of its exercise.

MERE ANGELIQUE ARNAULD

[God] is inclined to carry on His hidden dealings with the soul by means of what we should call very little things. He requires an absolute purity of heart in those with whom He expects to dwell, and a spirit of self-sacrifice which is ever ready to offer all things, however seemingly small, to Him.

ABBE GUILLORE

April 3

You owe me your very self.

PHILEMON 19 NIV

According to Christ's teaching, the priest and the Levite did not pay their debt to their Samaritan neighbor because they thought him a stranger with no claim on them. The rich man ignored his debt to Lazarus. We can all think of many debts—to the lonely whom we might visit, the misunderstood whom we might sympathize with, the ignorant whom we might teach. Is it not bewildering even to attempt to realize our debts? And yet, let us make a beginning, and all will be well. Let us steadily set ourselves to behave towards those whom we employ, or those who employ us, towards valets and shop assistants and others who minister to our convenience, as being men and women with the same right to courteous treatment, and to a real opportunity to make the best of themselves, as we have ourselves; let us thus realize our debts to our nearest "neighbors," and the whole idea of humanity, of brotherhood, will be deepened and made real to us. We will get a habit of considerateness and thoughtfulness for others as belonging to Christ, which will express itself habitually towards all.

CHARLES GORE

April 4

Let all who take refuge in you be glad; let them ever sing for joy. Spread your protection over them, that those who love your name may rejoice in you.

PSALM 5:11 NIV

I told them many things while I was with them in this world so they would be filled with my joy.

JOHN 17:13 NLT

God desires us to live as close as we can to the life that Jesus Christ lived. That is the broad avenue to perfect happiness. Most of us know by experience that in proportion as we have followed Him, we have found happiness. And we know by still larger experience that as we turn away from Him the world gets dark, and life ceases to be worth living.

GEORGE HODGES

Each soul has its own faculty; it can help in some way to make the world more cheerful and more beautiful. This is what makes life worth living. If we are living only for ourselves, our own amusement, luxury, advancement, life is not worth living. But if we are living as coworkers with Christ, as fellow-helpers with God, as part of the noble army of martyrs who bear witness to the truth in all time, then our lives are full of interest. This gives sweetness and strength to all our days.

JAMES FREEMAN CLARKE

April 5

It is good for me to draw near to God.

PSALM 73:28 KJV

And the sea of care grow still
In the shine of Your smile;
 And Your love's all-quickening ray
 Chases night and pain away,
That my heart grows light the while.

WOLFGANG CHRISTOPH DESSLER

If we believe that God is always at hand, always ready to hear,
surely we should take delight in telling Him all our little cares,
and woes, and hopes, as they flit by.

H. L. SIDNEY LEAR

If you have not much time at your disposal, do not fail to profit
by the smallest portions of time which are available to you. We do
not need much time in order to love God, to renew ourselves in His
Presence, to lift up our hearts towards Him, to worship Him in the
depths of our hearts, to offer Him what we do and what we suffer.

FRANÇOIS DE FÉNELON

April 6

We do not know how to pray as we should.

ROMANS 8:26 NASB

O Lord, hear; O Lord, forgive; O Lord, hearken and do; defer not, for thine own sake, O my God: for thy city and thy people are called by thy name.

DANIEL 9:19 KJV

Grant us not the ill
We blindly ask; in very love refuse
Whate'er You know our weakness would abuse.

JOHN KEBLE

We know not precisely what is best for us. We know not what will make us truly happy. We know not what will help us best in our struggle against temptations. And if *we* were to try to make a distinction between our mere passing wishes and that which our souls really needed, we should utterly fail. But we need not try. Let us take all our wishes, all our longings, all the promptings of our consciences, to the feet of our Father. He will hear and He will do. He will hear all we say. He will know what parts of our prayer are best for us to have, and what are not. And He will give us what His fatherly love will choose. And therefore to all our prayers we will add, "Your will be done in earth, as it is in heaven."

FREDERICK TEMPLE

April 7

When my spirit was overwhelmed within me, then You knew my path.

PSALM 142:3 NKJV

The work which we count so hard to do,
He makes it easy, for He works too;
The days that are long to live are His—
A bit of His bright eternities;
And close to our need His helping is.

SUSAN COOLIDGE

Do not yield to the temptation of looking at everything *at once,* as if everything would happen at once, and all the events of the day are crowded into an hour. Do not plan that way, but take each thing as it comes to you, and look upon it as the present expression of the will of God concerning you; then regard the next in the same way, and thus receive your day piece by piece from Him who will remember always when He gives you work to do, that you need strength to do it.

Often, when you have almost fainted in spirit, the thought comes, "If you have run with the footmen, and they have wearied you, what will you do with the horsemen?" Put it from you, it is a faithless thought; if you need more strength, you will have it, be sure of that, or the call to greater exertion may never come to you. Your business is with the present; leave the future in His hands, who will be sure to do the best, the very best for you.

PRISCILLA MAURICE

April 8

He is the Rock, his work is perfect: for all his ways are judgment: a God of truth and without iniquity, just and right is he.

DEUTERONOMY 32:4 KJV

We are his people, and the sheep of his pasture.

PSALM 100:3 KJV

Duties are ours, events are the Lord's; when our faith goes to meddle with events, and to hold a court (if I may so speak) upon God's providence, and begins to say, "How will You do this or that?" we lose ground; we have nothing to do there; it is our part to let the Almighty exercise His own office, and steer His own helm; there is nothing left us, but to see how we may be approved of Him, and how we may roll the weight of our weak souls, in well-doing, upon Him who is God omnipotent, and when what we try fails, it shall neither be our sin nor cross.

SAMUEL RUTHERFORD

Shall there be a mutiny among the flocks and herds, because their lord or their shepherd chooses their pastures, and allows them not to wander into deserts and unknown ways?

JEREMY TAYLOR

April 9

Ye know that he was manifested to take away our sins; and in him is no sin.

1 JOHN 3:5 KJV

They that sin are enemies to their own life.

TOBIT

To choose sin is to reject Christ; to be ashamed, for fear of man, to do what Christ commands is to deny Christ; to do, for fear of man, what Christ forbids, what is it but, with Pilate, to condemn Christ? For a Christian to be guilty of willful deadly sin, what is it but to crucify Christ afresh and put Him to an open shame? Do what you know to be pleasing to God, and avoid, by the grace of God, what you know will displease Him, and God will enliven your regret, and enlarge your faith, and brighten your hopes, and ignite your love. Only be *very* diligent, not knowingly doing anything which displeases God; be very diligent not to tamper with your conscience or do what you suspect may displease God.

EDWARD B. PUSEY

We can never cling to an impulsive sin with one hand, and grasp Jesus Christ with the other. Until you are content to reckon yourself dead indeed to every known form of sin, whether you think it small or great, you never can follow Jesus.

W. HAY M. H. AITKEN

April 10

Choose today whom you will serve.

JOSHUA 24:15 NLT

Barabbas and Jesus cannot both live within us. One must die. Yes, every emotion of selfishness or worldliness in every soul plays the part of Barabbas. Good influences may have prevailed for a time, and they, or perhaps motives of worldly regard, may have put Barabbas in prison, and under some restraint; but the decisive, the fatal question, remains, Shall he die? Yes, he or Jesus. Nor is it only on great occasions and in fearful crises that this question comes to us. Every hour, every moment, when we resist what we must know to be the influence of our Lord, and, casting that aside, give the victory, under whatever pretence or name, to that which is indeed our own Barabbas, we then do all that we are able to do to crucify our Lord afresh. Every emotion which tempts us to refuse obedience to Him, "to make insurrection," to suppress and overcome whatever sense of right conscience gives—is not that the robber, rebel, murderer, Barabbas? We may have, indeed, imprisoned him, we may have resolved that he should die— shall we now release him from restraint, and let him go free? If we do, we know now what must happen—we know between what alternatives we choose.

THEOPHILUS PARSONS

April 11

In Your name they rejoice all day long,
And in Your righteousness they are exalted.

PSALM 89:16 NKJV

Now first to souls who thus awake / Seems earth a fatherland
A new and endless life they take / With rapture from His hand.
The fears of death and of the grave / Are whelmed beneath the sea,
And every heart, now light and brave, / May face the things to be.

FRIEDRICH VON HARDENBERG

Happiness, let us understand this well, is as truly our portion here
as above; it cannot fail to fall within the lot of those who have
chosen for their portion Him whose nature is one with infinite,
unalienable joy. God, in communicating Himself to the soul, of
necessity communicates happiness; and all should, in union with
Him, have returned to their central rest, and are happy, in exact
proportion to the closeness and fullness of their union.

DORA GREENWELL

Happiness, heaven itself, is nothing else but a perfect conformity,
a cheerful and eternal compliance of all the powers of the soul with
the will of God.

SAMUEL SHAW

April 12

*Do not be afraid; I am the first and the last, and the living One;
and I was dead, and behold, I am alive forevermore, and I have
the keys of death and of Hades.*

REVELATION 1:17–18 NASB

Let all things seen and unseen,
    Their notes of gladness blend,
For Christ the Lord is risen,
    Our Joy that hath no end.

JOHN OF DAMASCUS

"The time of the singing of birds is come"—the time when nature
calls aloud to us and bids us awaken out of the deadness of
personal grief, and rejoice in the new manifestation of His beauty
that God is making to the world. "Behold, I am alive for evermore,
and the dead live to *Me*." Was not this the secret saying which the
new green growth was writing all over the hills, and which the
young pattering leaves and singing birds were repeating in music?
It must be well to have ears to hear and a heart that could respond
with a little flutter of returning joy and thankfulness.

ANNIE KEARY

The return of Easter should be to the Christian life the call of a
trumpet. It is the news of great victory. It is the solution of a great
perplexity. It is the assurance of a great triumph.

FREDERICK TEMPLE

April 13

You are controlled by the Spirit if you have the Spirit of God living in you. (And remember that those who do not have the Spirit of Christ living in them do not belong to him at all.)

ROMANS 8:9 NLT

What profits it that He is risen,
  If dead in sins you yet do lie?
If yet you cleave to your prison,
  What profit that He swells on high?
His triumph will avail you nought,
If you have ne'er the battle fought.

LYRA GERMANICA

Many, who often hear the gospel of Christ, are yet but little affected, because they are void of the Spirit of Christ. But whoever would fully and feelingly understand the word of Christ, must endeavor to make all their lives like, in its beauty, His. What will it benefit you to dispute profoundly the Trinity, if you are void of humility, and are therefore displeasing to the Trinity? Surely, lofty words do not make a man holy and just; but a virtuous life makes him dear to God. I had rather feel compunction than understand the definition of it. If you did know the whole Bible by heart and the sayings of all the philosophers, what would all that profit you without the love of God and without grace?

THOMAS À KEMPIS

April 14

Therefore, whether you eat or drink, or whatever you do,
do all to the glory of God.

1 CORINTHIANS 10:31 NKJV

Your glory alone, O God, be the end of all that I say;
Let it shine in every deed, let it kindle the prayers that I pray;
Let it burn in my innermost soul, till the shadows of self pass away.
And the light of Your glory, O God, be unveiled in the dawning
of day.

FREDERICK GEORGE SCOTT

We may stop at nothing short of all but our whole being. Doing,
thinking, willing, longing, having, loving, may be wrapped up,
gathered, and concentrated in the one will and good pleasure of
our God. Does any again ask, How can such little things be done to
the glory of God? Do them as you would do them if you saw Christ
by you.

EDWARD B. PUSEY

The time of labor does not with me differ from the time of prayer;
and, in the noise and confusion of the kitchen where I am at work,
while several persons are at the same time calling for different
things, I possess God in as great tranquility as if I were upon my
knees at the blessed sacrament.

BROTHER LAWRENCE

April 15

We know that when he appears, we shall be like him,
for we shall see him as he is.

1 John 3:2 niv

For if Christ be born within,
    Soon that likeness shall appear
Which the soul had lost through sin,
    God's own image fair and clear,
And the soul serene and bright
Mirror back His heavenly light.

Laurentius Laurenti

Lord, never was a magnet so powerful to draw to itself the hard
steel, as You, the Lord, lifted up on the cross, are powerful to draw
unto You the hearts of men. O beloved Lord, draw me through joy
and sorrow, from all that is in the world, to You and to Your cross;
form me, and shape me into Your image here below, that I may
enjoy You eternally in the glory whither You are gone.

Henry Suso

Think who Christ is, and what Christ is, and then think what His
personal influence must be—quite infinite, boundless, miraculous.
So that the very blessedness of heaven will not be merely the
sight of our Lord; it will be the being made holy, and kept holy,
by that sight.

Charles Kingsley

April 16

There are those who rebel against the light;
They do not know its ways
Nor abide in its paths.

JOB 24:13 NKJV

Your troops will be willing on your day of battle.

PSALM 110:3 NIV

See, in Your hands I lay them all—
My will that fails, my feet that fall,
My heart that wearies everywhere,
And finds Your yoke too hard to bear.

KATHARINE TYNAN HINKSON

The way may at times seem dark, but light will arise, if thou trust
in the Lord and wait patiently for Him. That light may sometimes
show hard things to be required, but do not be distressed if your
heart should rebel; bring your unwillingness and disobedience
to Him, in the faith that He will give the power to overcome, for
He cannot fail. "Greater is He that is in you, than he that is in
the world," so keep close to Him, and the victory will be won.
But do not, I beseech you, neglect anything that is required, for
disobedience brings darkness; and do not reason or delay, but
simply follow the leadings of the Holy Spirit, and He will guide you
into all peace.

ELIZABETH T. KING

April 17

Obey the commands of the LORD your God by walking in his ways and fearing him.

DEUTERONOMY 8:6 NLT

It came to pass, that, as they went, they were cleansed.

LUKE 17:14 KJV

God calls us to duty, and the only right answer is obedience. If it can be glad and willing and loving obedience, happy are we; but, in any case, whether we ourselves get enjoyment and blessing from the task or not, the call must be obeyed. The will of God must be done for the sake of God, not for the duty, and step by step God will provide the disposition.... Ideal obedience includes the whole will and the whole heart. We cannot begin with that. But we can begin with what we have. God calls. It is better to obey blunderingly than not to obey at all.

GEORGE HODGES

The test of love is not feeling, but obedience.

WILLIAM BERNARD ULLATHORNE

If one fights for good behavior, God makes one a present of the good feelings.

JULIANA H. EWING

April 18

Why are you in despair, O my soul?
And why are you disturbed within me?
Hope in God, for I shall again praise Him,
The help of my countenance and my God.

PSALM 43:5 NASB

In prayer we own You, Father, at our side,
Not always feel or taste You; and, 'tis well,
So, hour by hour, courageous faith is tried,
So gladlier will the morn all mists dispel.

JOHN KEBLE

Sometimes we are disturbed because we have no devout feelings;
but what we want is a devout will. We cannot always control the
imagination, but we can always do that which is our duty carefully
and patiently, with a view to pleasing God, and proving our love
to Him. We may feel cold and mechanical, but we cannot fulfill
our appointed duty without an exercise of the will, and therefore
all duties diligently performed testify a desire to love, and prove
our love.

H. L. SIDNEY LEAR

We must not allow ourselves to be cast down, nor to despair,
because our hearts seem colder at one time than another. The test
of the cold heart is the yielding to sin, and, if we are clinging to
Him, and to His will, we may be quite sure that what we take for
coldness of heart is a trial, not a treason.

FREDERICK TEMPLE

April 19

To do good and to communicate forget not: for with such sacrifices God is well pleased.

HEBREWS 13:16 KJV

Freely you have received, freely give.

MATTHEW 10:8 NKJV

Surely You have some work for me to do!
Oh, You, open my eyes,
To see how You would choose to have it done,
And where it lies!

ELIZABETH PRENTISS

Do not say you cannot gladden, elevate, and set free; that you have nothing of the grace of influence; that all you have to give is at the most only common bread and water. Give yourself to your Lord for the service of others with what you have. Cannot He change water into wine? Cannot He make stammering words to be instinct with saving power? Cannot He change trembling efforts to help into deeds of strength? Cannot He still, as of old, enable you in all your personal poverty to "make many rich"? God has need of you for the service of your fellow people. He has a work for you to do. To find out what it is, and then to do it, is at once your supremest duty and your highest wisdom. "Whatsoever He says unto you, do it."

GEORGE BODY

April 20

In the shelter of your presence you hide them.

PSALM 31:20 NIV

Let my life be hid in Thee,
    Life of life and light of light!
Love's illimitable sea,
    Depth of peace, of power the height!

Let my life be hid in Thee.
    From vexation and annoy;
Calm in Thy tranquility,
    All my mourning turned to joy.

JOHN BULL

It is small things that, just because of their smallness, distress and overset us. I mean the weight of daily care, which in their small details of personal expenditure, and in the careful routine of a household, and in the rearing of children, and in the society of friends, and in the outside duty, and in private affairs, singly and separately is sufficiently burdensome; but altogether, and on one set of shoulders, is sometimes felt to be more than the strength can bear. Those anxious lives, tempted to be fretful, and hasty, and self-important, and fussed with their incessant activities, may, if rightly interpreted, and manfully grasped, settle down into round and sunny centers of regular, and peaceful, and fruitful activities. Where there is prayer, there is a peace; and God, who makes every duty possible, knows, helps, and cares.

ANTHONY W. THOROLD

April 21

For the LORD your God is living among you.
He is a mighty savior.
He will take delight in you with gladness.
With his love, he will calm all your fears.
He will rejoice over you with joyful songs.

ZEPHANIAH 3:17 NLT

Made for Thyself, O God!
Made for Thy love, Thy service, Thy delight;
Made to show forth Thy wisdom, grace, and might;
Made for Thy praise, whom veiled archangels laud;
O strange and glorious thought, that we may be
A joy to Thee.

FRANCES RIDLEY HAVERGAL

It is not of God's severity that He requires much from us; it is of
His great kindness that He will have the soul to open itself wider,
to be able to receive much, that He may bestow much upon it. Let
no one think that it is hard to attain. Although it sounds hard,
and is hard at first, as touching the forsaking and dying to all
things, yet, when one has reached this state, no life can be easier,
or sweeter, of fuller of pleasures; for God is right diligent to be with
us at all seasons, and to teach us, that He may bring us to Himself,
when we are like to go astray. None of us ever desired anything
more ardently than God desires to bring men to the knowledge
of Himself.

J. TAULER

April 22

Look! I stand at the door and knock. If you hear my voice and open the door, I will come in, and we will share a meal together as friends.

REVELATION 3:20 NLT

O Love Divine!—whose constant beam
    Shines on the eyes that will not see,
And waits to bless us, while we dream
    Thou leavest us because we turn from Thee.

JOHN GREENLEAF WHITTIER

Unhappy spirit, cast down under your sins, multitudes of sins, years of sins!—heavily burdened as you are, and pierced through with sorrows, *you may look to God, and hope, for "He delights in mercy."* His mercy can make you a clean and beautiful, a happy and rejoicing spirit. God will be *"delighted"* to make you "equal to the angels." So humble, so loving is your God, and so earnestly does He long to bless you, that behold, *He stands at your door and knocks.*

JOHN PULSFORD

If God knocks continually at the heart of us, desiring to enter in and sup there, and to communicate to us His gifts, who can believe that when the heart opens and invites Him to enter, He will become deaf to the invitation, and refuse to come in?

LORENZO SCUPOLI

April 23

While your servant was busy here and there, he was gone.

1 KINGS 20:40 NKJV

Blessed are those who have regard for the weak;
the LORD delivers them in times of trouble.

PSALM 41:1 NIV

Comfort the fainthearted, uphold the weak, be patient with all.

1 THESSALONIANS 5:14 NKJV

It is decreed in the providence of God that, although the opportunities for doing good, which are in the power of every man, are beyond count or knowledge; yet, the opportunity once neglected, no man by any self-sacrifice can atone for those who have fallen or suffered by his negligence.

JULIANA H. EWING

Forgive us if this day we have done or said anything to increase the pain of the world. Pardon the unkind word, the impatient gesture, the hard and selfish deed, the failure to show sympathy and kindly help where we had the opportunity, but missed it; and enable us so to live that we may daily do something to lessen the tide of human sorrow, and add to the sum of human happiness.

F. B. MEYER

April 24

O Lord my God, I cried to You for help, and You healed me.

Psalm 30:2 nasb

It is sometimes a small matter that hinders and hides grace from us; at least if anything can be called small, and not rather a weighty matter, which obstructs so great a good.

And, if you remove this, be it great or small, and perfectly overcome it, you will have your desire.

For immediately, as soon as you give yourself to God from your whole heart, and seek neither this nor that, according to your own pleasure or will, but settle yourself wholly in Him, you will find yourself united and at peace; for nothing can bring so sweet a contentment, nothing be so delightful, as the good pleasure of the Divine Will.

Thomas à Kempis

If at any time this life of ours grows feeble, or low, or lonely, I know no other remedy than to return to its Eternal Source, to God Himself; and through Him all the means of grace become again living and true; and through Him all His creatures become again near and dear and accessible.

Elizabeth Rundle Charles

April 25

Truly I am full of power by the spirit of the LORD.

MICAH 3:8 KJV

You, who are kept by the power of God through faith unto salvation.

1 PETER 1:4–5 KJV

You must not look so much at the evil that is near, but rather at that which stands ready to pity and help—and which has pitied and helped your distressed soul, and will pity and help it again. Why is there a mercy-seat, but for the sinner to look towards in time of need? Be patient till the Lord's tender mercy and love visit you again; and then, look up to Him against this and such like snares, which would come between you and the appearance of the Lord's love that you may feel more of His presence with you, and of the sweet effects of that. For, these things are not to destroy you, but to teach you wisdom, which the Lord is able, through many exercises and sore trials, to bestow upon you; that your heart my be rid of all that burdens it. And filled with all it rightly desires after, in the proper season and goodness of the Lord.

ISAAC PENINGTON

April 26

Oh, that I had wings like a dove! For then would I fly away, and be at rest.

PSALM 55:6 KJV

They that wait upon the LORD shall renew their strength; they shall mount up with wings as eagles.

ISAIAH 40:31 KJV

Is there no way of escape for us when in trouble or distress? Must we just plod wearily through it all, and look for no relief? I rejoice to answer that there is a glorious way of escape for every one of us, if we will but mount up on wings, and fly away from it all to God. All creatures that have wings can escape from every snare that is set for them, if only they will fly high enough; and the soul that uses its wings can always find a sure "way to escape" from all that can hurt or trouble it. What then are these wings? Their secret is contained in the words "They that wait upon the Lord." The soul that waits upon the Lord is the soul that is entirely surrendered to Him, and that trusts Him perfectly. Therefore we might name our wings the wings of Surrender and of Trust. If we will only surrender ourselves utterly to the Lord, and will trust Him perfectly, we shall find our souls "mounting up with wings as eagles" to the "heavenly places" in Christ Jesus, where earthly annoyances or sorrows have no power to disturb us.

HANNAH WHITALL SMITH

April 27

The words of a wise man's mouth are gracious.

ECCLESIASTES 10:12 KJV

Worry weighs a person down;
an encouraging word cheers a person up.

PROVERBS 12:25 NLT

It would seem as if very few of us give this power of kind words the consideration which is due to it. So great a power, such a facility in the exercise of it, such a frequency of opportunities for the application of it, and yet the world still what it is, and we still what we are! It seems incredible. Take life all through, its adversity as well as its prosperity, its sickness as well as its health, its loss of its rights as well as its enjoyment of them, and we shall find that no natural sweetness of temper, much less any acquired philosophical equanimity, is equal to the support of the uniform habit of kindness. Nevertheless, with the help of grace, the habit of saying kind words is very quickly formed, and when once formed, it is not speedily lost. Sharpness, bitterness, sarcasm, acute observation, divination of motives—all these things disappear when a man is earnestly conforming himself to the image of Christ Jesus. The very attempt to be like our dearest Lord is already a wellspring of sweetness within us, flowing with an easy grace over all who come within our reach.

FREDERICK W. FABER

April 28

Jesus stood still, and commanded him to be called.

MARK 10:49 KJV

As we meet and touch, each day,
The many travelers on our way,
Let every such brief contact be
A glorious, helpful ministry;
The contact of the soil and seed,
Each giving to the other's need,
Each helping on the other's best,
And blessing, each, as well as blest.

SUSAN COOLIDGE

Do we not sometimes feel, in trial or perplexity, that others might
help us if they would only stop and listen? But they will not, and
in the constant hurry we know it is little use to speak. Let us note
the lesson for ourselves, and give what we ask—leisure to hear,
attentive, concentrated, not divided, calm, patient consideration.
It may be our busy work, as we think, for the master, which so
overcrowds our lives that we have not time for this "standing still."
Sad eyes meet ours, but we cannot stay to read their story. Some
look to us for help in battles which we fought long ago, but we
cannot turn aside to see how it fares with them in the strife, or to
whisper the secret of victory. But He would have said, even though
some plans of our own for His service were put aside, "Ye have
done it unto Me."

H. BOWMAN

April 29

Your kingdom come.
Your will be done
On earth as it is in heaven.

LUKE 11:2 NKJV

Thy Father reigns supreme above,
The glory of His name
Is grace and wisdom, truth and love,
His will must be the same.
And you have asked all joys in one,
In whispering forth, "Your will be done."

FRANCES RIDLEY HAVERGAL

In heaven God's will is *done*, and the Master teaches the child to ask that the will may be done on earth just as in heaven, in the spirit of adoring submission and ready obedience. Because the will of God is the glory of heaven, the doing of it is the blessedness of heaven. As the will is done, the kingdom of heaven comes into the heart.

ANDREW MURRAY

What is it you would have done, that He cannot do if He thinks fit? And if He thinks it is not fit, if you are one of His children, you will think with Him; you will reverence His wisdom, and rest satisfied with His will. This is believing indeed; the rolling all our desires and burdens over upon an almighty God; and where this is, it cannot choose but establish the heart in the midst of troubles, and give it a calm within in the midst of the greatest storms.

ROBERT LEIGHTON

April 30

Bless the LORD, O my soul,
And all that is within me, bless His holy name....
Who redeems your life from the pit,
Who crowns you with lovingkindness and compassion.

PSALM 103:1, 4 NASB

I desire that you should consider with firm faith that I, your most glorious God, who has created you for eternal blessedness, am eternal, sovereign, omnipotent.... You should seriously meditate that, in Me, your God, dwells the most perfect knowledge and infinite wisdom; so that in My overseeing of you, the heavens, and the earth, and the entire universe, I cannot be deceived in any way, or misled by any error. Were it otherwise, I should neither be all-wise, nor should I be God. Also consider attentively that, as I am your God, so am I infinitely good...love itself is My essence... therefore, I cannot will anything but that which is useful and beneficial to you and to all men; nor can I wish any evil to My creatures. Thus illuminated by the living light of faith, you will perceive that I, your God, have infinitely more knowledge, power, and preference to advance your happiness than you have. Therefore seek with all diligence to submit yourself totally to My will, so you shall live in continual tranquility of spirit, and shall have Me forever with you.

CATHERINE OF SIENA

MAY

Those who contemplate the beauty
of the earth find reserves of strength that will
endure as long as life lasts. There is symbolic
as well as actual beauty in the migration
of the birds, the ebb and flow of the tides,
the folded bud ready for the spring. There
is something infinitely healing in the repeated
refrains of nature—the assurance that dawn
comes after night, and spring after the winter.

RACHEL CARSON

May 1

He who says he abides in Him ought himself also to walk just as He walked.

1 John 2:6 nkjv

Since our way is troublesome and obscure, He commands us to notice His footsteps, tread where His feet have stood, and not only invites us forward by the argument of His example, but He has worn down much of the difficulty, and made the way easier and fit for our feet.

Jeremy Taylor

Do deeds of love for Him, to Him, following His steps.... Do the works of Christ, that your faith may live. You who say you abide in Christ ought to walk as He walked. If you seek your own glory, envy the prosperous, speak ill of the absent, do evil to him who injures you, this Christ did not do.

Edward B. Pusey

To know Christ is the way to grow in holiness. Christianity is not a religion of rules. It is the religion of the divine example. Try to follow the blessed steps of the most holy life. Take His advice. Ask yourself, in the moment of perplexity or temptation, what would He do if He were here? Nothing else will so surely lead us into the way of holy living.

George Hodges

May 2

But when the young man heard that saying, he went away sorrowful, for he had great possessions.

MATTHEW 19:22 KJV

We too, in our own way, have often a quiet impression that we are keeping all the commandments sufficiently, and inheriting the eternal life. One day a tremendous duty opens before us, and we are aghast at its hardness. What shall we do? What shall we answer? Is Christ deserving of everything from us, or only of part? It is a tremendous test which all cannot stand.

ANTHONY W. THOROLD

A great necessity is a great opportunity. Nothing is really lost by a life of sacrifice; everything is lost by failure to obey God's call. The opportunities of generously serving Jesus Christ are few; perhaps not more than one in a lifetime. They come, they do not return. What we do upon a great occasion will probably depend upon what we already are; what we are will be the result of previous years of self-discipline under the grace of Christ, or of the absence of it.

HENRY PARRY LIDDON

Things are not to be done by the effort of the moment, but by the preparation of past moments.

RICHARD CECIL

May 3

Who among you fears the LORD and obeys his servant?
If you are walking in darkness, without a ray of light,
trust in the LORD and rely on your God.

ISAIAH 50:10 NLT

The heart that yet can hope and trust,
And cry to You, though from the dust,
    Is all unconquered still.

PAUL GERHARDT

Stamp this upon your soul, for there is not such another charm
for all its fears and disquiet; therefore repeat it still with David,
sing this till it be stilled, and chide your distrustful heart into
believing: "Why are you cast down, O my soul, and why are you
disquieted within me? Hope in God, for I shall yet praise Him."
Though I am all out of tune for the present, never a right thing in
my soul, yet He will put forth His hand and change all, and *I shall
yet once again praise*, and therefore, even now, I will hope.

ROBERT LEIGHTON

Oh, that we could breathe out new hope, and new submission,
every day. Our waters are receding, and come neither to our
chin, nor to the stopping of our breath. I may see (if I would
borrow eyes from Christ) dry land, and it is near; why then should
we not laugh at adversity, and scorn our short-born and soon-
dying temptations?

SAMUEL RUTHERFORD

May 4

Nothing shall by any means hurt you.

LUKE 10:19 KJV

When you go through deep waters, I will be with you.
When you go through rivers of difficulty, you will not drown.
When you walk through the fire of oppression, you will not be
burned up; the flames will not consume you.

ISAIAH 43:2 NLT

Just as soon as we turn toward Him with loving confidence, and
say, "Your will be done," whatever chills or cripples or enslaves
our spirits, clogs their powers, or hinders their development, melts
away in the sunshine of His sympathy. He does not free us from
the pain, but from its power to dull the sensibilities; not from
poverty and care, but from their tendency to narrow and harden;
not from slander, but from the maddening poison in its sting; not
from disappointment, but from the hopelessness and bitterness
of thought which it so often brings about. We attain this perfect
liberty when we rise superior to adverse circumstances, triumph
over the pain and weakness of disease, over unjust criticism, the
wreck of sordid and selfish desire, every unhallowed longing, every
doubt of God's wisdom and love and kindly care, then we rise into
an atmosphere of undaunted moral courage, of restful content, of
child-like trust, of holy, all-conquering calm.

WILLIAM W. KINSLEY

May 5

My soul is in anguish. How long, O Lord, how long?
Turn, Lord, and deliver me; save me because of your
unfailing love.

Psalm 6:3–4 niv

I lay my head upon Your infinite heart,
I hide beneath the shelter of Your wing;
Pursued and tempted, helpless, I must cling
To You, my Father; bid me not depart,
For sin and death pursue, and Life is where You art!

Anonymous

Accustom yourself to commune with God, not with thoughts
deliberately formed to be expressed at a certain time, but with the
feelings with which your heart is filled. If you enjoy His presence,
and feel drawn by the attraction of His love, tell Him that you
delight in Him, that you are happy in loving Him, and that He is
very good to inspire so much affection in a heart so unworthy of
His love. But what shall you say in seasons of dryness, coldness,
weariness? Still say what you have in your heart. Tell God that
you no longer find His love within you, that you feel a terrible
void, that He wearies you, that His presence does not move you.
Say to Him, "O God, look upon my ingratitude, my inconstancy,
my unfaithfulness. Take my heart, for I cannot give it; and, when
You have it, oh, keep it, for I cannot keep it for You; and save me in
spite of myself."

François de Fénelon

May 6

Herein is love, not that we loved God, but that he loved us, and sent his Son to be the propitiation for our sins.

1 JOHN 4:10 KJV

I saw a little child, with bandaged eyes,
    Put up its hands to feel its mother's face;
She bent, and took the tender groping palms,
    And pressed them to her lips a little space.

I know a soul made blind by its desires,
    And yet its faith keeps feeling for God's face—
Bend down, O mighty Love, and let that faith
    One little moment touch Your lips of Grace.

ANNA J. GRANNISS

If I felt my heart as hard as a stone; if I did not love God, or man, or woman, or little child, I would yet say to God in my heart, "O God, see how I trust You, because You are perfect, and not changeable like me. I do not love You. I love nobody. I am not even sorry for it. You see how much I need You to come close to me, to put Your arm round me, to say to me, *my child*; for the worse my state, the greater my need of my Father who loves me. Come to me, and my day will dawn; my love will come back, and, Oh! How I shall love You, my God! And know that my love is Your love, my blessedness Your being."

GEORGE MACDONALD

May 7

The life of Jesus will be evident in our dying bodies.

2 Corinthians 4:11 NLT

The fretting friction of our daily life,
    Heart-weariness with loving patience borne;
The meek endurance of the inward strife,
    The painful crown of thorn,

Prepare the heart for God's own dwelling-place,
    Adorn with sacred loveliness His shrine,
And brighten every inconspicuous grace,
    For God alone to shine.

Mary E. Atkinson

God has a purpose for each one of us, a work for each one to do, a place for each one to fill, an influence for each one to exert, a likeness to His dear Son for each one to manifest, and then, a place for each one to fill in His holy Temple.

Arthur C. A. Hall

The surest method of arriving at a knowledge of God's eternal purposes about us is to be found in the right use of the present moment. God's will does not come to us in the whole, but in fragments, and generally in small fragments. It is our business to piece it together, and to *live* it into one orderly vocation.

F. W. Faber

May 8

It came to pass, while he blessed them, he was parted from them, and carried up into heaven.

LUKE 24:51 KJV

Lift up our thoughts, lift up our songs,
And let Your grace be given,
That while we linger here below,
Our hearts may be in heaven.

C. F. ALEXANDER

The parting blessing of our Lord was changed in the moment of its utterance into a pledge of eternal love, of unfailing and ever-watchful care for the well-being of His people.

JOHN ELLERTON

When the living presence of Jesus was taken away from His own, it was not that they were to have Him less, but in a lovelier, in a more divine way. For when He rose up to heaven, He took there with Him, all their hearts, and all their minds, and all their love. So is it with us. He is gone up to heaven, into the bosom of the Father, into the Father's heart of love, and we ascend up there with Him, with all our hearts, and all our love, and rest where He rests, in the Father's heart. *There* there is no separation, but one life, one existence, as He is one with the Father. And thus it is that being one with Him we can be as clear, bright mirrors that reflect His glory.

HENRY SUSO

May 9

If we live in the Spirit, let us also walk in the Spirit.

GALATIANS 5:25 KJV

No, my dear Lord, in following Thee,
Not in the dark, uncertainly,
    This foot obedient moves;
It is with a Brother and a King,
    Who many to His yoke will bring;
Who ever lives and ever loves.

JOHN GAMBOLD

If we are so led by the Spirit, where we go, and what we do,
is of comparatively little moment; we may be forced by the
circumstances of our life into surroundings that seem full of
peril, but if God sent us there, such surroundings can do us no
harm, though they may dull our *feeling* of happiness. Only let
us remember that if, by God's mercy, we are free agents, and
can choose our own way of life, then it is simple mockery to talk
of aspirations for the higher life, if we deliberately indulge our
baser nature by living in an atmosphere of worldliness, or by
doing something which is, perhaps, quite innocent for others, but
consciously works us harm.

GEORGE H. WILKINSON

May 10

For our citizenship is in heaven.

PHILIPPIANS 3:20 NASB

Green are the fields of the earth, holy and sweet her joys;
Take, and taste, and be glad—as fruit and blossom and bird,
But still as an exile, Soul; then, he, with a singing voice,
For the stars and sun and sweet heaven, whose ultimate height is in
the Lord!
Ripe, lovely, and glad, you shall grow in the light of His face and
His word.

KATHARINE TYNAN HINKSON

Stand still awhile, and seriously consider the noble end for which
you were created, and for which God has placed you in this world!
You were not created for time and the creature, but for God and
eternity, and to employ yourself with God and eternity. And you
are in the world, to the end that you may give blessedness, from
which you have turned yourself away by sin; in order that you may
become thoroughly sanctified and enlightened, and that God may
have joy, delight, peace, and pleasure in you, and you in God.

GERHARD TERSTEEGEN

[Pray] that prayer taught by the saints, "Make me reach, my God,
the degree of holiness to which You did call me in creating me!"

LADY GEORGIANA FULLERTON

May 11

I know whom I have believed, and am persuaded that he is able to keep that which I have committed unto him against that day.

2 TIMOTHY 1:12 KJV

Let me Thy power, Thy beauty see;
So shall the hopeless labor cease,
And my free heart shall follow Thee
Through paths of everlasting peace.
My strength Thy gift—my life Thy care—
I shall forget to seek elsewhere
The wealth to which my soul is heir.

ANNA L. WARING

To give heart and mind to God, so that they are ours no longer, to do good without being conscious of it, to pray ceaselessly and without effort as we breathe, to love without stopping to reflect upon our feelings—such is the perfect forgetfulness of self, which casts us upon God, as a babe rests upon its mother's breast.

JEAN NICOLAS GROU

Abiding in Jesus is not a work that needs each moment of the mind to be engaged, or the affections to be directly and actively occupied with it. It is an entrusting of oneself to the keeping of the Eternal Love, in the faith that it will abide near us, and with its holy presence watch over us and ward off the evil, even when we have to be most intently occupied with other things. And so the heart has rest and peace and joy in the consciousness of being kept when it cannot keep itself.

ANDREW MURRAY

May 12

Who gave himself for us, that he might redeem us from all iniquity, and purify unto himself a peculiar people, zealous of good works.

TITUS 2:14 KJV

Love only can the conquest win,
    The strength of sin subdue;
Come, O my Savior, cast out sin,
    And from my soul anew.

CHARLES WESLEY

Living and victorious faith is found when Christ dwells in our hearts. But Christ will not dwell in our hearts if we fill our hearts with things which He hates. Yet, is there then no victory, nor real faith, when the world holds a struggle with us, sometimes overcoming us, sometimes overcome? In some things victory should be complete at once. Sins of infirmity there may be; sins against light there should not be. To do willfully and knowingly what God hates destroys faith, and hope, and love. But so you are fighting against your besetting sin, if you are conquering yourself, you are still Christ's soldier, even though in thought, word, or deed, you are, from time to time, in lesser things surprised. This, then, is a matter of faith, that if we will, we can, by the grace of God, prevail over every temptation.

EDWARD B. PUSEY

May 13

Your statutes are my heritage forever; they are the joy of my heart.

PSALM 119:111 NIV

Bound with the love of God on every side,
Breathing that love as heaven's own healing air,
I work or wait, still following my Guide,
Braving each foe, escaping every snare.

HORATIUS BONAR

The Lord preserves us near to Himself, out of that which separates from Him and weakens; and nothing shall be able to interrupt our joy in the Lord, nor our delight and pleasure in His will.

ISAAC PENINGTON

It is easy to make great sacrifices when God does not ask them, but to give up our own will in each detail of life is something far harder. And this is what He *does* ask: To hold ourselves ever in readiness for His bidding, to count no token of it too slight—such is His call to each. Thus only shall we be ready for further service if He sees fit to lead us on to it.

H. BOWMAN

To live in the Spirit is the right condition of man, his normal condition; and to live in the Spirit is to live with God—hearing Him, and knowing Him, and loving Him, and delighting to do His will.

THOMAS ERSKINE

May 14

O my people, trust in him at all times. Pour out your heart to him, for God is our refuge.

PSALM 62:8 NLT

From tedious toil, from anxious care,
Dear Lord, I turn again to Thee;
Thy presence and Thy smile to share
Makes every burden light to me.

RAY PALMER

It is a good thing to have fixed seasons for lifting up the heart to God, not merely the appointed hours of prayer, but a momentary act before and after meals, beginning any occupation, entering into society, leaving the house, etc. Especially it is a help to make such brief acts after having said or done anything either wrong or foolish, after any trifling irritation or disappointment, when the spirit feels, it may be, wounded or desolate, or when one's vanity is annoyed at having been guilty of some little folly or blunder. Sometimes we are more really troubled and sore at trivialities of this sort than at far weightier things. But if all such things were met with a momentary uplifting of the heart to God, all these little frailties and worries would tend to mold the character more and more to God's pattern, and they would assuredly lose their sting; for he who thinks much of God will daily think less of himself.

H. L. SIDNEY LEAR

May 15

You have been my defense and refuge in the day of my trouble.

PSALM 59:16 NKJV

Commit your way to God, / The weight which makes you faint;
Worlds are to Him no load, / To Him breathe your complaint.
Up! Up! The day is breaking, / Say to thy cares, good-night!
Your troubles from you shaking, / Like dreams in day's fresh light.

PAUL GERHARDT

When you find yourself, as I dare say you sometimes do,
overpowered as it were by melancholy, the best way is to go out,
and do something kind to somebody or other.

JOHN KEBLE

Do not give way to depression, but resign yourself to our dear
Lord with the object of bearing bravely the discomforts and petty
contradictions of this life.

CHARLES DE CONDREN

Never suffer yourself to be subdued by melancholy; it is amongst
the things that will most injure you. It is impossible to persevere in
the path of holiness, if we give not ourselves to it with joy. The love
of God should impart peace to the soul.

MADAME GUYON

May 16

My flesh and my heart may fail,
But God is the strength of my heart and my portion forever.

PSALM 73:26 NASB

O, little heart of mine! shall pain
    Or sorrow make you moan,
When all this God is all for you,
    A Father and your own.

FREDERICK W. FABER

Make allowance for infirmities of the flesh, which are purely
physical. To be fatigued, body and soul, is not sin; to be in
"heaviness" is not sin. Christian life is not a feeling; it is a
principle. When your hearts will not *fly*, let them *go*, and if they
"will neither fly nor go," be sorry for them and patient with them,
and take them to Christ, as you would carry your little lame child
to a tender-hearted, skillful surgeon. Does the surgeon, in such a
case, upbraid the child for being lame?

ELIZABETH PRENTISS

When you feel ill and indisposed, and when in this condition your
prayer is cold, heavy, filled with despondency, and even despair,
do not be disheartened or despairing, for the Lord knows your
sick and painful condition. Struggle against your infirmity, pray
as much as you have strength to, and the Lord will not despise the
infirmity of your flesh and spirit.

JOHN ILYICH SERGIEFF

May 17

Through God we will do valiantly,
For it is He who shall tread down our enemies.

PSALM 60:12 NKJV

Create in me a clean heart, O God; and renew a right spirit
within me.

PSALM 51:10 KJV

If any man compares his own soul with the picture drawn in
the New Testament of what a Christian ought to be; if any man
fixes his eye on the pattern of self-sacrifice, of purity, of truth, of
tenderness, and measures his own distance from the standard,
he might be ready to despair. But fear not, because you are far
from being like the pattern set before you; fear not, because your
faults are painful to think of; continue the battle and fear not. If
indeed you are content with yourself, and are making no endeavor
to rise above the poor level at which you now stand, then there
is reason to fear. But if you are fighting with all your might, fear
not, however often you may have fallen, however deeply, however
ungratefully, however inexcusably. This one thing we can give, and
this is what He asks: hearts that shall never cease from this day
forward, till we reach the grave, to strive to be more like Him; to
come nearer to Him; to root out from within us the sin that keeps
us from Him. To such a battle, brethren, I call you in His name.

FREDERICK TEMPLE

May 18

May the Lord make you increase and abound in love to one another and to all, just as we do to you.

1 Thessalonians 3:12 NKJV

If we love God, we know what loving is,
    For love is God's, He sent it to the earth,
        Half-human, half-divine, all glorious—
Half-human, half-divine, but wholly His;
    Not loving God, we know not love's true worth,
        We taste not the great gift He gave to us.

Maurice Francis Egan

Let us see that whenever we have failed to be loving, we have also failed to be wise; that whenever we have been blind to our neighbor's interests, we have also been blind to our own; whenever we have hurt others, we have hurt ourselves still more. Let us, at this blessed time of Pentecost, ask forgiveness of God for all acts of malice and uncharitableness, blindness and hardness of heart; and pray for the spirit of true charity, which alone is true wisdom. And let us come to Holy Communion in charity with each other and with all; determined henceforth to feel for each other, and with each other; to put ourselves in our neighbors' places; to see with their eyes, and to feel with their hearts, so much so that God shall give us that great grace; determined to make allowances for their mistakes and failings; to give and forgive, even as God gives and forgives, for ever, that so we may be indeed the children of our Father in heaven, whose name is Love.

Charles Kingsley

May 19

Be renewed in the spirit of your mind, and...put on the new man which was created according to God, in true righteousness and holiness.

Ephesians 4:23–24 NKJV

Be constant, O happy soul, be constant, and of good courage; for, however intolerable you are to yourself, yet you will be protected, enriched, and beloved by that greatest Good, as if He had nothing else to do than to lead you to perfection by the highest steps of love; and if you do not turn away, but persevere constantly, know that you offer to God the most acceptable sacrifice. If, from the chaos of nothing, His omnipotence has produced so many wonders, what will He do in your soul, created after His own image and likeness, if you keep constant, quiet, and resigned?

Miguel de Molinos

Would you feel your soul's rest in Christ? You must know His voice, hear it, learn daily of Him, become His disciple; take up, from *His* nature, what is contrary to *your* nature. And then, as your nature is worn out, and His nature comes up in you, you will find all easy, all that is of life easy, and transgression hard— unbelief hard. Yes, you will find it very hard and unnatural, when His nature is grown up in you, either to distrust the Lord or listen to His enemy.

Isaac Penington

May 20

He hath chosen us in Him before the foundation of the world,
that we should be holy and without blame before Him in love.

EPHESIANS 1:4 KJV

O Love, who formed me to wear
    The image of Thy Godhead here;
Who sought me with tender care
    Through all my wanderings wild and drear;
        O Love! I give myself to Thee,
        Thine ever, only Thine to be.

JOHANN SCHEFFLER

We live not for ourselves, but for God, for some purpose of His,
for some special end to be accomplished, which He has willed to
be accomplished by oneself, and not by another; something which
will be left undone, if we do it not, or not be done as it would have
been done, if the one ordained to it had done it. We live gifted with
certain forms of spiritual grace embodied in us, for some purpose
to Divine Love to be fulfilled by us, some idea of the Divine Mind
to be imaged forth in our creaturely state. To devote oneself to
God is to concentrate the powers of one's being to their ordained
end, and therefore to have the happiest and truest life; happiest,
because happiness must be in accordance of these powers with the
law of their creation, and truest, because the attainment of the
highest glory must be in the accomplishment of the end for which
we were created.

T. T. CARTER

May 21

God...will render to each person according to His deeds: to those who by perseverance in doing good seek for glory and honor and immortality, eternal life.

ROMANS 2:5–7 NASB

Thus would I press on to the glory,
    A knight in the army of God,
Whose march will be onward and forward,
    Because of the foes on the road.
Before me the guerdon You give,
    My glorious eternal reward,
And with me Your peace and Your wisdom,
    Because of the Cross of the Lord.

HENRY SUSO

If He calls you to a kind of service which is according to His will but not according to your taste, you must not go to it with less, rather with more courage and energy than if your taste coincided with His will. The less of self and self-will there is in anything we do, the better. You must not amuse yourself with going from side to side, when duty calls you straight on; nor make difficulties, when the real thing is to get over them. Let your heart be full of courage, and then say, "I shall succeed. Not I, but the grace of God which is with me."

FRANCIS DE SALES

May 22

Never be lazy, but work hard and serve the Lord enthusiastically.

ROMANS 12:11 NLT

Let us begin from this moment to acknowledge Him in all our ways, and do everything, whatsoever we do, as service to Him and for His glory, depending upon Him alone for wisdom, and strength, and sweetness, and patience, and everything else that is necessary for the right accomplishing of all our living. It is not so much a change of acts that will be necessary, as a change of motive and of dependence. The house will be kept, or the children cared for, or the business transacted, perhaps, just the same as before as to the outward, but inwardly God will be acknowledged, and depended on, and served; and there will be all the difference between a life lived at ease in the glory of His Presence, and a life lived painfully and with effort apart from Him. There will result also from this bringing of God into our affairs a wonderful accession of divine wisdom in the conduct of them, and a far greater quickness and dispatch in their accomplishment, a surprising increase in the fertility of resource, and an enlargement on every side that will amaze the formerly cramped and confined soul.

HANNAH WHITALL SMITH

May 23

When I sit in darkness, the LORD shall be a light unto me.

MICAH 7:8 KJV

When doubts disturb my troubled breast,
    And all is dark as night to me,
Here, as on solid rock, I rest—
    That so it seemeth good to Thee.

RAY PALMER

When trouble, restless fears, anxious fretfulness strive to overpower the soul, our safety is in saying, "My God, I believe in Your perfect goodness and wisdom and mercy. What You do I cannot now understand, but I shall one day see it all plainly. Meanwhile I accept Your will, whatever it may be, unquestioning, without reserve." There would be no restless disturbance, no sense of utter discomfort and discomposure in our souls, if we were quite free from any—it may be almost unconscious—opposition to God's will. But we do struggle against it, we do resist; and so long as that resistance endures we cannot be at peace. Peace, and even joy, are quite compatible with a great deal of pain—even mental pain— but never with a condition of antagonism of resistance.

H. L. SIDNEY LEAR

Let him set his heart firmly upon this resolution: "I will bear it inevitably, and I will, by God's grace, do it nobly."

JEREMY TAYLOR

May 24

Show me where to walk, for I give myself to you.

PSALM 143:8 NLT

I will counsel you with My eye upon you.

PSALM 32:8 NASB

Teach me to do the thing that pleases You;
You are my God, in You I live and move;
Oh, let Your loving Spirit lead me forth
Into the land of righteousness and love.

J. S. B. MONSELL

The minds that are alive to every word from God give constant
opportunity for His divine interference with a suggestion that may
alter the courses of their lives; and, like the ships that turn when
the steersman's hand but touches the helm, God can steer them
through the worst dangers by the faintest breath of feeling, or the
lightest touch of thought.

RICHARD H. HUTTON

It is no delusion, no dream of a fevered brain, no error of a too
confiding soul that has made the children of God delight to trust
in His Providential aid. When God, in deed and in truth, is *present*
and *dominant* in the soul of man, He can, and He will, give to
that soul a real guidance. He will guide it, with the guidance of
an eye that sees and foresees—that knows what is best for us and
the world, and leads us in that way where, for our sakes, and the
world's, it is best for us to go.

HENRY SEPTIMUS SUTTON

May 25

Serve the LORD with gladness.... For the LORD is good; His mercy is everlasting, and His truth endures to all generations.

PSALM 100:2, 5 NKJV

Teach me Thy love to know;
    That this new light which now I see,
May both the work and workman show:
    Then by a sunbeam I will climb to Thee.

GEORGE HERBERT

Why should we not rejoice in the things of God? If the day is pure and serene, we enjoy its gladness. Why should we not rejoice in the serene light of truth that shines from heaven upon us? We find a joy in the presence and cheerful greeting of our friends. Why should we not look up to heaven whence so many pure and most loving faces look upon us with divine affection, and with most tender desires to cheer and help us? Having an almighty and most loving Father, in whom we live, and move, and have our being, let us rejoice in Him. Having a most loving Savior who has made Himself our brother, and feeds us with His life, we ought surely to rejoice in Him. Having the Holy Spirit of God with us, making us His temples, and pouring His love into our hearts, we ought certainly to answer His love, and rejoice in His overflowing goodness. "Rejoice in the Lord always, and again I say Rejoice."

WILLIAM BERNARD ULLATH

*Blessed are all who fear the L*ORD*, who walk in obedience to him....*
Blessings and prosperity will be yours.

PSALM 128:1–2 NIV

We think it a gallant thing, to be fluttering up to heaven with our
wings of knowledge and speculation; whereas the highest mystery
of a divine life here, and of perfect happiness hereafter, consists
in nothing but mere obedience to the divine will. Happiness is
nothing but that inward sweet delight, which will arise from the
harmonious agreement between our wills and the will of God.
There is nothing in the whole world able to do us good or hurt, but
God, and our own will: neither riches nor poverty, nor disgrace nor
honor, nor life nor death, nor angels nor devils; but willing, or not
willing, as we ought.

RALPH CUDWORTH

The one misery of man is self-will, the one secret of blessedness
is the conquest over our own wills. To yield them up to God is
rest and peace. What disturbs us in this world is not "trouble,"
but our opposition to trouble. The true source of all that worries
and irritates, and wears away our lives, is not in external things,
but in the resistance of our wills to the will of God expressed by
external things.

ALEXANDER MACLAREN

May 27

O LORD, You are our Father,
We are the clay, and You our potter;
And all of us are the work of Your hand.

ISAIAH 64:8 NASB

To be conformed to the image of his Son.

ROMANS 8:29 KJV

He who has appointed you your task will proportion it to your strength, and your strength to the burden which He lays upon you. He who makes the seed grow you know not how, and see not, will, you know not how, ripen the seed which He has sown in your heart, and raise you by the secret workings of His good Spirit. You may not see the change yourself, but He will gradually change you, make you another person. Only yield yourself to His molding hand, as clay to the potter, having no wishes of your own, but seeking in sincerity, however faint, to have His will fulfilled in you, and He will teach you what to pray for, and will give you what He teaches you. He will retrace His own image on you line by line, erasing by His grace and gracious discipline the marks and spots of sin which have defaced it.

EDWARD B. PUSEY

May 28

A new commandment I give to you, that you love one another;
as I have loved you, that you also love one another.

JOHN 13:34 NKJV

One with our brethren here in love,
  And one with saints that are at rest,
And one with angel hosts above,
  And one with God forever blest.

ISAAC WILLIAMS

All extreme sensitivities, fastidiousness, suspicion, readiness to
take offense, and tenacity of what we think our due, come from
self-love, as does the unworthy secret gratification we sometimes
feel when another is humbled or mortified; the cold indifference,
the harshness of our criticism, the unfairness and hastiness of
our judgments, our bitterness towards those we dislike, and
many other faults must more or less rise up before most men's
conscience when they question…how far they do indeed love their
neighbors as Christ has loved them. He will root out all dislikes
and aversions, all readiness to take offense, all resentments, all
bitterness, from the heart which is given up to His guidance. He
will infuse His own tender love for mankind into His servant's
mind, and teach them to "love one another as [Christ] has
loved you."

JEAN NICOLAS GROU

May 29

They are before the throne of God and serve him day and night in his temple; and he who sits on the throne will spread his tent over them.

REVELATION 7:15 NIV

So many worlds, so much to do,
    So little done, such things to be,
    How know I what had need of thee,
For thou were strong as thou were true?

ALFRED, LORD TENNYSON

You are still in the quarry and not complete, and therefore to you, as once to us, much is inexplicable. But you are destined for a higher building and one day you will be placed in it by hands not human, a living stone in a heavenly temple.

L. B. COWMAN

God has a will to be done not in earth only, but also in heaven; they are not dismissed from the King's business who are called from the camp to the Court, from being common soldiers to being the most trusted advisors.

ABRAHAM CHEARE

May 30

We pray always for you, that our God would count you worthy of this calling, and fulfil all the good pleasure of his goodness, and the work of faith with power.

2 Thessalonians 1:11 KJV

Thou settest us each task divine,
We bless that helping hand of Thine,
    That strength by Thee bestowed.
Thou minglest in the glorious fight;
Thine own the cause! Thine own the might!
    We serve the Living God.

Thomas H. Gill

Every hard effort generously faced, every sacrifice cheerfully submitted to, every word spoken under difficulties, raises those who speak or act or suffer to a higher level; endows them with a clearer sight of God; braces them with a will of more strength and freedom; warms them with a generous and large and tender heart.

Henry P. Liddon

A man's best desires are always the index and measure of his possibilities; and the most difficult duty that a man is capable of doing is the duty that above all he should do.

Charles H. Brent

May 31

When you call, the LORD will answer. "Yes, I am here," he will quickly reply.

ISAIAH 58:9 NLT

Ever quickly Thou do hear
    Thy children's feeble cry,
And do keep them everywhere
    Beneath Thy watchful eye;
And 'midst the worlds that lean on Thee
Thou has faithful thoughts of me.

ANONYMOUS

"He will be very gracious unto thee at the voice of thy cry." That has comforted me often, more than any promise or answer; it includes answers, and a great deal more besides; it tells us what He is towards us, and that is more than what He will *do*. And the "cry" is not long, connected, thoughtful prayers; a cry is just an *unworded dart upwards* of the heart, and at *that* "voice" He will be very gracious. What a *smile* there is in these words!

FRANCES RIDLEY HAVERGAL

He that has not yet tempted you above your strength will continue so to the end. If, for a time, He hides His face from you, yet He does it but for a moment, to make you the more heartily to cry to Him; and surely He will hear you, not only when you are in crying, but also while you are in thinking how to cry. He is with you in trouble, and will indeed deliver you.

JOHN BRADFORD

JUNE

Not every day of our lives is overflowing with
joy and celebration. But there are moments
when our hearts nearly burst within us
for the sheer joy of being alive. The first sight
of our newborn babies, the warmth of love
in another's eyes, the fresh scent of rain
on a hot summer's eve—moments like these
renew in us a heartfelt appreciation for life.

GWEN ELLIS

June 1

Until now you have not asked for anything in my name.
Ask and you will receive, and your joy will be complete.

JOHN 16:24 NIV

God's "ask"
Means all fullness and all grace,
Access in every time and place;
        Yet we
To whom this mercy is so free,
    This privilege of light to bask
In the full sunshine of His face,
    Regard prayer even as a task.

ANNA E. HAMILTON

There is some power we have not yet discovered, some secret as yet
unknown—but oh! what a marvelous power! what a blessed secret!
that can make the Christian life a life of love, and trust, and bright
serenity; something different from the duty-life, which, though
real, does not satisfy; having all the activity and earnestness of
the duty-life, but having with it the peace and joy which many and
many a soul is craving.

WILLIAM R. HUNTINGTON

We do not value as we ought our inestimable privilege of being
allowed to worship God. We do not prize our heavenly prerogative
of being permitted to keep His commandments. We look at that as
an obligation which is more properly a boon.

FREDERICK W. FABER

June 2

You will be considered worthy of the kingdom of God,
for which indeed you are suffering.

2 THESSALONIANS 1:5 NASB

Fear not, for He has sworn;
    Faithful and true His name;
The glorious hours are onward born;
    'Tis lit, th'immortal flame;
It glows *around* you; kneel, and strive, and win
Daily one living ray—'twill brighter glow within.

JOHN KEBLE

Count that day lost (though you may have dispatched much
business) in which you have neither gained some victory over your
own evil inclinations and your self-will, nor returned thanks to
your Lord for His mercies.

LORENZO SCUPOLI

Between dawn and dark there is time enough for collisions of
disinterestedness with selfishness in our dealings with our fellow-
creatures, in the life of our own homes; time enough to meet or to
evade the demands of homely faithfulness in our various work,
time enough to confront the sturdy rebellion of passions and
besetting sins against our spiritual nature, time enough to win or
to lose heaven in.

HENRY WILDER FOOTE

June 3

All things are yours; whether Paul, or Apollos, or Cephas,
or the world, or life, or death, or things present, or things to come;
all are yours; and ye are Christ's; and Christ is God's.

1 CORINTHIANS 3:21–23 KJV

Mark those people whose life is hidden in God, so that of
themselves they make no account. Thus can they delight
themselves fully and freely in all that which God is doing, apart
from the thought of themselves; and to them therefore it is true
that heaven and earth are theirs, and all things are theirs, and
fulfill their will, because the will of God is their will. And their cup
overflows with joy even here below, because in all things they have
a joy and delight that is steadfast and full. While they walk with
God, all is peace. For in Him sorrow is not sorrow, and pain is not
pain, but all is peace and rest, all that God wills, to them is sweet
and pleasant. Or is it only that to them the will of God is sweet?
It is more than this. For to them He gives the fair sunshine of His
comfort, and the blessed joy of heaven, even here below. So that
they live already as it were in heaven.

HENRY SUSO

June 4

Blessed are those who trust in the LORD and have made the LORD their hope and confidence.

JEREMIAH 17:7 NLT

Thus will I live and walk from day to day,
     Contented, trustful, satisfied, and still;
What life so shielded, or what life so free,
     As that within the center of Your will!

JANE WOODFALL

Follow Christ in the denial of *all that wills of self,* and then all is put away that separates you from God; the heaven-born new creature will come to life in you, which alone knows and enjoys the things of God.

WILLIAM LAW

Divine tranquility grows from the life of God in the soul, which is the same as the life of pure love. Why should a soul be otherwise than tranquil, which seeks for nothing but what comes in the providence of God; and which, forgetful of self, has nothing to do but to love? It has an innate conviction, strong as the everlasting foundations, that, if there is a God above us, all is well, *all must be well.*

THOMAS C. UPHAM

June 5

Now I urge you to take heart.

ACTS 27:22 NKJV

I will be glad and rejoice in you; I will sing praise to your name, O Most High.

PSALM 9:2 NIV

If you have a murmuring spirit, you cannot have true cheerfulness; it will generally show in your countenance and your voice. Some little fretfulness or restlessness of tone will betray it. Your cheerfulness is forced, it does not spring up freely and healthily out of your heart, which it can only do when that is truly at rest in God; when you are satisfied with His ways, and wishing no change in them. When this is truly your case, then your heart and mind are free, and you can rejoice in spirit.

PRISCILLA MAURICE

Let us seek the grace of a cheerful heart, an even temper, sweetness, gentleness, and brightness of mind, as walking in His light, and by His grace. Let us pray to Him to give us the spirit of ever-abundant, ever-springing love, which overpowers and sweeps away the vexations of life by its own richness and strength, and which, above all things, unites us to Him who is the fountain and the center of all mercy, loving kindness, and joy.

JOHN HENRY NEWMAN

June 6

I will run the course of Your commandments,
for You shall enlarge my heart.

PSALM 119:32 NKJV

I honor and love your commands. I meditate on your decrees.

PSALM 119:48 NLT

Love is higher than duty. But the reason is that love in reality contains duty in itself. Love without a sense of duty is a mere delusion, from which we cannot too soon set ourselves free. Love is duty and something more.

FREDERICK TEMPLE

Think not anything little, wherein we may fulfill His commandments. It is in the midst of common and ordinary duties that our life is placed; common occupations make up our lives. By faith and love we obey; but by obedience are the faith and love, which God gives us, strengthened. Then shall we indeed love our Lord, when we seek to please Him in all things, [when we] speak or are silent, sleep or wake, labor or rest, do or suffer with a single eye to His service. God gives us grace so to love Him, that we may in all things see Him; in all, obey; and, obeying, see Him more clearly and love Him less unworthily; and so, in that blissful harmony of obedience and of love, be prepared to see Him "face to face."

EDWARD B. PUSEY

June 7

I pray that out of his glorious riches he may strengthen you with power through his Spirit in your inner being, so that Christ may dwell in your hearts through faith.

Ephesians 3:16–17 NIV

May we not only be delivered from the outward act or word that grieves Thee, but may the very springs of our nature be purified!

F. B. Meyer

Take the last fleeting swell of petty impatience, or of unkind criticism; things which to the unawakened conscience look so small, to the awakened conscience so large. There is not one that need have taken place. Had I been walking that moment with God, abiding that moment in Christ, drawing that moment on the sanctifying Spirit's power, I should not have lost my temper, I should not have thought unkindly—[much less] *looked* impatient, or indulged in needless severity of *words*. The occasion for the very feeling would have been as if it were not, being neutralized in Jesus Christ. And if that might have been true for the last five minutes, why should it not be true for the next five, for the present minute? "I can do all things," I have resources for all circumstances, "in Him that strengthened me."

Handley C. G. Moule

June 8

As those who have been chosen of God, holy and beloved, put on a heart of compassion, kindness, humility, gentleness and patience; bearing with one another, and forgiving each other, whoever has a complaint against anyone; just as the Lord forgave you, so also should you.

COLOSSIANS 3:12–13 NASB

The discord is within, which jars
    So sadly in life's song;
'Tis we, not you who are in fault,
    When others seem so wrong.

FREDERICK W. FABER

Self-preoccupation, self-broodings, self-interest, self-love— these are the reasons why you go jarring against your fellows. Turn your eyes off yourself; look up, and out! There are men, your brothers, and women, your sisters; they have needs that you can aid. Listen for their confidences; keep your heart wide open to their calls, and your hands alert for their service. Learn to give, and not to take; to drown your own hungry wants in the happiness of lending yourself to fulfill the interests of those nearest or dearest. Look up and out, from this narrow, confined self of yours, and you will rattle no longer; you will fret no more, you will provoke no more; but you will, to your own glad surprise, find the secret of "the meekness and the gentleness of Jesus"; and the fruits of the Spirit will all bud and blossom from out of your life.

HENRY SCOTT HOLLAND

June 9

The LORD bless you and keep you;
The LORD make His face shine upon you,
And be gracious to you;
The LORD lift up His countenance upon you,
And give you peace.

NUMBERS 6:24–26 NKJV

The eternal God is thy refuge, and underneath are the
everlasting arms.

DEUTERONOMY 33:27 KJV

You will in time experience that you do belong not only to this life, but also are capable of enjoying and beholding God and eternal things, to your perfect contentment and rest. You will then fix your eyes, like a little innocent child, upon the face of God, steadfastly and joyfully; and He in return, like a faithful and loving mother, will keep His eyes upon thee, by which you will be made holy through and through, and transformed into the same image from glory to glory. All your delight, joy, and bliss will be in God, and God, in return, will have His joy and good pleasure in you. He will rest and dwell in you, as in His serene throne or peace; and your spirit, that had so long gone astray, like a friendless child in a foreign land, will again sweetly repose in its true rest and home, in undisturbed peace. And so you will become a clear heaven of the ever-blessed God, in which He will dwell, and which He will fill with His divine light and love, and in which He will be glorified in time and in eternity.

GERHARD TERSTEEGEN

June 10

Now the God of hope fill you with all joy and peace in believing, that ye may abound in hope, through the power of the Holy Ghost.

ROMANS 15:13 KJV

Do, I entreat you, drive away all these anxious thoughts which hinder your soul, and try to serve God cheerfully. Be resolute in overcoming self, and in bearing with your mental troubles, whatever they be, leaving all to God and doing whatever you know to be His will, quickly and heartily; be gentle, patient, humble, and courteous to all, but especially be gentle and patient with yourself. I think that many of your troubles arise from an exaggerated anxiety, a secret impatience with your own faults; and this restlessness, when once it has got possession of your mind, is the cause of numberless trifling faults, which worry you, and go on adding to your burden until it becomes unbearable. I would have you honest in checking and correcting yourself, but at the same time patient under the consciousness of your frailty. Remember that Jesus our Lord loves to dwell within a quiet heart, and to come to those who are at peace with themselves; restlessness and anxiety hinder our seeing Him, even when He is beside us and speaking to us.

PERE HYACINTHE BESSON

June 11

Though I walk in the midst of trouble, you preserve my life.

PSALM 138:7 NIV

It is very helpful to make a habit of offering, morning by morning, the troubles of the day just beginning to our dear Lord, accepting His will in all things, especially in all little personal trials and vexations. Some persons have found great benefit from making, when first they wake, the act...[of] accepting "all things tolerable and intolerable" for love of Christ; then at midday, a moment's inward search to see whether there had been any voluntary slackening of submission, any deliberate opposition to God's will, any hesitation in resisting the distaste or worry, the impatience of discouragement we are tempted to feel when things go contrary to our own will and likings, [then] making a fresh resolution to go on heartily; and, at night, a quick review of the day's failures for which to ask pardon, and strength to go on better anew. Some such habit as this is a great check to that terrible hindrance of the spiritual life which, terrible though it be, is so apt to steal upon many good and earnest souls—a complaining, grumbling, self-pitying spirit.

H. L. SIDNEY LEAR

June 12

That Christ may dwell in your hearts by faith.

EPHESIANS 3:17 KJV

Christ in you, the hope of glory.

COLOSSIANS 1:27 KJV

> Enter my opening heart;
> Fill it with love and peace and light from heaven;
> Give me Yourself—for all in You is given;
> Come—never to depart.

THOMAS WILLIAM WEBB

Wherever you go, whatever you do at home, or abroad, in the field, or at church, do all in a desire of union with Christ, in imitation of His attitudes and inclinations, and look upon all as nothing, but that which exercises and increases the spirit and life of Christ in thy soul. From morning to night keep Jesus in your heart, long for nothing, desire nothing, hope for nothing but to have all that is within you changed into the spirit and attitude of the holy Jesus. This new birth in Christ, thus firmly believed and continually desired, will do everything that you want to have done in you; it will dry up all the springs of vice, stop all the workings of evil in your nature, and it will bring all that is good into you, it will open all the gospel within you, and you will know what it is to be taught of God.

WILLIAM LAW

June 13

The LORD God is a sun and shield: the LORD will give grace and glory; no good thing will he withhold from them that walk uprightly.

PSALM 84:11 KJV

Just to trust Him, this is all!
    Then the day will surely be
Peaceful, whatsoe'er befall,
    Bright and blessed, calm and free.

FRANCES RIDLEY HAVERGAL

What we should do is really, very often, to be still. And if we want something to make us more active and energetic, watchful and holy, I know but one thought, that is *faith*—faith producing love. More trust and confidence and joy in God would be the secret— the only true or successful secret—of more goodness. And this should come quietly and calmly, not in great effort; this kingdom of God has come not with observation. Rest and quiet growth are what you want.

JAMES HINTON

Open wide every avenue of your being to receive the blessed influences your Divine Husbandman may bring to bear upon you. Bask in the sunshine of His love. Drink in of the waters of His goodness. Keep your face upturned to Him. You need make no efforts to grow. But let your efforts instead be all concentrated on this, that you abide in the Vine.

HANNAH WHITALL SMITH

June 14

From this day will I bless you.

HAGGAI 2:19 KJV

Every day is a fresh beginning;
Listen, my soul, to the glad refrain,
And spite of old sorrow and older sinning,
And puzzles forecasted and possible pain,
Take heart with the day, and begin again.

SUSAN COOLIDGE

Every temptation to an evil attitude which can assail us today will be an opportunity to decide the question [of] whether we shall gain calmness and the rest of Christ, or whether we shall be tossed by the restlessness and agitation of the world. No, the very diversity of the seasons, day and night, heat and cold, affecting us variably, and producing exhilaration or depression, are so contrived as to advance us towards the being which we become, and to help us decide whether we shall be masters of ourselves, or whether we shall be swept away at the mercy of accident and circumstance, miserably susceptible of merely outward influences.

F. W. ROBERTSON

Why will you defer your good purpose from day to day? Arise, and begin in this very instant, and say, "Now is the time to be doing; now is the time to be striving; now is the right time to amend myself." Unless you do earnestly force yourself, you shall never get the victory over sin.

THOMAS À KEMPIS

June 15

Lying lips are abomination to the LORD: but they that deal truly are his delight.

PROVERBS 12:22 KJV

Stop telling lies. Let us tell our neighbors the truth, for we are all parts of the same body.

EPHESIANS 4:25 NLT

It seems to me, that the shortest way to curb the darker forms of deceit is to set watch more scrupulously against those which have mingled, unwatched and unchecked, with the current of our life. Do not let us lie at all. Do not think of one falsity as harmless, and another as slight, and another as unintended. Cast them all aside; they may be light and accidental, but they are an ugly soot from the smoke of the pit, for all that, and it is better that our hearts should be swept clean of them, without over care as to which is largest or blackest. Speaking truth is like writing well, and comes only by practice; it is less a matter of will than of habit, and I doubt if any occasion can be trivial which permits the practice and formation of such a habit.

JOHN RUSKIN

If you tell the truth, you have infinite power *supporting you*; but if not, you have infinite power against you.

CHARLES GEORGE GORDON

June 16

My God shall supply all your need according to his riches in glory by Christ Jesus.

PHILIPPIANS 4:19 KJV

How must the pilgrim's load be borne?
    With staggering limbs and look forlorn?
His Guide chose all that load within;
    There's need of everything but sin.

So, trusting Him whose love He knows,
    Singing along the road he goes;
And nightly of his burden makes
    A pillow, till the morning breaks.

LUCY LARCOM

They live contented with what they have, whether it be little or much, because they know that they receive as much as is profitable for them; little, if little be profitable, and much, if much be profitable; and that they cannot tell what is profitable for them, but the Lord only can, who has an eternal end in view in all things which He provides.

EMANUEL SWEDENBORG

I hope you will learn, what I am always hoping to learn, to rejoice in God continually, knowing that He is really ordering all your circumstances to the one end of making you a partaker of His own goodness, and bringing you within His own sympathy.

THOMAS ERSKINE

That ye sorrow not, even as others who have no hope.

1 THESSALONIANS 4:13 KJV

Is God's comfort too little for you?

JOB 15:11 NLT

What shall make trouble? Not the holy thought
    Of the departed; that will be a part
Of those undying things His peace has wrought
    Into a world of beauty in the heart.

SARAH J. WILLIAMS

She spoke of those who had walked with her long ago in her garden, and for whose sake, now that they had all gone into the world of light, every flower was double dear. Would it be a true proof of loyalty to them if she lived gloomily or despondently because they were away? She spoke of the duty of being ready to welcome happiness as well as to endure pain, and of the strength that endurance wins by being grateful for small daily joys, like the evening light, and the smell of roses, and the singing of birds. She spoke of the faith that rests on the Unseen Wisdom, and Love like a child on its mother's breast, and the melting away of doubts in the warmth of an effort to do some good in the world.

HENRY VAN DYKE

June 18

That they might be called trees of righteousness,
the planting of the LORD, that he might be glorified.

ISAIAH 61:3 KJV

The entrance into the eternal kingdom of our Lord and Savior
Jesus Christ will be abundantly supplied to you.

2 PETER 1:11 NASB

Have you a sense of the way to the Father? Then be careful that
your spirit daily bows before Him, that He would continue His
mercy to you; making your way more and more clear before you
every day—yes, and supporting you in all the exercises and trials
which may befall you, in every kind; that, by His secret working
in your spirit, and helping you with a little help from time to
time, you may still be advancing nearer and nearer towards the
kingdom; until you find the Lord God open an entrance for you,
and give you an inheritance of life, joy, righteousness, and peace;
which is strength to the soul against sin and death.

ISAAC PENINGTON

Probably the greatest result of the life of prayer is an unconscious
but steady growth into the knowledge of the mind of God and into
conformity with His will; for after all, prayer is not so much the
means by which God's will is bent to man's desires, as it is that
man's will is bent to God's desires.

CHARLES H. BRENT

June 19

Has anyone said to God…
"Teach me what I do not see;
If I have done iniquity,
I will not do it again"?

JOB 34:31–32 NASB

Yes, take my heart, and in it rule,
Direct it as it pleases Thee;
I will be silent in Thy school,
And learn whate'er Thou teaches me.

GERHARD TERSTEEGEN

People cannot become perfect by effort of hearing or reading about perfection. The chief thing is not to listen to yourself, but silently to listen to God. Talk little and do much, without caring to be seen. God will teach you more than all the most experienced persons or the most spiritual books can. You already know a great deal more than you practice. You do not need the acquirement of fresh knowledge half so much as to put in practice that which you already possess.

FRANÇOIS DE FÉNELON

To speak with the tongues of men or angels on religious matters is a much less thing than to know how to keep the mind upon God, and abide with Him in the closet of our hearts, observing, loving, adoring, and obeying His holy power within us.

WILLIAM LAW

June 20

Love each other with genuine affection, and take delight in honoring each other.

ROMANS 12:10 NLT

Love as brothers, be compassionate and humble.

1 PETER 3:8 NIV

Let your religion make you more considerate, more loving and attractive, more able to think of and enter into the pleasure and interests of others.

ARTHUR C. A. HALL

Love one another in spite of your differences, in spite of your faults. Love one another, and make the best of one another, as He loved us, who, for the sake of saving what was good in the human soul, forgot, forgave, put out of sight what was bad—who saw and loved what was good even in the tax collector Zaccheus, even in the penitent Magdalen, even in the dying thief at the cross, even in the heretical Samaritan, even in the Pharisee Nicodemus, even in the heathen soldier, even in the outcast Caananite. It is very easy to fix our attention only on the weak points of those around us, to magnify them, to irritate them, to aggravate them; and, by so doing, we can make the burden of life unendurable, and can destroy our own and others' happiness and usefulness wherever we go. But this is not the new love wherewith we are to love one another.

ARTHUR P. STANLEY

June 21

Justice, and only justice, you shall pursue, that you may live and possess the land which the LORD your God is giving you.

DEUTERONOMY 16:20 NASB

The LORD your God commands you this day to follow these decrees and laws; carefully observe them with all your heart and with all your soul.

DEUTERONOMY 26:16 NIV

Never pass by or barter with the clear voice of conscience, with the plain command of duty; never let it be doubtful to your own soul whether you belong to the right side or wrong, whether you are a true soldier or a false traitor. Never deliberate about what is clearly wrong, and try to persuade yourself that it is not.

FREDERICK TEMPLE

The first resolve of one who gives himself wholly to God must be never to give way deliberately to any fault whatever; never to act in defiance of conscience, never to refuse anything God requires, never to say of anything, It is too small for God to heed. Such a resolution as this is an essential foundation in the spiritual life. I do not mean that in spite of it we shall fall into inadvertencies, infirmities, errors; but we shall rise up and go on anew from such fault—because they are involuntary, the will has not consented to them.

JEAN NICOLAS GROU

June 22

Take therefore no thought for the morrow.

MATTHEW 6:34 KJV

I will not leave you nor forsake you. Be strong and of good courage.

JOSHUA 1:5–6 NKJV

I have laid help upon one that is mighty.

PSALM 89:19 KJV

Why should we, then, burden ourselves, with superfluous cares, and fatigue and weary ourselves in the multiplicity of our ways? Let us rest in peace. God Himself invites us to cast our cares, our anxieties up to Him.

MADAME GUYON

If we may take one test or sign by which to judge in advance the spiritual life, it would be this—whether more and more calmness is being maintained in the midst of all the disturbances and troubles which are wont to come, which may ever be looked for in some form or other—whether there be peacefulness of mind, and order of thought in the midst of all that once too much distracted and agitated the soul.

T. T. CARTER

June 23

Behold the fowls of the air.... Consider the lilies of the field.

MATTHEW 6:26, 28 KJV

I was in the act of kneeling down before the Lord my God, when a little bird came and perched near my window, and thus preached to me: "O you grave man, look on me, and learn something, if not the deepest lesson, then a true one. Your God made me, and those like me; and, if you can conceive it, loves me and cares for me. *You* study Him in great problems, which oppress and confound you: you lose sight of one half of His ways. Learn to see your God not in great mysteries only, but in me also. His burden on me is light, His yoke on me is easy; but you make burdens and yokes for yourself which are very hard to bear. Things as deep as hell and high as heaven you consider overmuch; but you do not 'consider the lilies' sufficiently. If *you* could be as a lily before God, for at least one hour in the twenty-four, it would do you good; I mean, if you could cease to will and to think, and *be* only. Consider, the lily is as real from God as you are, and is a figure of something *in Him*—the like of which should also be in you. You have longest to grow, but the lily grows without longing, yes, without even thinking or willing, *grows* and *is* beautiful both to God and man."

JOHN PULSFORD

June 24

In God I will praise his word, in God I have put my trust;
I will not fear what flesh can do unto me.

PSALM 56:4 KJV

Do not fear circumstances. They cannot hurt us, if we hold fast by God and use them as the voices and ministries of His will. Trust Him about every one and everything, for all times and all needs, earth and heaven, friends and children, the conquest of sin, the growth of holiness, the cross that chafes, the grace that stirs.

ANTHONY W. THOROLD

I find that it is not the circumstances in which we are placed, but the spirit in which we meet them that constitutes our comfort; and that this may be undisturbed, if we seek for and cherish a feeling of quiet submission, whatever may be the deprivations allotted us.

ELIZABETH T. KING

Wherever God may lead you, there you will find Him, in the most harassing business, as in the most tranquil prayer.

FRANÇOIS DE FÉNELON

June 25

Teach me Your way, O LORD;
I will walk in Your truth;
Unite my heart to fear Your name.

PSALM 86:11 NKJV

If thou but suffer God to guide thee,
    And hope in Him through all thy ways,
He'll give thee strength, whate'er betide thee,
    And bear thee through the evil days;
Who trusts in God's unchanging love,
Builds on the rock that nought can move.

GEORG NEUMARK

If we seek, indeed, that all our ways may be His ways, if we resolve
and pray that we will keep to the path of obedience, of trust, of
duty, then we know that His angels are in charge of us, and that
they can bear us nowhere beyond our Father's eye, His hand,
His care. Then we know that all worlds are His, all souls are His;
we can trust to Him those He has taken from us, and know that
when He has called them to pass out of our sight, He is with them
still, to keep them in all their ways, even in that hidden path over
which the dark shadow lies, until the day breaks and the shadows
flee away.

JOHN ELLERTON

June 26

In the multitude of my anxieties within me, Your comforts delight my soul.

PSALM 94:19 NKJV

Oh, listen then, Most Pitiful!
　　To Thy poor creature's heart;
It blesses Thee that Thou art God,
　　That Thou art what Thou art!

FREDERICK W. FABER

What the particular thoughts or temptations are that disquiet you, I know not; but, whatsoever they are, look above them, and labor to fix your eye on that infinite goodness, which never fails them that, by faith, do absolutely rely and rest upon it; and patiently wait upon Him, who has pronounced them all, without exception, blessed that do so.

ROBERT LEIGHTON

Thoughts that disturb and trouble us seldom come from God. It is generally best to put them away, and throw oneself, with increased trust in Him and mistrust of self, at His feet. And never forget, amid whatever may befall you—dryness, coldness, desolation, and disappointment, consciousness of many faults, of great weakness, and want of faith—that where love is, there God is sure to be. He never yet has suffered any soul to fall wholly from Him which, amid all its frailties and falls, clings to Him in love.

H. L. SIDNEY LEAR

June 27

You shall go to all to whom I send you,
And whatever I command you, you shall speak.

JEREMIAH 1:7 NKJV

Be assured of this, you do not know God in truth, and have no true peace, if you are depending upon times and places. Remember that whatever God gives you to do, from moment to moment, that is the very best thing you could possibly be doing, and you little know where and when the Lord will meet you. He who does not seek and find God everywhere, and in everything, finds Him nowhere and in nothing. And He who is not at the Lord's service in everything is at His service in nothing.

JOHN TAULER

God must be sought and seen in His providences; it is not our actions in themselves considered which please Him, but the spirit in which they are done, more especially the constant ready obedience to every discovery of His will, even in the minutest things, and with such a suppleness and flexibility of mind as not to adhere to anything, but to turn and move in any direction where He shall call.

MADAME GUYON

June 28

You will show me the path of life; in Your presence is fullness of joy; at Your right hand are pleasures forevermore.

PSALM 16:11 NKJV

Lord, it is not life to live,
    If Thy presence Thou deny,
Lord, if Thou Thy presence give,
    'Tis no longer death to die.
Source and Giver of repose,
Singly from Thy smile it flows;
Peace and happiness are Thine;
Mine they are, if Thou art mine.

AUGUSTUS TOPLADY

We live from day to day, as it were, by chance, and forget that human life itself is as much an art, governed by its own rules and precepts of perfection, as the most complicated profession by which that life is maintained or adorned.

W. ARCHER BUTLER

The art of life consists in taking each event which befalls us with a contented mind, confident of good. This makes us grow younger as we grow older, for youth and joy come from the soul to the body more than from the body to the soul. With this method and art and temper of life, we live, though we may be dying. We rejoice always, though in the midst of sorrows, and possess all things, though destitute of everything.

JAMES FREEMAN CLARKE

June 29

Let not your hearts faint, fear not, and do not tremble, neither be ye terrified because of them.

DEUTERONOMY 20:3 KJV

Son of the living God! Oh, call us / Once and again to follow Thee,
And give us strength, whate'er befall us, / Thy true disciples still
to be.
And if our coward hearts deny Thee, / In inmost thought, or deed,
or word,
Let not our hardness still defy Thee, / But with a look subdue us,
Lord.

HENRY A. MARTIN

Half our difficulty in doing anything worthy of our high calling is
the shrinking anticipation of its possible after-consequences. But
if Peter had tarried, and cast up all that was to come, the poverty,
and wandering, and solitude, and lonely old age, the outcast life,
and chance of fearful death, it may be he would have been neither
an apostle nor a Christian.

HENRY EDWARD MANNING

Some men will follow Christ on certain conditions—if He will not
lead them through rough roads—if He will not bring them any
painful tasks—if the sun and wind do not annoy them—if He will
remit a part of His plan and order. But the true Christian, who
has the spirit of Jesus, will say, as Ruth said to Naomi, "Whither
thou goest I will go," whatever difficulties and dangers may be in
the way.

RICHARD CECIL

June 30

If we love our Christian brothers and sisters, it proves that we have passed from death to life. But a person who has no love is still dead.

1 John 3:14 nlt

For who has aught to love and loves aright,
　　Will never in the darkest strait despair,
For out of love exhales a living light,
　　The light of love, that spends itself in prayer.

Hartley Coleridge

Love is life, and lovelessness is death. As the grace of God changes a man's heart and cleanses and sanctifies him, this is the great evidence of the change, this is the great difference which it makes: that he begins to grow in love, to lay aside self-seeking, and to live for others—and so he may know that he has passed from death to life. He may know it even here and now—yes, that great discovery or love, that learning to live for others and finding the grace and gentleness that God is keeping up all over the world—even now it is the way from death to life. Even now it changes homes, it lightens every burden, it brings peace and gladness into the hardest days; it alters even the tone of a man's voice and the very look of his face. But all this, blessed and surpassing as it is, far above all else in the world, still is but the beginning. For that life into which we pass, as God's dear grace of love comes in us and about us, is the very life of heaven.

Francis Paget

JULY

Look back from where we have come.

The path was at times an open road of joy,

At others a steep and bitter track of stones and pain.

How could we know the joy without the suffering?

And how could we endure the suffering but that we

are warmed and carried on the breast of God?

DESMOND M. TUTU

July 1

*You, O L*ORD, *have made me glad by what You have done,*
I will sing for joy at the works of Your hands.

PSALM **92:4** NASB

Consider it
(This outer world we tread on) as a harp—
A gracious instrument on whose fair strings
We learn those airs we shall be set to play
When mortal hours are ended.

JEAN **I**NGELOW

Every year has been to me a softening of the impressible nature,
and a clearing of the eye in all the fields of divine goodness, quite
irrespective of the hard, hot, choking work of the external world
and its attacks. I feel more and more how all right spirit life is a
gladness and a glory increasing; how divine goodness is speaking
in all tones that reach the heart with joy or sorrow, awe or ecstasy,
everywhere and in all things, if we can but hear it; how completely
the spirit within can be in communion with light, independent of
external circumstances; and yet how external circumstances and
creation are the medium through which God speaks. And if it is
indeed a speech of God, an ever present incarnation of the divine
mind, then the power of reading the divine mind can only exist for
those who are in accordance with it.

EDWARD **T**HRING

July 2

In this was manifested the love of God toward us, because that God sent his only begotten Son into the world, that we might live through him.

1 JOHN 4:9 KJV

Thy love to me, O God,
    Not mine, O Lord, to Thee
Can rid me of this dark unrest,
    And set my spirit free.

HORATIUS BONAR

The spirit of prayer is a pressing forth of the soul out of this earthly life, it is a stretching with all its desire after the life of God, it is a leaving, as far as it can, all its own spirit, to receive a spirit from above, to be one life, one love, one spirit with Christ in God. For the love which God bears to the soul, His eternal, never-ceasing desire to enter into it, and to dwell in it, stays no longer than till the door of the heart opens for Him. For nothing does, or can keep God out of the soul, or hinder His holy union with it, but the desire of the heart turned from Him.

WILLIAM LAW

Holiness is the beauty of the Lord God of hosts. You cannot separate the one from the other. To have it, you must have Him. Nor will it be hard to obtain either; for He longs to enter into your being. Your longing is the faint response of your heart to His call.

F. B. MEYER

July 3

Continue in prayer, and watch in the same.

COLOSSIANS 4:2 KJV

But if distractions manifold prevail,
And if in this we must confess we fail,
Grant us to keep at least a prompt desire,
Continual readiness for prayer and praise,
An altar heaped and waiting to take fire
With the least spark, and leap into a blaze.

RICHARD CHENEVIX TRENCH

When the set time comes round for prayer, it may be, and often is, the case that the mind is depressed, and finds it a hard struggle to raise up to communion with God. Your purpose is to hold communion with the Infinite Wisdom and Infinite Love; can you do this, or even attempt this, without coming away from the exercise brighter, calmer, happier, stronger against evil? Make a vigorous effort to throw your whole soul into some very short petition, and the spirit of inertness and heaviness shall be exorcised. But if not, and your mind is dry to the end, do not worry yourself. If only you make a sincere effort to draw near to God, all shall be well. He sees that you have a will to pray, and accounts the will for the deed.

EDWARD MEYRICK GOULBURN

Pray hardest when it is hardest to pray.

CHARLES H. BRENT

July 4

*If anyone is in Christ, he is a new creation; the old has gone,
the new has come!*

2 CORINTHIANS 5:17 NIV

His perfect peace has swept from sight
The narrow bounds of time and space,
And, looking up with still delight,
We catch the glory of His face.

AUGUSTA LARNED

In every moment of our days, when once our hearts are yielded
to His service, God is working in us and through us. Until now,
perhaps, our little world has only been large enough to hold self
and the present. But, gradually, through tender leadings and
unfoldings, and, it may be, through pain and suffering, we come
to learn life's lesson—that it is God's world, not ours; that our
existence is not finished and rounded off here, but forms part of
one vast scheme to which mind and heart and spirit expand and
grow, while all the horizon round them grows and expands too,
until it touches the shore of the endless future. Then we become
conscious that earth and heaven are not so far separated but that
the first is but the vestibule of the second—imperfect, cloudy, full
of broken fragments, but still part of the same temple of God as
that to which we shall pass in by and by.

H. BOWMAN

July 5

All things are possible to him who believes.

MARK 9:23 NKJV

My grace is sufficient for thee: for my strength is made perfect in weakness.

2 CORINTHIANS 12:9 KJV

It is possible, I dare to say, for those who will indeed draw on their Lord's power for deliverance and victory, to live a life in which His promises are taken as they stand, and found to be true. It is possible to cast *every* care on Him, daily, and to be at peace amidst the pressure. It is possible to see the will of God in everything, and to find it, as one has said, no longer a sigh, but a song. It is possible, in the world of inner act and motion, to put away, to get put away, *all* bitterness, and wrath, and anger, and evil speaking, daily and hourly. It is possible, by unreserved resort to divine power, under divine conditions, to become strongest, through and through, at our weakest point; to find the thing which yesterday upset all our obligations to patience, or to purity, or to humility, an occasion today, through Him who loves us, and works in us, for a joyful consent to His will, and a delightful sense of His presence and sin-annulling power. These are things divinely possible.

HANDLEY C. G. MOULE

July 6

But we all, with open face beholding as in a glass the glory of the Lord, are changed into the same image from glory to glory.

2 Corinthians 3:18 KJV

Your life in me be shown!
Lord! I would henceforth seek
    To think and speak
Your thoughts, Your words alone;
    No more my own.

Frances Ridley Havergal

Nothing short of the life of the eternal Son of God—the holiness, the purity of God, is the standard at which we are to aim; *that* is to be reproduced in our circumstances; the divine perfections are to be translated, reproduced in *our* life, *our* home, *our* trials, *our* difficulties, *our* age of the world. Let us ask ourselves, What is the special likeness of Christ that He would reproduce in *me*? What are the features of His life that He calls *me* to imitate? What pattern would He set before me in my work, my circumstances, my difficulties? What are the inspirations of grace that He would urge me to cultivate and cherish?

Arthur C. A. Hall

The Christian life must be in its own degree something like the Master's own life, luminous with His hope, and surrounded by a bracing atmosphere which uplifts all who even touch its outer fringe.

Hugh Black

July 7

Work willingly at whatever you do, as though you were working for the Lord rather than for people.

Colossians 3:23 NLT

If you love Him as I want you to do, you will offer Him the whole use of your day, as you open your eyes to the light of each morning, to be spent in active service or silent suffering, according to His good pleasure. You will not select the most agreeable task, but *His* task, whatever it may be; you will not disdain humble service, or be ambitious for distinguished service; you will lie, like a straw, on the current of His will, to be swept away and be forgotten, if it pleases Him, or to be caught up by His mighty hand and transformed thereby into a thunderbolt.

Elizabeth Prentiss

Let us pray for Him, therefore, to cast in us the mind that was in Christ, that we may offer up ourselves to be disposed of as He sees best, whether for joy or sorrow; to be slighted, or esteemed; to have many friends, or to dwell in a lonely home; to be passed by, or called to serve Him and His kingdom in our own land, or among people of a strange tongue; to be, to go, to do, to suffer even as He wills, even as He ordains, even as Christ endured, "who, through the eternal Spirit, offered Himself without spot to God."

Henry Edward Manning

July 8

Behold, I...will reveal unto them the abundance of peace and truth.

JEREMIAH 33:6 KJV

Glory, honor, and peace to everyone who works what is good.

ROMANS 2:10 NKJV

True peace is when the soul revolves around its center, almighty God, craving for nothing but what God continually supplies, its passions subdued to itself, itself lovingly loyal to God, in harmony with its God and His laws. God made the soul for Himself, to have its bliss in His infinite, unchanging, exhaustless love. The soul then "...be restless, until it repose in Him." Everything, whether it belongs to the keenest intellect, or the lowest senses, is an idol if the soul rests in it, apart from God. The soul's craving for peace is its natural yearning for its End, its Maker, and its God. Since the soul is large enough to contain the infinite God, nothing less than Himself can satisfy or fill it.

EDWARD B. PUSEY

With those who have made ready to receive Him in peaceful trust, He will come and dwell in love and joy; and great is their rest and blessedness.

ABBE GUILLORE

July 9

We have come to know and have believed the love which God has for us. God is love, and the one who abides in love abides in God, and God abides in him.

1 John 4:16 NASB

As flame streams upward, so my longing thought
    Flies up to Thee,
Thou God and Savior, who hast truly wrought
Life out of death, and to us, loving, brought
A fresh, new world; and in Thy sweet chains caught,
    And made us free!

Maurice Francis Egan

What a blessed and glorious thing human existence would be if we fully realized that the infinitely wise and infinitely powerful God loves each one of us, with an intensity infinitely beyond what the most fervid human spirit ever felt towards another, and with a concentration as if He had none else to think of! And this love has brought us into being, just that we might be taught to enter into *full sympathy* with Him, receiving His—giving our own—thus entering into the joy of our Lord. This is the hope, the sure and certain hope, set before us—sure and certain for "the mountains shall depart, and the hills be removed; but my kindness shall not depart from thee, neither shall the covenant of my peace be removed, saith the Lord that has mercy on thee."

Thomas Erskine

July 10

Therefore I will boast all the more gladly about my weaknesses, so that Christ's power may rest on me.

2 Corinthians 12:9 NIV

The Lord stood with me, and strengthened me.

2 Timothy 4:17 KJV

To His own the Savior gives
    Daily strength;
To each troubled soul that lives,
    Peace at length.

Karl Rudolph Hagenbach

Remember that your work comes only moment by moment, and as surely as God calls you to work, He gives the strength to do it. Do not think in the morning, "How shall I go though this day? I have such-and-such work to do, and persons to see, and I have not strength for it." No, you have not, for you do not need it. Each moment, as you need it, the strength will come, only do not look forward an hour; circumstances may be very different from what you expect. At any rate you will be borne through each needful and right thing "on eagles' wings." Do not worry yourself with misgivings; take each thing quietly.

Priscilla Maurice

God does not demand impossibilities.

Augustine of Hippo

July 11

Do all things without complaining and disputing.

PHILIPPIANS 2:14 NKJV

He that hath no rule over his own spirit is like a city that is broken down, and without walls.

PROVERBS 25:28 KJV

Behold, the paths of life are ours—we see
Our blest inheritance where'er we tread;
Sorrow and danger our security,
And disappointment lifting up our head.

ANNA L. WARING

One valuable way of practicing self-control is in controlling grumbling, and an unnecessary display of irritation at petty inconveniences. A workman has fulfilled his task imperfectly, some order is wrongly executed, someone keeps you waiting unreasonably; people are careless or forgetful, or do what they have to do badly. Try not to be disturbed; be just, and show the persons to blame where they are wrong, even (if it is needful) make them do the thing over again properly; but refrain from extended or vehement expressions of displeasure. A naturally quick, impetuous person will find that to cultivate a calm external habit is a great help towards gaining the inward even spirit he needs.

H. L. SIDNEY LEAR

July 12

Do not withhold good from those who deserve it, when it is in your power to act. Do not say to your neighbor, "Come back later; I'll give it tomorrow"—when you now have it with you.

PROVERBS 3:27–28 NIV

Do not only take occasions of doing good when they are thrust upon you, but study how to do all the good you can, as those "that are zealous of good works." Zeal of good works will make you plot and contrive for them; consult and ask advice for them; it will make you glad when you meet with a hopeful opportunity; it will make you do it largely and not sparingly, and by the halves; it will make you do it speedily, without unwilling backwardness and delay; it will make you do it constantly to your lives' end. It will make you labor in it as your trade, and not only consent that others do good at your charge. It will make you glad, when good is done, and not to grudge at what it cost you. In a word, it will make your neighbors to be to you as yourselves, and the pleasing of God to be above yourselves, and therefore to be as glad to do good as to receive it.

RICHARD BAXTER

July 13

*The steps of a good man are ordered by the L*ORD,
and He delights in his way.

PSALM **37:23** NKJV

So her life was full of sunshine, for in toiling for the Lord
She had found the hidden sweetness that in common things
lies stored;
He has strewn the earth with flowers, and each eye their
brightness sees;
But He filled their cups with honey for His humble working bees.

FRANCESCA **A**LEXANDER

The occupations of every day seem often trifling, we may do them
without thinking as ordinary things, yet they are the scenes of our
appointed lot—appointed by God for you and me. The ordering,
the application of these ordinary occupations, is the appointing
of the divine purpose; it is for ourselves to carry them out. And
secretly our character forms according as we handle them. Give
your heart to God eternal, since you are yourself eternal. Join
your heart to what He has given you to do. Join your heart to His
teaching, and become of a will like His own will. Nothing comes
by pure accident, not even the interruptions in our busy day. And
such as follow on to know God's will see in all events what may
lead to good, and so trust grows into a habit, as habit grows by
perpetual use, till every circumstance may be seen to be but a
fresh manifestation of the will of God working itself out in us.

T. T. CARTER

July 14

Are not five sparrows sold for two farthings, and not one of them is forgotten before God?

LUKE 12:6 KJV

So do not fear; you are more valuable than many sparrows.

MATTHEW 10:31 NASB

The trees of the LORD are full of sap; the cedars of Lebanon, which he hath planted; where the birds make their nests: as for the stork, the fir trees are her house.

PSALM 104:16–17 KJV

It was a beautiful sight to see the herons come home, rising into the golden sunlight above the hills I could not tell from whence, and sailing on the glorious arches of their wings, on and on— always alone, and each as he came down with outstretched neck and pendent legs ready to settle, taking one last sweep down, then up, on to the summit of the tall Scotch fir, to take a survey of the realm, and, as another approached, plunging into the thick heads of lower trees with a loud good-night to his neighbors, and to all the fair land and water round about him, and a Deo Gratias for all his day's happiness, pleasant unto the ear of his dear God, if not consciously addressed to Him.

My heavenly Father cares for them; I am of more value than many herons.

EDWARD WHITE BENSON

July 15

In thy presence is fulness of joy.

PSALM 16:11 KJV

O rest of rests! O peace serene, eternal!
> You ever live, and You change never;
And in the secret of Your presence dwells
> Fullness of joy, forever and forever.

HARRIET BEECHER STOWE

I have no home, until I am in the realized presence of God. This holy presence is my inward home, and, until I experience it, I am a homeless wanderer, a straying sheep in a waste howling wilderness.

ANONYMOUS

Heaven consists in nothing else than walking, abiding, resting in the Divine Presence. There are souls who enter into this heaven before leaving the body. If you believe that your God, found, felt, and rested in, is heaven, why not, under the gracious help which He grants to you in His Son, *begin at once to discipline and qualify your soul for this heaven*? If this is your chief good, why turn away from it, as though it were a thing not to be desired? If it is the very end of your being, the only right, good, and blessed end, why postpone your qualification for it, as though it were a bitter necessity? Suffer your soul, so noble in its origins, to be withdrawn from dust, noise, multitudes, vain treasures, and vain pleasures, to find its sweetness and fullness in God.

JOHN PULSFORD

July 16

Lord, are you not from everlasting? My God, my Holy One, we will not die.

Habakkuk 1:12 niv

My meditation of him shall be sweet: I will be glad in the Lord.

Psalm 104:34 kjv

The more our ideas about God are multiplied, the more various our thoughts, and images, and recollections of things which have to do with Him, of course the more our minds and hearts are engrossed with Him, and so it becomes easier to live all day in His sensible presence. And is not the practice of the presence of God one half of holiness? And so, weary with work or foiled with disappointment, when the dark night is closing in, bringing with it to our sick spirits a sense of imprisonment, and when the dismal rain curtains us round, and we fret to be at liberty and at large, there is the very freedom of a sovereign to a soul traversing this boundless empire of God and Jesus, angels, saints, humans, and the blameless creatures, and rejoicing in that never-ceasing sacrifice of praise which is rising up from every nook and corner of creation to the dear Majesty of our most loving God and Father.

Frederick W. Faber

Delight in the happiness of God.

Lorenzo Scupoli

July 17

Trust ye in the LORD forever: for in the LORD JEHOVAH is everlasting strength.

ISAIAH 26:4 KJV

Come, children, let us go!
    Our Father is our guide;
And when the way grows steep and dark,
    He journeys at our side.
        Our spirits He would cheer,
The sunshine of His love
Revives and helps us as we rove,
        Ah, blest our lot e'en here!

GERHARD TERSTEEGEN

He [God] knows everything about us. And He cares about everything. Moreover, He can manage every situation. And He loves us! Surely this is enough to open the wellsprings of joy.... And joy is always a source of strength.

HANNAH WHITALL SMITH

Some of us believe that God is all mighty and may do all; and that He is all wisdom, and can do all; but that He is all love, and will do all, there we fail.

JULIAN OF NORWICH

July 18

For today the Lord will appear unto you.

Leviticus 9:4 kjv

Behold, now is the accepted time; behold, now is the day of salvation.

2 Corinthians 6:2 kjv

Do not let your growth in holiness depend upon surrounding circumstances, but minister to your growth. Beware of looking onward, or out of the present in any way, for the sanctification of your life. The only thing you can really control is the present—the actual moment that is passing by. Sanctify *that* from hour to hour, and you sanctify your whole life; but brood over the past, or project yourself into the future, and you will lose all. The little act of obedience, love, self-restraint, meekness, patience, devotion, actually offered to you, is all you can do now, and if you neglect that to fret about something else at a distance, you lose your real opportunity of serving God. A moment's silence, when some irritating words are said by another, may seem a very small thing; yet at that moment it is your one duty, your one way of serving and pleasing God, and if you break [the silence], you have lost your opportunity.

H. L. Sidney Lear

July 19

Use your freedom to serve one another in love. For the whole law can be summed up in this one command: "Love your neighbor as yourself."

GALATIANS 5:13–14 NLT

A man who habitually pleases himself will become continually more selfish and sordid, even among the most noble and beautiful conditions which nature, history, or art can furnish; and, on the other hand, anyone who will try each day to live for the sake of others will grow more and more gracious in thought and bearing, however dull and even run-down may be the outward circumstances of his soul's probation.

FRANCIS PAGET

It is the habit of making sacrifices in small things that enables us to make them in great, *when it is asked of us.* Temper, love of preeminence, bodily indulgence, the quick retort, the sharp irony—in checking these let us find our cross and carry it. Or, when the moment comes for some really great service, the heart will be petrified for it, and the blinded eyes will not see the occasion of love.

ANTHONY W. THOROLD

July 20

Do to us whatever seems best to You; only deliver us this day, we pray.

JUDGES 10:15 NKJV

Dear Lord, whose mercy veileth all
That may our coming day befall,
Still hide from us the things to be,
But rest our troubled hearts in Thee.

HARRIET McEWEN KIMBALL

Peace of heart lies in perfect resignation to the will of God. What you need is true simplicity, a certain calmness of spirit which comes from certain surrender to all that God wills, patience and toleration for your neighbor's faults, and a certain candor and childlike docility in acknowledging your own faults. The trouble you feel about so many things comes from your not accepting everything which may happen to you, with sufficient resignation to God. Put all things, then, in His hands, and offer them beforehand to Him in your heart as a sacrifice. From the moment when you cease to want things to be according to your own judgment, and accept unconditionally whatever He sends, you will be free from all your uneasy retrospection and anxieties about your own concerns.

FRANÇOIS DE FÉNELON

July 21

The LORD will do what is good in his sight.

2 SAMUEL 10:12 NIV

The best will is our Father's will,
And we may rest there calm and still;
Oh! Make it hour by hour your own,
And wish for nought but that alone
    Which pleases God.

PAUL GERHARDT

"Thy will be done." For instance, when you wish, and by every means endeavor, to be well, and yet remain ill—then say, "Thy will be done." When you undertake something, and your undertaking does not succeed, say, "Thy will be done." When you do good to others, and they repay you with evil, say, "Thy will be done." Or when you would like to sleep, and are overtaken by sleeplessness, say, "Thy will be done." In general, do not become irritated when anything is not done in accordance with your will, but learn to submit in everything to the will of the heavenly Father.

JOHN ILYICH SERGIEFF

Try to make an instantaneous act of conformity to God's will, at everything which vexes you.

EDWARD B. PUSEY

July 22

Look, the highest heavens and the earth and everything in it all belong to the LORD your God.

DEUTERONOMY 10:14 NLT

High King of heaven, my victory won,
May I reach heaven's joys, O bright heaven's Sun!
Heart of my own heart, whatever befall,
Still be my Vision, O Ruler of all.

MARY BYRNE AND ELEANOR HULL

The immediate result of the coming of these good tidings of great joy to me was no outward change in anything, but an inward change of everything, making everything translucent with the light within and beyond. The sum of it all was always that the universe is full of God, and God is love. We are His, and all things are His; therefore in Him all things are ours. In the home, in society, in nature, our beloved moors and woods, and rivers and glens and seas, there was the touch, the breath of God's living, real presence.

ELIZABETH RUNDLE CHARLES

He is so infinitely blessed, that every perception of His blissful presence imparts a vital gladness to the heart. Every degree of approach to Him is, in the same proportion, a degree of happiness. And I often think that were He always present to our mind, as we are present to Him, there would be no pain, nor sense of misery.

SUSANNA WESLEY

July 23

I will bring the blind by a way that they knew not; I will lead them in paths that they have not known: I will make darkness light before them, and crooked things straight. These things will I do unto them, and not forsake them.

ISAIAH 42:16 KJV

When over dizzy heights we go,
    One soft hand blinds our eyes,
The other leads us, safe and slow,
    O Love of God most wise!

ELIZA SCUDDER

The simple thought of a life which is to be the unfolding of a divine plan is too beautiful, too captivating, to suffer one indifferent or heedless moment. Living in this manner, every turn of your experience will be a discovery to you of God, every change a token of His fatherly counsel. Whatever obscurity, defeats, losses, injuries; your outward state, employment, relations; what seems hard, unaccountable, severe, or, as nature might say, distressing—all these you will see are parts or central elements in God's beautiful and good plan for you, and, as such, are to be accepted with a smile. Take your burdens, and troubles, and losses, and wrongs, if come they must and will, as your opportunities, knowing that God has girded you for greater things than these.

HORACE BUSHNELL

July 24

Seek the LORD, and his strength: seek his face evermore.

PSALM 105:4 KJV

O Jesus Christ, grow Thou in me,
    And all things else recede;
My heart be daily nearer Thee,
    From sin be daily freed.

Make this poor self grow less and less,
    Be Thou my life and aim;
Oh, make me daily, through Thy grace,
    More worthy of Thy name.

J. C. LAVATER

As, on rising, we should hear Him saying to us, "Take this yoke upon thee, My child, today," "Bear this burden for Me and with Me today." So, before retiring to rest, and collecting our mind for our evening prayer, it is well to put these questions to our conscience, "Have I, in a single instance this day, denied myself either in temper or appetite, and so submitted myself to the Savior's yoke?" And again, "Have I, in a single instance, shown sympathy or considerateness for others, accepted their faults or weaknesses of character, given time or taken trouble to help them, or be of use to them?" If so, I have gained ground; I have made an advance in the mind of Christ today, if it be only a single step. Let me thank God, and take courage. A single step is so much clear gain.

EDWARD MEYRICK GOULBURN

July 25

Because of his great love for us, God, who is rich in mercy, made us alive with Christ even when we were dead in transgressions.

EPHESIANS 2:4–5 NIV

Lord, to Thy call of me I bow,
  Obey like Abraham;
Thou lov'st me because Thou art Thou,
  And I am what I am.

Doubt whispers, *"Thou art such a blot*
  He cannot love poor thee."
If what I am He loveth not,
  He loves what I shall be.

GEORGE MACDONALD

We may hate ourselves when we come to realize failings we have not recognized before, and feel that there are probably others which we do not yet see as clearly as other people see them, but this kind of impatience for our perfection is not felt by those who love us, I am sure. It is one's greatest comfort to believe that it is not even felt by God. Just as a mother would not love her child the better for its being turned into a model of perfection at once, but does love it the more dearly every time it tries to be good, so I do hope and believe our Great Father does not wait for us to be good and wise to love us, but loves us, and loves to help us in the very thick of our struggles with folly and sin.

JULIANA H. EWING

July 26

And he said to them all, If any man will come after me, let him deny himself, and take up his cross daily, and follow me.

LUKE 9:23 KJV

We pray Thee, grant us strength to take
    Our daily cross, whate'er it be,
And gladly for Thine own dear sake
    In paths of pain to follow Thee.

WILLIAM WALSHAM HOW

The more you accept daily crosses as daily bread, in peace and simplicity, the less they will injure your frail, delicate health; but forebodings and worries would soon kill you.

FRANÇOIS DE FÉNELON

We speak of the crosses of daily life, and forget that our very language is a witness against us, how meekly we ought to bear them, in the blessed steps of our holy Lord; how in "every cross and care," we ought not to acquiesce simply, but to take them cheerfully—not cheerfully only but joyfully; yes, if they should even deserve the name of "tribulation," to "joy in tribulation" also, as seeing in them our Father's hand, our Savior's cross.

EDWARD B. PUSEY

July 27

Blessed are all they that wait for him.

ISAIAH 30:18 KJV

I will trust again His love, His power,
Though I cannot feel His hand today;
To His help anew I will betake me,
Though His countenance seems turned away!
Though without one smile, one gracious token,
Through the flames and floods my path must go,
When the fires subside the waves pass over,
My Deliverer I again shall know.

JOACHIM LANGE

In the night of distress, feel as some—which may quiet and stay
your heart till the next springing of the day—the sun will arise,
which will scatter the clouds. And in the day of His power you will
find strength to walk with Him; yes, in the day of your weakness
His grace will be sufficient for you.

ISAAC PENINGTON

My times are in Your hand, O Lord! And, surely, that is the best.
Were I to choose, they should be in no other hands, neither mine
own, nor any others. When He withholds mercies or comforts for
a season, it is but the due season. Therefore it is our wisdom and
our peace to resign all things into His hands, to have no will nor
desires, but only this: that we may still *wait for Him.* Never was
any one who *waited for Him* miserable with disappointment.

ROBERT LEIGHTON

July 28

You open Your hand and satisfy the desire of every living thing.

PSALM 145:16 NKJV

There's not a craving in the mind
    You do not meet and still;
There's not a wish the heart can have
    Which You do not fulfill.

FREDERICK W. FABER

You will see the truth about the eternal life soon; I don't think it is possible to live up to the highest point of duty *and of happiness* without this. I know one can go on doing one's duty thoroughly under clouds of doubt, and even in complete unbelief; there are many who do, and they are dear to God, but the duty is done sadly, without the spring of life and joy that we are meant to have. That fountain of life and strength is hid in God. Christ showed us the way to it, and we get it into our souls when we utterly trust Him and give up our hearts, and our lives, and our aspirations to Him as to a faithful Creator, who will not leave unsatisfied any of the longings of the souls He has made; who will not let love die, or disappoint finally the cravings for joy, for perfection, for light, and knowledge that He has implanted, and that are parts of Himself, immortal as He is.

ANNIE KEARY

July 29

I have made the earth, and created man upon it: I, even my hands, have stretched out the heavens, and all their host have I commanded. I have raised him up in righteousness, and I will direct all his ways.

ISAIAH 45:12–13 KJV

He who suns and worlds upholdeth
    Lends us His upholding hand;
He the ages who unfoldeth
    Do our times and ways command.
       God is for us;
    In His strength and stay we stand.

THOMAS H. GILL

You have trusted Him in a few things, and He has not failed you. Trust Him now for everything, and see if He does not do for you exceedingly abundantly above all that you could ever have asked or thought, not according to your power or capacity, but according to His own mighty power, that will work in you all the good pleasure of His most blessed will. You find no difficulty in trusting the Lord with the management of the universe and all the outward creation, and can your case be any more complex or difficult than these, that you need to be anxious or troubled about His management of it?

HANNAH WHITALL SMITH

July 30

He rescued us from the domain of darkness, and transferred us to the kingdom of His beloved Son.

COLOSSIANS 1:13 NASB

It is right that we should have an aim of our own, determined by our individuality and our surroundings; but this may readily degenerate into exclusive narrowness, unless it has for a background the great thought that there is a kingdom of God within us, around us, and above us, in which we, with all our powers and aims, are called to be conscious workers. Toward the forwarding of this silent ever-advancing kingdom, our little work, whatever it is, if good and true, may contribute something. And this thought lends to any calling, however lowly, a consecration which is wanting even to the loftiest self-chosen ideals. But even if our aim should be frustrated and our work come to naught, yet the failure of our most cherished plans may be more than compensated. In the thought that we are members of this kingdom, already begun, here and now, yet reaching forward through all time, we shall have a reserve of consolation better than any which success without this could give.

JOHN CAMPBELL SHAIRP

July 31

The world and its desires pass away, but the man who does the will of God lives forever.

1 John 2:17 NIV

I am Yours, save me.

Psalm 119:94 NASB

Take, O Lord, and receive all my liberty, my memory, my understanding, and my will, all that I have and possess. You have given it to me; to You, O Lord, I restore it; all is Yours, dispose of it according to Your will. Give me Your love and Your grace, for this is enough for me.

Ignatius Loyola

Recognize the love of God in everything He has given us—and He has given us everything. Every breath we draw is a gift of His love, every moment of existence is a gift of grace, for it brings with it immense graces from Him.

Thomas Merton

There is no restraint so strong as an unreserved abandonment of self into God's hand.

H. L. Sidney Lear

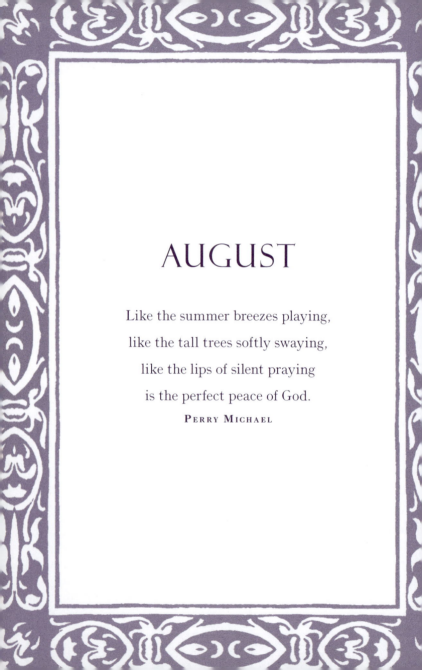

AUGUST

Like the summer breezes playing,

like the tall trees softly swaying,

like the lips of silent praying

is the perfect peace of God.

PERRY MICHAEL

August 1

I have sinned; for I have transgressed the commandment of the Lord, *and thy words: because I feared the people, and obeyed their voice.*

1 Samuel 15:24 kjv

Listen to Me, you who know righteousness, you people in whose heart is My law: Do not fear the reproach of men, nor be afraid of their insults.

Isaiah 51:7 nkjv

You must not follow the crowd in doing wrong.

Exodus 23:2 nlt

All timidity, indecision, fear of ridicule, weakness of purpose, such as the apostles showed when they deserted Christ, and Peter especially when he denied Him, are to be numbered among the tempers of mind which are childish as well as sinful; which we must learn to despise.

John Henry Newman

You, who have yielded so readily to your friend's persuasion, and have joined him in doing wrong, you know not how many times a very little resistance would have saved both him and yourself; you know not how many times he was hesitating already, and would have drawn back altogether if you had but given him an opening to do so; you know not how often, at the very time he was arguing with you, he was in reality arguing against his own conscience, and might have been turned back with ease if you had not given way.

Frederick Temple

August 2

You shall follow the LORD your God and fear Him; and you shall keep His commandments, listen to His voice, serve Him, and cling to Him.

DEUTERONOMY 13:4 NASB

God visits a soul when He brings before it a new vision of truth or duty, a new range of opportunities, a new endowment of force as well as insight, at some time to which all that precedes has led up, and from which all that follows depends in its solemn history. No divine visitation leaves us where it found us; it always leaves us better or worse; if not better, then certainly worse.

HENRY PARRY LIDDON

The issues are with God, and His servants know not the word disappointment, for they are incapable of reading His designs. Only this they know, that the slightest hesitation in obeying what they believe to be a divine impulse produces a suffering more intense than any consequences which may accrue to them from the world.

LAURENCE OLIPHANT

Never shrink from deep devotion, because you fear its trials or its sacrifices. Paul, in martyrdom, was unspeakably happier than God's half-hearted servants.

WILLIAM R. HUNTINGTON

August 3

If only you had paid attention to my commands, your peace would have been like a river, your righteousness like the waves of the sea.

ISAIAH **48:18** NIV

It is so easy to become more thick-skinned in conscience, more tolerant of evil, more hopeless of good, more careful of one's own comfort and one's own property, more self-satisfied in leaving high aims and great deeds to enthusiasts, and then to believe that one is growing older and wiser. And yet those high examples, those good works, those great triumphs over evil, which single hands effect sometimes, we are all grateful for, when they are done, whatever we may have said of the doing. But we speak of saints and enthusiasts for good, as if some special gifts were made to them in middle age which are withheld from other men. Is it not rather that some few souls keep alive the lamp of zeal and high desire which God lights for most of us while life is young?

JULIANA H. EWING

To live with a high ideal is a successful life. It is not what one does, but what one tries to do, that makes the soul strong and fit for a noble career.

E. P. TENNEY

August 4

The LORD is like a father to his children, tender and compassionate to those who fear him.

PSALM 103:13 NLT

God only knows the love of God:
Oh, that it now were shed abroad
    In this poor stony heart;
For love I sigh, for love I pine;
This only portion, Lord, be mine,
    Be mine this better part.

CHARLES WESLEY

Don't measure God's mind by your own. It would be a poor love that depended not on itself, but on the feelings of the person loved. A crying baby turns away from its mother's breast, but she does not put it away till it stops crying. She holds it closer. For my part, in the worst mood I am ever in, when I don't feel I love God at all, I just look up to His love. I say to Him, "Look at me. See what state I am in. Help me!" Ah! You would wonder how that makes peace. And the love comes of itself; sometimes so strong, it nearly breaks my heart.

GEORGE MACDONALD

He does not love us because we are so lovely, but because He always loves what He pities.

ELIZABETH PRENTISS

August 5

We pray this so that the name of our Lord Jesus may be glorified in you, and you in him, according to the grace of our God and the Lord Jesus Christ.

2 THESSALONIANS 1:12 NIV

Clothe yourself with the presence of the Lord Jesus Christ.

ROMANS 13:14 NLT

Send down Your likeness from above,
    And let this my adorning be:
Clothe me with wisdom, patience, love,
    With lowliness and purity.

JOACHIM LANGE

Evidently, in order to be a manifestation of Christ we must be in some way like Him. He is a Christian who follows Christ, who measures all things by the standard of His sanction, who would not willingly say a word which he would not like to have Christ hear, nor do an act which he would not like to have Christ see. He is a Christian who tries to be the kind of citizen Christ would be, and who asks himself in all the alternatives of his business life, and his social life, and his personal life, what would the Master do in this case? The best Christian is he who most reminds the people with whom he lives of the Lord Jesus Christ. He who never reminds anybody of the Lord Jesus Christ is not a Christian at all.

GEORGE HODGES

August 6

[Jesus] was transfigured before them: and his face did shine as the sun, and his raiment was white as the light.

MATTHEW 17:2 KJV

Master, it is good for us to be here.

MARK 9:5 KJV

Master, it is good to be
Entranced, enwrapt, alone with Thee;
Watching the glistering raiment glow,
Whiter than Hermon's whitest snow;
The human lineaments that shine
Irradiant with a light divine:
Till we do too change from grace to grace,
Gazing on the transfigured face.

A. P. STANLEY

The Transfiguration has lived on through ages, and has brought the past into union with the present. The "decease which He should accomplish at Jerusalem" has been owned as the bond of fellowship between those who walk the earth and suffer in it, and those who are departed from it. In the light of that "countenance which was altered, of that raiment which was white and glistering," all human countenances have acquired a brightness, all common things have been transfigured. A glimpse of the divine beauty has broken through the darkness, and has cheered the humblest pilgrims.

FREDERIC DENISON MAURICE

August 7

With You is the fountain of life; in Your light we see light.

PSALM 36:9 NKJV

How beautiful our lives may be; how bright
In privilege; how fruitful of delight!
And lo! All round us His bright servants stand;
Events, His duteous ministers and wise,
With frowning brows, perhaps, for their disguise,
But with such wells of love in their deep eyes,
And such strong rescue hidden in their hands!

HENRY SEPTIMUS SUTTON

We see always what we are looking for, and if our mind has become
trained to look for trouble and difficulty and all dark and dreary
things, we find just what we seek. On the other hand, it is quite as
easy to form the habit of looking always for beauty, for good, for
happiness, for gladness, and here, too, we shall find precisely what
we seek.

J. R. MILLER

I never knew her fail to find happiness wherever she was
placed, and good in whomever she came across. Whatever her
circumstances might be, they always yielded to her causes for
thankfulness, and work to be done with a ready and hopeful heart.

HORATIA K. F. EDEN

August 8

Blessed is he who trusts in the LORD.

PROVERBS 16:20 NASB

This world of ours is a happy world, so that God is our end, so that we can say to Him, "You are my God." Then everything takes new hues of joy and love. Our daily comforts have a new soul in them, for they abound in thanksgiving; our daily infirmities or crosses have a special joy in them, because they are so tenderly fitted to us by the medicinal hand of our God; the commonest acts of life are full of deep interest, because their end is God; daily duties are daily joys, because they are something which God gives us to offer unto Him, to do to our very best, in acknowledgment of His love. It is His earth we walk on; His air we breathe; His sun, the emblem of His all-penetrating love, which gladdens us. Eternity! Yes, that too is present to us, and is part of our joy on earth. God has given us faith to make our future home as certain to us as this our spot of earth; and hope, to aspire strongly to it; and love, as a foretaste of the all-surrounding, ever-unfolding, almighty love of our own God.

EDWARD B. PUSEY

August 9

Bring joy to your servant, for to you, O Lord, I lift up my soul.

PSALM 86:4 NIV

Ah, dearest Lord! To feel that You are near,
Brings deepest peace, and hushes every fear;
To see Your smile, to hear Your gracious voice,
Makes soul and body inwardly rejoice
    With praise and thanks!

CHRISTIAN GREGOR

Prayer is a habit, and the more we pray the better we shall pray.
Sometimes [it means] to go to be alone with God and Christ in
the fellowship of the Spirit, just for the joy and blessedness of it;
to open, with reverent yet eager hands, the door into the presence
chamber of the great King, and then to fall down before Him, it
may be, in silent adoration; our very attitude an act of homage,
our merely being there, through the motive that prompts it, being
the testimony of our soul's love. To have our set day-hours of close
communion, with which no other friends shall interfere, and which
we learn to look forward with a living gladness, on which we look
back with satisfaction and peace—this indeed is prayer.

ANTHONY W. THOROLD

August 10

Make me walk in the path of Your commandments,
for I delight in it.

PSALM 119:35 NKJV

Peace I leave with you, my peace I give unto you: not as the world
giveth, give I unto you. Let not your heart be troubled, neither let
it be afraid.

JOHN 14:27 KJV

Then may Your glorious, perfect will
    Be evermore fulfilled in me,
And make my life an answering chord
    Of glad, responsive harmony.

JEAN SOPHIA PIGOTT

Christ is the embodied harmony of God, and he that receives Him
settles into harmony with Him. "My peace I give unto you" are the
Savior's words; and this peace of Christ is the equanimity, dignity,
firmness, serenity, which made His outwardly afflicted life appear
to flow in a calmness so sublime. The soul is such a nature that, no
sooner is it set in peace with itself, than it becomes an instrument
in tune, a living instrument, discoursing heavenly music in its
thoughts, and chanting melodies of bliss, even in its dreams.
We may even say that when a soul is in this harmony, no fires of
calamity, no pains of outward torment can for one moment break
the sovereign spell of its joy. It will turn the fires to freshening
gales, and the pains to sweet instigations of love and blessing.

HORACE BUSHNELL

August 11

You have given a banner to those who fear You, that it may be displayed because of the truth.

PSALM 60:4 NASB

The strife is o'er, the battle done,
The victory of life is won.
The song of triumph has begun.
    Alleluia!

FRANCIS POTT, TRANSLATOR

You can fight with confidence where you are sure of victory. With Christ and for Christ, victory is certain.

BERNARD OF CLAIRVAUX

My son, you are never secure in this life, but, as long as you live, you shall always need spiritual armor.

You ought honorably to go through all, and to use a strong hand against whatever resists you.

For to him that overcomes is manna given, and for the indolent there remains much misery.

Dispose not yourself for much rest, but for great patience.

Wait for the Lord, behave yourself honorably, and be of good courage; do not distrust Him, do not leave your place, but steadily offer both body and soul for the glory of God.

THOMAS À KEMPIS

August 12

Our heart shall rejoice in him, because we have trusted in his holy name.

PSALM 33:21 KJV

On our way rejoicing as we homeward move,
Hearken to our praises, O Thou God of love!
Is there grief or sadness? Thine it cannot be!
Is our sky beclouded? Clouds are not from Thee!
On our way rejoicing as we homeward move,
Hearken to our praises, O thou God of love!

J. S. B. MONSELL

My position has come to this, Am I living near my Savior? Then I am as happy as the day is long, and as light-hearted as a child. It may be that I have plenty of annoyances, but they don't trouble me when His presence is with me. Am I downcast and worried? Then I am away from God.

JOHN KENNETH MACKENZIE

We may sing beforehand, even in our winter storm, in the expectation of a summer sun at the turn of the year; no created powers can mar our Lord Jesus' music, nor spill our song of joy. Let us then be glad and rejoice in the salvation of our Lord; for faith had never yet cause to have wet cheeks, and hanging-down brows, or to droop or die.

SAMUEL RUTHERFORD

August 13

I will delight in your decrees and not forget your word.

PSALM 119:16 NLT

Which also sat at Jesus' feet, and heard his word.

LUKE 10:39 KJV

Lo! At Your feet I wait Your will,
Let that alone my being fill,
All earthly passions calm and still.

C. S.

Whatever happens let us not be too busy to sit at Jesus' feet. We shall not really lose time by enjoying this; nay, we shall redeem the time; for there is usually much more time and strength forfeited by friction than by toil, and we shall gain in blessedness and enjoyment of our work, and gain in the quality of our work; and, above all, we shall gain in that we shall give Him pleasure where otherwise we might only grieve Him. And this is indeed the crown of all our endeavors. He who pleases Him does not live in vain.

W. HAY M. H. AITKEN

A low standard of prayer means a low standard of character and a low standard of service. Those alone labor effectively among men who impetuously fling themselves upward towards God.

CHARLES H. BRENT

August 14

There is a spirit in man: and the inspiration of the Almighty giveth them understanding.

JOB 32:8 KJV

If you then, being evil, know how to give good gifts to your children, how much more will your heavenly Father give the Holy Spirit to those who ask Him!

LUKE 11:13 NKJV

We have a Father in heaven who is almighty, who loves His children as He loves His only-begotten Son, and whose very joy and delight it is to succor and help them at all times and under all circumstances.

GEORGE MÜLLER

In the fellowship which is established in prayer between man and God we are brought into personal union with Him in whom all things have their being. In this lies the possibility of boundless power; for when the connection is once formed, who can lay down the limits of what man can do in virtue of the communion of his spirit with the infinite Spirit?

BROOKE FOSS WESTCOTT

August 15

Be strong and very courageous.

JOSHUA 1:7 NASB

Go forward, Christian soldier, / Beneath His banner true!
The Lord Himself, thy Leader, / Shall all thy foes subdue.
His love foretells thy trials: / He knows thine hourly need;
He can with bread of heaven / Thy fainting spirit feed.

LAWRENCE TUTTIETT

While there is left in you a trace of ill-temper, or of vanity, or
pride, or of selfishness; while there is left in you a single sin, or
germ of sin, you must not rest from battle. God does not require
from you to be sinless when you come before Him, but He does
require you to be unceasing in your perseverance. He does not
require that you shall never have fallen; but he does require
unwearied efforts. He does not require you to win, but He does
require you to fight.

FREDERICK TEMPLE

Still fight resolutely on, knowing that, in this spiritual combat,
none is overcome but he who ceases to struggle and to trust in God.

LORENZO SCUPOLI

August 16

Then my enemies will turn back when I call for help.
By this I will know that God is for me.

PSALM 56:9 NIV

Soul! Would you from the battle shrink,
  And flee before the foe?
Do you beneath the burden sink,
  And in the dust lie low?
Oh! Waste not there vain tears and sighs:
  The trumpet sounds are clear;
O'ercome, and to My glory rise!
  O'ercome, and triumph here!

THOMAS H. GILL

Be not discouraged because of your soul's enemies. Are you
troubled with thoughts, fears, doubts, imaginations, reasonings?
Do you see, yet, much in you, excited to the power of life? Oh! Do
not fear it; do not look at it, so as to be discouraged by it, but look
to Him! Look up to the power which is over all their strength;
wait for the descending of the power upon you; abide in faith of
the Lord's help, and wait in patience till the Lord arise; and see if
His arms do not scatter what yours could not. So, be still before
Him, and, in stillness, believe in His name; yes, enter not into the
hurryings of the enemy, though they fill the soul; for, there is yet
some places to which they cannot enter, from where patience, faith,
and hope will spring up in you, even in the midst of all they can do.

ISAAC PENINGTON

August 17

We always carry around in our body the death of Jesus, so that the life of Jesus may also be revealed in our body.

2 Corinthians 4:10 NIV

But we as in a glass espy
    The glory of His countenance,
Not in a whirlwind hurrying by
    The too presumptuous glance,
But with mild radiance every hour,
    From our dear Savior's face benign
Bent on us with transforming power
    Till we, too, faintly shine.

John Keble

If we are faithful and humble, God will increase our faith by enabling us to obey more faithfully, and will strengthen our sight by enabling us to do what we now see. As in our daily walk we come nearer towards heaven, He will open to us more of heaven. And so the veil which sin laid upon our sight being taken away, "we all, with open face, beholding, as in a glass, the glory of the Lord," studying His countenance, watching His looks, seeking to have His gracious and compassionate look cast upon us in the midst of our frailties and infirmities, may catch some faint reflections of its brightness, and be changed into the image upon which we gaze, which we love, which, in our weakness, we would long to copy and transfuse into ourselves; [that] we too may be "changed into the same image, from glory to glory, as by the Spirit of the Lord."

Edward B. Pusey

August 18

*From where the sun rises to where it sets, you inspire shouts
of joy.... You crown the year with a bountiful harvest.*

PSALM 65:8, 11 NLT

I sing because Your works are fair, / Your glory makes me glad,
The garments bright of praise I wear, / For You are brightly clad.

Full triumph does my soul possess, / Because Your ways are right;
The glory of Your righteousness / Makes it my dear delight.

THOMAS H. GILL

The fullness of joy is to behold God in all; for by the same blessed
might, wisdom, and love, that He made all things, to the same end
our good Lord leads it continually, and there to Himself shall bring
it, and, when it is time, we shall see it.

JULIAN OF NORWICH

God gives us richly all things to enjoy, while He Himself is His own
best gift, and to be enjoyed not in a way of duty, but in the simple,
natural realizing correctly of what we possess in Him.

JOHN McLEOD CAMPBELL

August 19

It is required in stewards, that a man be found faithful.

1 Corinthians 4:2 kjv

Too many people are not faithful in little things. They are not to be absolutely depended upon. They do not always keep their promises. They break engagements. They fail to pay their debts promptly. They come late to appointments. They are neglectful and careless in little things. In general they are good people, but their life is honeycombed with small failures. One who can be positively depended upon, who is faithful in the least things as well as the greatest, whose life and character are true through and through, gives out a light in this world which honors Christ and blesses others.

J. R. Miller

Duties retire evermore from the observation of those who slight them.

Sarah W. Stephen

Great thoughts go best with common duties. Whatever therefore may be your responsibility regard it as a fragment in an immeasurable ministry of love.

Brooke Foss Westcott

August 20

*I do not regard myself as having laid hold of it yet; but one thing
I do: forgetting what lies behind and reaching forward to what lies
ahead, I press on toward the goal for the prize of the upward call
of God in Christ Jesus.*

PHILIPPIANS 3:13–14 NASB

> Till, as each moment wafts us higher,
> By every gush of pure desire,
> And high-breathed hopes of joys above,
> By every sacred sigh we heave,
> Whole years of folly we outlive,
> In His unerring sight, who measures life by love.

JOHN KEBLE

What we can *do* is a small thing; but we can...aspire to great
things. Thus if a man cannot be great, he can yet be good in will;
and what he, with his whole heart and mind, love and desire, wills
to be, that without doubt he most truly is. It is little we can bring
to pass; but our will and desire may be large. Nay, they may grow
till they lose themselves in the infinite abyss of God. And if you
cannot be as entirely His as you willingly would be, be His as
much as you possibly may; but, whatever you are, be that truly
and entirely; and what you cannot be, be contented not to be, in
a sincere spirit of resignation, for God's sake and in Him. So shall
you in some way possess more of God in lacking than in having.

JOHN TAULER

August 21

The God of Israel is He that giveth strength and power unto His people. Blessed be God.

PSALM 68:35 KJV

I will meet distress and pain,
I will greet e'en Death's dark reign,
I will lay me in the grave
With a heart still glad and brave;
    Whom the Strongest does defend,
    Whom the Highest counts His friend,
    Cannot perish in the end.

PAUL GERHARDT

Could we but live more entirely in the unseen Presence, and trust to the unseen support—and if lonely, or disappointed, or depressed, turn more quickly to God, fully confident of His all-embracing care, believing in His perfect love, the tender sympathy with which He ever regards us, how different life would be from what it ordinarily is! Yet we doubt not that divine support is assured to us, if we seek to do what is pleasing in His sight. If the end we desire comes not, yet there is rest in the assurance that we have told Him all, and left it to Him to do what He wills.

T. T. CARTER

August 22

Therefore, since Christ suffered for us in the flesh, arm yourselves also with the same mind, for he who has suffered in the flesh has ceased from sin.

1 Peter 4:1 NKJV

Take your whole portion with your Master's mind—
  Toil, hindrance, hardness, with His virtue take—
And think how short a time your heart may find
  To labor or to suffer for His sake.

Anna L Waring

Your portion is to love, to be silent, to suffer, to sacrifice your inclinations, in order to fulfill the will of God, by molding yourself to that of others. Happy indeed you are then to bear a cross laid on you by God's own hands, by order of His providence. The discipline which we choose for ourselves does not destroy our self-love like that which God assigns us Himself each day. All we have to do is to give ourselves up to God day by day, without looking further. He carries us in His arms as a loving mother carries her child. In every need let us look with love and trust to our heavenly Father.

François de Fénelon

The loving heart which seeks to offer all, even disappointments and vexations which touch the tenderest places, to God, will be more likely to grow in generosity of spirit than one who bears grudgingly what cannot be averted.

H. L. Sidney Lear

August 23

By his divine power, God has given us everything we need for living a godly life. We have received all of this by coming to know him, the one who called us to himself by means of his marvelous glory and excellence.

2 PETER 1:3 NLT

We often try in vain to cut up our errors by the roots, to fight evil hand to hand on its own ground, where it has us at a disadvantage, when our most sure way to victory is by developing and fortifying the good that is in us. We have but a certain measure of strength and activity; as much of this as is added to the good is taken from the evil.

MADAME SWETCHINE

I think you will find that it is not by making resolutions in a difficulty that you will conquer a fault—tackling it, I mean— but much more by opening a window to almighty God, and letting Him speak to you. As long as we are young we set so much importance on our own efforts, whereas often, if we will just do nothing but listen quietly to what God has to say to us, we shall find that He sets us thinking and mending our faults by a quiet way which looks as though it had nothing to do with it; and then, when we come to about where our fault used to be, we find it gone, imperceptibly as it were, by our having been strengthened in another direction which lay, though we did not know it, at the real root of the matter.

HENRIETTA KERR

August 24

I have heard the murmurings of the children of Israel.

EXODUS 16:12 KJV

Save our blessings, Master, save
  From the blight of thankless eye,
Teach us for all joys to crave
  Benediction pure and high,
Own them given, endure them gone,
Shrink from their hardening touch, yet prize them won,
Prize them as rich odors meet
For love to lavish at His sacred feet.

JOHN KEBLE

Nothing so hinders us in what we are doing as to be longing after
something else; in so doing, we leave off tilling our own field, to
drive the plough through our neighbor's land, where we must
not look to reap a harvest; and this is mere waste of time. If our
thoughts and hopes are elsewhere, it is impossible for us to set our
faces steadily towards the work required of us.

FRANCIS DE SALES

One thing is indisputable: the chronic mood of looking longingly at
what we have not, or thankfully at what we have, realizes two very
different types of character. And we certainly can encourage the
one or the other.

LUCY C. SMITH

August 25

*"For the mountains shall depart
And the hills be removed,
But My kindness shall not depart from you,
Nor shall My covenant of peace be removed,"
Says the L*ORD*, who has mercy on you.*

ISAIAH **54:10** NKJV

Not one word has failed of all the good promises he gave.

1 KINGS **8:56** NIV

There is a persuasion in the soul of man that he is here for a cause, that he was put down in this place by the Creator to do the work for which He inspires him, that thus he is an overmatch for all antagonists that could combine against him.

RALPH **W**ALDO **E**MERSON

It is impossible for that man to despair who remembers that his Helper is omnipotent and can do whatever He pleases. Let us rest there awhile—He can, if He please: He is infinitely loving, willing enough; and He is infinitely wise, choosing better for us than we can do for ourselves. God invites and cherishes the hopes of men by all the variety of His providence. He that believes does not make haste, but waits patiently, till the times of refreshment come, and dares trust God for the morrow. He is no more solicitous for the next year than he is for that which is past.

JEREMY **T**AYLOR

August 26

Blessed be the God and Father of our Lord Jesus Christ, the Father of mercies and God of all comfort, who comforts us in all our affliction so that we will be able to comfort those who are in any affliction with the comfort with which we ourselves are comforted by God.

2 CORINTHIANS 1:3–4 NASB

The spirit of gracious and *expressed* affection. Ah, let no one shrink from expressing it! The heart has strange abysses of gloom, and often yearns for just one word of love to help. And it is just when the manner may be drier and less genial than usual that the need may be greatest.

LUCY C. SMITH

God puts within our reach the power of helpfulness, the ministry of pity: He is ever ready to increase His grace in our hearts, that as we live and act among all the sorrows of the world we may learn by slow degrees the skill and mystery of consolation. "If you know these things, happy are you if you do them." There is no surer way of steadfast peace in this world than the active exercise of pity; no happier state of mind and work than the lowly watching to see if we can lessen any misery that is about us: nor is there any better way of growth in faith and love.

FRANCIS PAGET

August 27

Lay up for yourselves treasures in heaven...for where your treasure is, there will your heart be also.

MATTHEW 6:20–21 KJV

> Since I am coming to that holy room
> Where with the choir of saints forevermore
> I shall be made Your music, as I come
> I tune the instrument here at the door,
> And, what I must do then, think here before.

JOHN DONNE

To lay up treasure in heaven is to do acts which promote, or belong to, the kingdom of God; and what our Lord assures us of is that any act of our hands, any thought of our heart, any word of our lips, which promotes the divine kingdom by the ordering whether of our own life or of the world outside—all such activity, though it may seem for the moment to be lost, is really stored up in the divine treasure-house. And when the heavenly city, the New Jerusalem, shall at last appear, that honest effort of ours, which seemed so ineffectual, shall be found to be a brick built into that eternal and celestial fabric.

CHARLES GORE

We cannot remove the conditions under which our work is to be done, but we can transform them. They are the elements out of which we must build the temples where we serve.

BROOKE FOSS WESTCOTT

August 28

If you keep My commandments, you will abide in My love.

JOHN 15:10 NKJV

This did not once so trouble me,
That better I could not love Thee;
    But now I feel and know
That only when we love, we find
How far our hearts remain behind
    The love they should bestow.

RICHARD CHENIVIX TRENCH

Our Lord gives the answer to a difficulty continually perplexing
honest Christians—"How am I to learn to *love* God? I want to do
my duty, but I do not feel as if I loved God." Our Lord gives the
answer, "Where your treasure is, there will your heart be also."
Act for God, do and say the things that He wills, direct your
thoughts and intentions God-ward; and, depend upon it, in the slow
process of nature, all that belongs to you—your instincts, your
intelligence, your affections, your feelings—will gradually follow
along the line of your action. Act for God; you are already *showing*
love to Him and you will learn to *feel* it.

CHARLES GORE

They who, continuing faithful to divine grace, however partially
communicated, serve God with their whole lives, will never fail
of that one reward, the greatest which even He has to bestow, the
being made able to love Him with their whole hearts.

DORA GREENWELL

August 29

My problems go from bad to worse. Oh, save me from them all!

PSALM 25:17 NLT

Low at His feet lay your burden of carefulness,
    High on His heart He will bear it for thee,
Comfort thy sorrows, and answer thy prayerfulness,
    Guiding thy steps as may best for thee be.

J. S. B. MONSELL

The greatest burden we have to carry in life is self. The most
difficult thing we have to manage is self. Our own daily living, our
moods and feelings, our especial weaknesses and temptations, and
our peculiar temperaments—our inward affairs of every kind—
these are the things that perplex and worry us more than anything
else, and that bring us oftenest into bondage and darkness. In
laying off your burdens, therefore, the first one you must get
rid of is yourself. You must hand yourself and all your inward
experiences, your temptations, your temperament, your moods and
feelings, all over into the care and keeping of your God, and leave
them there. He made you and therefore He understands you, and
knows how to manage you, and you must trust Him to do it.

HANNAH WHITALL SMITH

August 30

*I am the L*ORD *your God, who teaches you to profit,*
Who leads you by the way you should go.

ISAIAH 48:17 NKJV

Just as God leads me I would go;
    I would not ask to choose my way;
Content with what He will bestow,
    Assured He will not let me stray.
So as He leads, my path I make,
And step by step I gladly take,
    A child in Him confiding.

LAMPERTUS GEDICKE

He has not made us for nothing; He has brought us thus far, in
order to bring us further, in order to bring us on to the end. He will
never leave us nor forsake us, so that we may boldly say, "The Lord
is my Helper; I will not fear what flesh can do unto me." We "may
cast all our care upon Him who cares for us." What is it to us how
our future path lies, if it is but His path? What is it to us where it
leads us, so that in the end it leads to Him? What is it to us what
He puts upon us, so that He enables us to undergo it with a pure
conscience, a true heart, not desiring anything of this world in
comparison of Him? What is it to us what terror befalls us, if He is
but at hand to protect and strengthen us?

JOHN HENRY NEWMAN

August 31

Behold, the LORD's hand is not shortened, that it cannot save; neither his ear heavy, that it cannot hear: but your iniquities have separated between you and your God, and your sins have hid his face from you.

ISAIAH 59:1–2 KJV

One thing alone, dear Lord! I dread—
    To have a secret spot
That separates my soul from Thee,
    And yet to know it not.

FREDERICK W. FABER

It is a condition of enjoying continued insight into the laws which govern spiritual truth, that we should conform our moral being to that measure of truth which we already see. A deliberate rejection of duty prescribed by already recognized truth cannot but destroy, or at least impair most seriously, the clearness of our mental vision. A single act may thus involve grave inward deterioration; it may land the soul upon a lower level of moral life, where passion is more imperious, and principle is weaker; where a man is less his own master, and more readily enslaved to the circumstances and beings around him.

H. P. LIDDON

It is strange but inflexible spiritual law, that those who aim at anything short of the best according to their conception, as God has given them light, will sooner or later come to grief. It is merely a matter of time.

CHARLES H. BRENT

SEPTEMBER

Friendships, family ties, the companionship
of little children, an autumn forest flung
in prodigality against a deep blue sky,
the intricate design and haunting fragrance
of a flower, the counterpoint of a Bach fugue
or the melodic line of a Beethoven sonata,
the fluted note of bird song, the glowing glory
of a sunset: the world is aflame with things
of eternal moment.

E. MARGARET CLARKSON

September 1

Do not fret—it leads only to evil.

PSALM 37:8 NIV

To anxious, prying thoughts,
    And weary, fretting care,
The Highest yieldeth nought;
    He giveth all to prayer.

PAUL GERHARDT

Do not be disquieted about your faults. Love without ceasing, and much will be forgiven you, because you have loved much. Faults perceived in peace, in the spirit of love, are immediately consumed by love itself; but faults perceived in an angry fit of self-love disturb peace, interrupt the presence of God, and the exercise of perfect love. Vexation at a fault is generally more of a fault than the fault itself.

FRANÇOIS DE FÉNELON

Fight like a good soldier; and if you sometimes fall through frailty, take again greater strength than before, trusting in My more abundant grace.

THOMAS À KEMPIS

This alone is your concern: to fight honorably, and never, however extensive your wounds, to lay down your arms, or to take to flight.

LORENZO SCUPOLI

September 2

"Let not a wise man boast of his wisdom, and let not the mighty man boast of his might, let not a rich man boast of his riches; but let him who boasts boast of this, that he understands and knows Me, that I am the LORD who exercises lovingkindness, justice and righteousness on earth; for I delight in these things," declares the LORD.

JEREMIAH 9:23–24 NASB

What do you fear? His wisdom reigns
    Supreme confessed;
His power is infinite; His love
Your deepest, fondest dreams above—
    So trust and rest.

ADELAIDE A. PROCTER

The firm belief of, and resting on, His power and wisdom, and love, gives a clear, satisfying answer to all doubts and fears. It does us no good to stand to jangle with each trifling, grumbling objection, but carries all before it, makes day in the soul, and so chases away those fears that vex us only in the dark.

ROBERT LEIGHTON

I feel that goodness, and truth, and righteousness are realities, eternal realities, and that they cannot be abstractions, or vapors floating in a spiritual atmosphere, but that they necessarily imply a living, personal will, a good, loving, righteous God, in whose hands we are perfectly safe, and who is guiding us by unfailing wisdom.

THOMAS ERSKINE

September 3

As a shepherd seeketh out his flock in the day that he is among his sheep that are scattered; so will I seek out my sheep, and will deliver them out of all places where they have been scattered in the cloudy and dark day.

EZEKIEL 34:12 KJV

The life which I now live in the flesh I live by the faith of the Son of God, who loved me, and gave himself for me.

GALATIANS 2:20 KJV

Perverse and foolish, oft I strayed,
    But yet in love He sought me,
And on His shoulder gently laid,
    And home rejoicing brought me.

SIR HENRY W. BAKER

Try to feel, by imagining what the lonely Syrian shepherd must feel towards the helpless things which are the companions of his daily life, for whose safety he stands in jeopardy every hour, and whose value is measured to him not by price, but by his own jeopardy. Then we have reached some notion of the love which Jesus meant to represent; that eternal tenderness which bends over us, and knows the name of each and trials of each, and thinks for each with a separate solicitude, and gave itself for each with a sacrifice as special, and a love as personal, as if in the whole world's wilderness there were none other but that one.

FREDERICK W. ROBERTSON

September 4

Make my joy complete by being of the same mind, maintaining the same love, united in spirit, intent on one purpose.... Have this attitude in yourselves which was also in Christ Jesus.

PHILIPPIANS 2:2, 5 NASB

Jesus, Your all-victorious love
    Shed in my heart abroad;
Then shall my feet no longer rove,
    Rooted and fixed in God.
My steadfast soul, from falling free,
    Shall then no longer move,
While Christ is all the world to me,
    And all my heart is love.

CHARLES WESLEY

Let our temper be under the rule of the love of Jesus: He can not alone curb it—*He can* make us gentle and patient. Let the vow, that not an unkind word of others shall ever be heard from our lips, be laid trustingly at His feet. Let the gentleness that refuses to take offence, that is always ready to excuse, to think and hope the best, mark our communication with all. Let our life be one of self-sacrifice, always studying the welfare of others, finding our highest joy in blessing others. And let us, in studying the divine art of doing good, yield ourselves as obedient learners to the guidance of the Holy Spirit. By His grace, the most commonplace life can be transfigured with the brightness of a heavenly beauty, as the infinite love of the divine nature shines out through our frail humanity.

ANDREW MURRAY

September 5

You yourselves are taught by God to love one another.

1 Thessalonians 4:9 NKJV

If we love one another, God lives in us and his love is made complete in us.

1 John 4:12 NIV

This is the great business and meaning of our life on earth: that we should more and more yield up our hearts to God's great grace of love; that we should let it enter ever more fully and more freely into us, so that it may even fill our whole heart and life. We must day after day be driving back, in His strength, the sin that does so easily beset us, and the selfishness that sin has fastened in our hearts; and then His love will day by day increase in us.

Prayer will win and keep it; work will strengthen and exercise it; the Bible will teach us how to know and prize it, how to praise God for it.... And so (blessed be God!) love and joy and peace will grow in us, beyond all that we can ask or think; and He will forgive us, for love's sake, all the failures, all the faults in whatever work He has given us to do; and will bring us at last into the fullness of that life which even here He has suffered us to know; into that one eternal home, where love is perfect, and unwearied, and unending; and where nothing ever can part us from one another or from Him.

Francis Paget

September 6

Bringing into captivity every thought to the obedience of Christ.

2 Corinthians 10:5 kjv

"I will lift up mine eyes unto the hills." The vision of God unseals
the lips of man. Herein lies strength for conflict with the common
enemy of the praying world known as wandering thoughts. If
the eye is fixed on God, thought may roam where it will without
irreverence, for every thought is then converted into a prayer.
Some have found it a useful thing when their minds have wandered
off from devotion and been snared by some good but irrelevant
consideration, not to chase away the offending thought as the
eyes are again lifted to the Divine Face, but to take it captive,
carry it into the presence of God, and weave it into a prayer before
putting it aside and resuming the original topic. This is to lead
captivity captive.

Charles H. Brent

Each wish to pray is a breath from heaven, to strengthen and
refresh us; each act of faith, done to amend our prayers, is wrought
in us by Him, and draws us to Him, and His gracious look on us.
Neglect nothing which can produce reverence.

Edward B. Pusey

September 7

Let me live forever in your sanctuary, safe beneath the shelter of your wings!

PSALM 61:4 NLT

Would it not be possible for every man to double his intellectual force by keeping much in the company of Infinite Wisdom?

E. P. TENNEY

I cannot help the thought which grows steadily upon me, that the better part of prayer is not the asking, but the kneeling where we can ask, the resting there, the staying there, drawing out the willing moments in heavenly communion with God, within the closet, with the night changed into the brightness of the day by the light of Him who all the night was in prayer to God. Just to be there, at leisure from ourselves, at leisure from the world, with our souls at liberty, with our spirit feeling its kinship to the Divine Spirit, with our life finding itself in the life of God—this is prayer. Would it be possible that one could be thus with God, listening to Him, speaking to Him, reposing upon His love, and not come out with a shining face, a gladdened heart, an intent more constant and more strong to give to the waiting world which so sadly needs what has been taken from the heart of God?

ALEXANDER MCKENZIE

September 8

*Sing unto the LORD, O ye saints of his, and give thanks
at the remembrance of his holiness.*

PSALM 30:4 KJV

Glad with Your light, and glowing with Your love,
So let me ever speak and think and move
    As fits a soul new-touched with life from heaven;
That seeks but so to order all her course
As most to show the glory of that Source
    By whom alone her strength, her life, are given.

C. J. P. SPITTA

Our Christianity is apt to be of a very "dutiful" kind. We mean to
do our duty, we attend church and go to our communions. But our
hearts are full of the difficulties, the hardships, the obstacles which
the situation presents, and we go on our way sadly, downhearted
and despondent. We need to learn that true Christianity is
inseparable from deep joy; and the secret of that joy lies in a
continual looking away from all else—away from sin and its ways,
and from the various hindrances to the good we would do—up to
God, His love, His purpose, His will. In proportion as we do look
up to Him we shall rejoice, and in proportion as we rejoice in the
Lord will our religion have tone and power and attractiveness.

CHARLES GORE

September 9

*Just as the Father has loved Me, I have also loved you;
abide in My love.*

JOHN 15:9 NASB

Abide in Me: These words are the command of love, which is ever
only a promise in a different shape. Think of this until all feeling
of burden and fear and despair pass away, and the first thought
that comes as you hear of abiding in Jesus is one of bright and
joyous hope.

ANDREW MURRAY

When love is heard inviting more trust, more love, the
encouragement to trust, to love, goes beyond the rebuke that our
love is so little, and we take heart to confide in the love that is
saying, "Give me thine heart," expecting that it will impart itself
to us, and enable us to give the response of love which it desires.
For indeed it must be with the blessed purpose to enable us to love
Him that our God bids us love Him; for He knows that no love but
what He Himself quickens in us can love Him.

Therefore always feel the *call to love a gracious promise* of
strength to love, and marvel not at your own deadness, but trust
in Him who quickens the dead.

JOHN MCLEOD CAMPBELL

September 10

And above all these things put on charity, which is the bond of perfectness.

COLOSSIANS 3:14 KJV

You hate hatred's withering reign;
    In souls that discord maketh dark
    Do You rekindle love's bright spark,
And make them one again.

PAUL GERHARDT

We have cause to suspect our religion if it does not make us gentle, and forbearing, and forgiving; if the love of our Lord does not so flood our hearts as to cleanse them of all bitterness, and spite, and wrath. If a man is nursing anger, if he is letting his mind become a nest of foul passions, malice, and hatred, and evil wishing, how dwells the love of God in him?

HUGH BLACK

Love me always, boy, whatever I do or leave undone. And— God help me—whatever you do or leave undone, I'll love you. There shall never be a cloud between us for a day; no, sir, not for an hour. We're imperfect enough, all of us, we needn't be so bitter; and life is uncertain enough at its safest, we needn't waste its opportunities.

JULIANA H. EWING

September 11

Love does no harm to a neighbor; therefore love is the fulfillment of the law.

ROMANS 13:10 NKJV

In her tongue is the law of kindness.

PROVERBS 31:26 KJV

The worst kinds of unhappiness, as well as the greatest amount of it, come from our conduct to each other. If our conduct, therefore, were under the control of kindness, it would be nearly the opposite of what it is, and so the state of the world would be almost reversed. We are for the most part unhappy because the world is an unkind world. But the world is only unkind for the lack of kindness in us who compose it.

FREDERICK W. FABER

You feel in some families as if you were living between the glasses of a microscope. Manner, accent, expression, all that goes to make up your "personality," all that you do or leave undone, is commented upon and found fault with.

H. BOWMAN

If you would be loved as a companion, avoid unnecessary criticism upon those with whom you live.

ARTHUR HELPS

September 12

Yes indeed, it is good when you obey the royal law as found in the Scriptures: "Love your neighbor as yourself."

JAMES 2:8 NLT

Do you feel yourself alone and empty-hearted? Then you have necessity indeed for fortitude and brave endurance, but above all and before all you must get out of your solitude. You cannot command for yourself the love you would gladly receive; it is not in our power to do that; but that noble love which is not asking but giving—that you can always have. Wherever your life touches another life, there you have opportunity. To mix with men and women in the ordinary forms of social association becomes a sacred function when one carries into it the true spirit. To give a close, sympathetic attention to every human being we touch; to try to get some sense of how he feels, what he is, what he needs; to make in some degree his interest our own—that disposition and habit would deliver any one of us from isolation or emptiness.

GEORGE S. MERRIAM

She did not try to set others right; she only listened to and loved and understood her fellow-creatures.

ELIZA KEARY

September 13

The peace of God, which passeth all understanding,
shall keep your hearts and minds through Christ Jesus.

PHILIPPIANS 4:7 KJV

I take You for my Peace, O Lord,
    My heart to keep and fill;
Your own great calm, amid earth's storms,
    Shall keep me always still,
And as Your kingdom does increase,
So shall Your ever-deepening peace.

ANNIE W. MARSTON

Remember this, busy and burdened disciple; man or woman tried
by uncertain health; immersed in secular duties; forced to a life
of almost ceaseless publicity: Here is written an assurance, a
guarantee, that not at holy times and welcome intervals only, not
only in the dust of death, but in the dust of life: there is prepared
for you the peace of God, able to keep your hearts and thoughts in
Christ Jesus. It is found in Him, it is cultivated by connection with
Him. It is "the secret of His presence." Amidst the circumstances
of your life, which are the expression of His will, He can maintain
it, He can keep you in it. Nay, it is not passive; it "shall keep" you
alive, and loving, and practical, and ready at His call.

HANDLEY C. G. MOULE

September 14

I will walk within my house with a perfect heart.

PSALM 101:2 KJV

Teach me, O God, Your holy way,
    And give me an obedient mind;
    That in Your service I may find
My soul's delight from day to day.

WILLIAM TIDD MATSON

As far as human frailty will permit, each little trifling piece of duty
which presents itself to us in daily life, if it is only a compliance
with some form of social courtesy, should receive a consecration,
by setting God—His will, word, and providence—before us in it,
and by lifting up our hearts to Him in spoken prayer, while we
are engaged in it. The idea must be thoroughly worked into the
mind, and woven into the texture of our spiritual life, that the
minutest duties which God prescribes to us in the order of His
providence—a casual visit, a letter of sympathy, and obligation of
courtesy, are not by any means too humble to be made means of
spiritual advancement, if only the thing be done "as to the Lord,
and not to men."

EDWARD MEYRICK GOULBURN

Learn to commend your daily acts to God, so the dry everyday
duties of common life become steps to heaven, and lift your
heart there.

EDWARD B. PUSEY

September 15

Deliver those who are being taken away to death, and those who are staggering to slaughter, Oh hold them back. If you say, "See, we did not know this," does He not consider it who weighs the hearts? And does He not know it who keeps your soul? And will He not render to man according to his work?

PROVERBS 24:11–12 NASB

What we value for ourselves we must seek to spread to others; and what we shrink from ourselves—depressing surroundings, a tainted atmosphere, what we shrink to think of those nearest and dearest to us being exposed to—let us do all we can to remove from others. "Lead *us* not into temptation. Deliver *us* from evil." Do what you can to sweeten the mental and moral atmosphere that surrounds you.

ARTHUR C. A. HALL

We have a more or less true ideal of what our own human life ought to be—of what opportunities we ought to have for the development of our faculties, of what home and school and college, youth and married life and old age, work and rest ought to mean for ourselves and our families. We are to be as truly zealous and active for other groups or other individuals as we are for our own group or our own family or ourselves.

CHARLES GORE

September 16

I will mention the lovingkindnesses of the LORD, and the praises of the LORD, according to all that the LORD hath bestowed on us.

ISAIAH 63:7 KJV

Be content with what you have.

HEBREWS 13:5 NIV

My God shall supply all your need according to his riches in glory by Christ Jesus.

PHILIPPIANS 4:19 KJV

Begin with thanking Him for some little thing, and then go on, day by day, adding to your subjects of praise; thus you will find their numbers grow wonderfully; and, in the same proportion, will your subjects of murmuring and complaining diminish, until you see in everything some cause for thanksgiving. If you cannot begin with anything positive, begin with something negative. If your whole lot seems only filled with causes for discontent, at any rate there is some trial that has *not* been appointed you, and you may thank God for its being withheld from you. It is certain that the more you try to praise, the more you will see how your path and your lying down are beset with mercies, and that the God of love is ever watching to do you good.

PRISCILLA MAURICE

September 17

The meek shall inherit the earth; and shall delight themselves in the abundance of peace.

PSALM 37:11 KJV

Joy is Your gift, O Father!
    You would not have us pine;
In darkest hours Your comfort
    Does aye most brightly shine;
Ah, then how oft Your voice
    Has shed its sweetness o'er me,
    And opened heaven before me,
And bid my heart rejoice!

PAUL GERHARDT

I perceive we postpone all our joys of Christ, till He and we be in our own house above, thinking that there is nothing of it here to be sought or found, but only hope and fair promises; and that Christ will give us nothing here but tears, sadness, crosses; and that we shall never feel the smell of the flowers of that high garden of paradise above, till we come there. No, but I find it possible to find young glory, and a young green paradise of joy even here. We dream of hunger in Christ's house while we are here, although He allows feasts to all the children within God's household.

SAMUEL RUTHERFORD

September 18

Now to Him who is able to do exceedingly abundantly above all that we ask or think, according to the power that works in us, to Him be glory in the church by Christ Jesus to all generations, forever and ever. Amen.

EPHESIANS 3:20–21 NKJV

All the simplest, most living, and most genuine Christians of our own time are such as rest their souls, day by day, on this confidence and promise of accruing power, and make themselves responsible, not for what they have in some inherent ability, but for what they can have in their times of stress and peril, and in the continual raising of their own personal quantity and power. Instead of gathering in their souls timidly beforehand upon the little sufficiency they possess, they look upon the great world God has made, and all the greater world of the Savior's kingdom in it, as being friendly and complementary, ready to pour in help, minister light, and strengthen them to victory, just according to their faith. And so they grow in courage, confidence, personal volume, efficiency of every kind, and instead of slinking into their graves out of impotent lives, they lie down in the honors of heroes.

HORACE BUSHNELL

Expect great things from God; attempt great things for God.

WILLIAM CAREY

September 19

*He who dwells in the shelter of the Most High will rest
in the shadow of the Almighty.*

PSALM 91:1 NIV

As soon as I woke in the morning I threw myself into the arms of
Divine Love as a child does into its father's arms. I rose to serve
Him, and to perform my daily labor simply that I might please
Him. If I had time for prayer, I fell on my knees in His divine
presence, consecrated myself to Him, and begged Him that He
would accomplish His holy will perfectly in me and through me,
and that He would not permit me to offend Him in the least thing
all through the day. I occupied myself with Him and His praise
as long as my duties permitted. Very often, I had not leisure to
say even so much as the Lord's Prayer during the day; but that
did not trouble me. I thought it as much my duty to work for Him
as to pray to Him, for He Himself had taught me, that all that I
should do for love of Him would be a true prayer. I loved Him and
rejoiced in Him. If my occupations required all my attention, I had
nevertheless my heart turned towards Him; and, as soon as they
were finished, I ran to Him again, as to my dearest Friend. When
evening came, and every one went to rest, I found mine only in the
Divine Love, and fell asleep, still loving and adoring Him.

ARMELLE NICOLAS

September 20

Those who love Your law have great peace,
And nothing causes them to stumble.

PSALM 119:165 NASB

In Your might all things I bear,
    In Your love find bitter sweet,
And with all my grief care,
    Sit in patience at Your feet.

A. H. FRANCKE

What you need to do is to put your character over completely in the hands of your Lord, surrendering to Him the entire control of it. Say, "Yes, Lord, YES!" to everything, and trust Him so to work in you to choose, as to bring your whole wishes and affections into conformity with His own sweet, and lovable, and most lovely will. It is wonderful what miracles God works in choices that are utterly surrendered to Him; He turns hard things into easy, and bitter things into sweet. It is not that He puts easy things in the place of the hard, but He actually changes the hard thing into an easy one.

HANNAH WHITALL SMITH

It has been well remarked, it is not said that *after* keeping God's commandments, but *in* keeping them there is great reward. God has linked these two things together, and no man can separate them—obedience and peace.

F. W. ROBERTSON

Choose life...that you may love the LORD your God, that you may obey His voice, and that you may cling to Him, for He is your life and the length of your days.

DEUTERONOMY 30:19–20 NKJV

God gently calls us every day;
Why should we then our bliss delay?
He calls to heaven and endless light;
Why should we love the dreary night?

Praise, Lord, to Thee for Matthew's call,
At which he rose and left his all;
Thou, Lord, e'en now are calling me;
I will leave all, and follow Thee.

WILLIAM WALSHAM HOW

Obey His blessed call now, and, having obeyed it once, never again disobey any call within you to do His will. While we mourn our neglect of past calls, our sorrow, which is still His gift and call within us, will draw down His gladdening look, [and] again call us to Him. If we pass by no call which, however indistinctly, we may have, He will cheer us with clearer and gladlier calls. Our very sorrow and fear will be our joy and hope; our very stumblings our strength, and dimness our light, while stumbling or in darkness we feel after Him who is our Stay, our Light, our Joy.

EDWARD B. PUSEY

September 22

Dear friends, don't be surprised at the fiery trials you are going through, as if something strange were happening to you. Instead, be very glad—for these trials make you partners with Christ in his suffering.

1 PETER 4:12–13 NLT

Not more than I can bear I know
    You dearest Lord, wilt on me lay,
And I can learn of You to go
    Unfearing on my way.

HARRIET MCEWEN KIMBALL

It is a tremendous moment when first one is called upon to join the great army of those who suffer. That vast world of love and pain opens suddenly to admit us one by one within its fortress. We are afraid to enter into the land, yet you will, I know, feel how high is the call. It is as a trumpet speaking to us that cries aloud, "it is your turn—endure." Play your part. As they endured before you, so now close up the ranks—be patient and strong as they were. Since Christ, this world of pain is no accident disturbing or sinister, but a lawful department of life, with experiences, interests, adventures, hopes, delights, secrets of its own. These are all thrown open to us as we pass within the gates—things that we could never learn or know or see, so long as we were well. God help you to walk through this world now opened to you, as through a kingdom, royal, and wide and glorious.

HENRY SCOTT HOLLAND

September 23

Take heed, and be quiet; fear not, neither be fainthearted.

ISAIAH 7:4 KJV

Though everything outside fall into confusion, and though your body be in pain and suffering, and your soul in desolation and distress, yet let your spirit be unmoved by it all, placid and serene, delighted in and with its God inwardly, and with His good pleasure outwardly.

GERHARD TERSTEEGEN

To say each morning, "I must have things exhausting, painful, to bear today, and they shall all be offered up beforehand as my heart's sacrifice; they shall be, not fought against, but received calmly and as welcome, for His sake who suffers them to come," gives a dignity, a purpose, no, a very joy to what otherwise is all cheerless annoyance.

H. L SIDNEY LEAR

As soon as anything presents itself to your mind as a suffering, and you feel a repugnance to it, resign yourself immediately to God with respect to it; give yourself up to Him in sacrifice, and you will find that, when the cross arrives, it will not be so very burdensome, because you had disposed yourself to a willing reception of it.

MADAME GUYON

September 24

Wait for the Lord; be strong and let your heart take courage; yes, wait for the Lord.

Psalm 27:14 nasb

I ask not that my course be calm and still;
No, here too, Lord, be done Thy holy will:
    I ask but for a quiet childlike heart;
Though thronging cares and restless toil be mine,
Yet may my heart remain forever Thine;
    Draw it from earth, and fix it where Thou art.

B. J. P. Spitta

True union with God is to do His will without ceasing, in spite of all our natural disinclination, in all the wearisome and painful duties of our condition.

François de Fénelon

When persons have learned to look upon the daily course of their ordinary life, with its duties and troubles, however commonplace, as their offering to God, and as the safest school for themselves of perfection, they will have made a very important step in the spiritual life. Another step, so simple that it is often despised, is to do everything, however ordinary, as well as it can possibly be done, for God's sake. A third is to be always pressing forward; when a mistake is made, or a fault committed, to face and admit it freely; but having asked God to supply the deficiency caused by our own infirmity, to go on steadfastly and hopefully.

H. L. Sidney Lear

September 25

If you serve Christ with this attitude, you will please God,
and others will approve of you, too.

ROMANS 14:18 NLT

Then shall I not be ashamed, when I have respect unto all
thy commandments.

PSALM 119:6 KJV

True fidelity consists in obeying God in all things, and in following
the light that points out our duty, and the grace which guides
us; taking as our rule of life the intention to please God in all
things, and to do always not only what is acceptable to Him,
but, if possible, what is *most* acceptable; not trifling with petty
distinctions between sins great and small, imperfections and faults,
for, though there may be such distinctions, they should have no
weight with the soul that is determined to do *all* His will. To this
sincere desire to do the will of God, we must add a cheerful spirit,
that is not overcome when it has failed, but begins again and again
to do better; hoping always to the very end to be able to do it;
bearing with its own involuntary weakness, as God bears with it;
waiting with patience for the moment when it shall be delivered
from it; going straight on in singleness of heart, according to the
strength that it can command; losing no time by looking back, nor
making useless reflections upon its falls, which can only embarrass
and retard its progress.

FRANÇOIS DE FÉNELON

September 26

Commit thy way unto the LORD; trust also in him, and he shall bring it to pass.

PSALM 37:5 KJV

Plan not, nor scheme—but calmly wait;
    His choice is best.
While blind and erring is thy sight,
His wisdom sees and judges right,
    So trust and rest.

ADELAIDE A. PROCTER

"Great peace have they which love My law." They see that from Me, the sovereign Ruler of the world, order, and love, nothing but good can spring; and that I can take care of them and their affairs far better and more successfully than they could of themselves. Thus, considering that all that happens to them comes from Me, they are strong with an invincible patience, and bear all things, not only with resignation, but with cheerfulness and joy, tasting in all things that befall them externally or internally the sweetness of My incredible love. And this is to believe, and meditate with a cheerful and grateful spirit, even in the midst of tribulations and difficulties, that it is I who sweetly dispose all things, and that whatever happens springs from the inexhaustible fountain of My goodness.

CATHERINE OF SIENA

September 27

Therefore, there is now no condemnation for those who are in Christ Jesus.

ROMANS 8:1 NIV

It may be that recollections of the past hinder you, but you must reject them; anxious thoughts may arise, put them away; your faults seem to raise up a barrier, but no past faults can separate a loving heart from God.

H. L. SIDNEY LEAR

Do not scrutinize so closely whether you are doing much or little, ill or well, so long as what you do is not sinful, and that you are heartily seeking to do everything for God. Try as far as you can to do everything well, but when it is done do not think about it; try rather to think of what is to be done next. Go on simply in the Lord's way, and do not torment yourself. We ought to hate our faults, but with quiet, calm hatred, not petulantly at them, and win through them the grace of self-deprecation and humility. Be constant and courageous, and rejoice that He has given you the will to be wholly His.

FRANCIS DE SALES

September 28

Even to your old age I will be the same, and even to your graying years I will bear you! I have done it, and I will carry you; and I will bear you and I will deliver you.

ISAIAH 46:4 NASB

The chariots of God are twenty thousand, even thousands of angels; the Lord is among them, as in Sinai, in the holy place.

PSALM 68:17 KJV

I have not a shadow of doubt that if all our eyes could be opened today, we should see our homes, and our places of business, and the streets we traverse, filled with the "chariots of God." There is no need for any one of us to walk for lack of chariots. That cross inmate of your household, who has hitherto made life a burden to you, and who has been the juggernaut car to crush your soul into the dust, may henceforth be a glorious chariot to carry you to the heights of heavenly patience and long-suffering. That misunderstanding, that mortification, that unkindness, that disappointment, that loss, that defeat—all these are chariots waiting to carry you to the very heights of victory you have so longed to reach. Mount into them, then, with thankful hearts, and lose sight of all second causes in the shining of His love who will carry you in His arms safely and triumphantly over it all.

HANNAH WHITALL SMITH

September 29

Are they not all ministering spirits, sent forth to minister for them who shall be heirs of salvation?

HEBREWS 1:14 KJV

Angels descending, bring from above
Echoes of mercy, whispers of love.

FANNY J. CROSBY

With every evil overcome, and every new likeness of Christ inwardly put on, you are brought more completely within the circle of the great cloud of witnesses, the myriads of angels in full assembly, and the spirits of good men made perfect; their strength passes mightily into your soul and their peace is laid brightly within the heart. This is one of the essential elements of our strength when we are supported and buoyed up in doing the divine will. You are not marching alone. You feel it; you know it. Visible or invisible, a mighty host is with you; you are marching with them in countless and congested numbers; one spirit moves the whole and lifts their feet, and they keep step to the same music.

EDMUND H. SEARS

September 30

You must not fear them, for the LORD your God Himself fights for you.

DEUTERONOMY 3:22 NKJV

Oh, for trust that brings the triumph
    When defeat seems strangely near!
Oh, for faith that changes fighting
    Into victory's ringing cheer—
Faith triumphant, knowing not defeat or fear!

HERBERT BOOTH

Hopefulness of final victory is ours, if we only remember that we are fighting God's battles. And can He know defeat? He who is the God of the great world around us is the God of the little world within. It is He who is contending in you; you are but His soldier, guided by His wisdom, strengthened by His might, shielded by His love. Keep your will united to the will of God, and the final defeat is impossible, for He is invincible.

GEORGE BODY

Courage, it shall be well. We follow a conquering general; yes, who has conquered already; and He that has conquered for us shall ever conquer in us.

ROBERT LEIGHTON

OCTOBER

Sunshine spills through autumn-colored
leaves, lighting up their brilliance
like stained-glass windows
in a great cathedral,
expressing the wonder of God's love,
declaring His glory.

October 1

Nevertheless I am continually with You; You have taken hold of my right hand.

PSALM 73:23 NASB

Faith is a grasping of almighty power;
The hand of man laid on the arm of God;
    The grand and blessed hour
In which the things, impossible to me,
Become the possible, O Lord, through Thee.

ANNA E. HAMILTON

Nothing is necessary for you in maintaining a triumphant Christian life, but just stay by the helm, and put yourself in where the power is. Come unto God, unite yourself to God, and the doing power you have is infinite!—and is none the less yours because it is His. Trim your ship steadily to the course, and God's own gales will waft it.

HORACE BUSHNELL

Gaze intently with the eye of faith at the infinite wisdom and omnipotence of God, to whom nothing is impossible or difficult, and consider that His goodness is unbounded, and unspeakable His willingness to give, hour by hour, and moment by moment, all things needful for the spiritual life, and for complete victory over self, if we will throw ourselves with confidence into His arms.

LORENZO SCUPOLI

October 2

In every work that he began in the service of the house of God,
and in the law and in the commandments, to seek his God,
he did it with all his heart. So he prospered.

2 CHRONICLES 31:21 NKJV

In waiting we begin to get in touch with the rhythms of life—
stillness and action, listening and decision. They are the rhythms
of God. It is in the everyday and the commonplace that we learn
patience, acceptance, and contentment.

RICHARD J. FOSTER

There is no other way in which one's life will be so surely, so
quickly, transfigured as in the faithful, happy, cheerful doing of
everyday tasks. We need to remember that this world is not so
much a place for doing things as for making character. Right in the
midst of what some people call drudgery is the very best place to
get the transformed, transfigured life. The doing of common tasks
patiently, promptly, faithfully, cheerfully, makes the character
beautiful and bright. But we must take heed always that we do our
tasks, whatever they are, with love in our heart. Doing any kind of
work unwillingly, with complaint and murmuring, hurts the life.

J. R. MILLER

God weighs more how much love a man works, than how much
he does. He does much that loves much. He does much that does
a thing well.

THOMAS À KEMPIS

October 3

These things I have spoken to you, so that in Me you may have
peace. In the world you have tribulation, but take courage;
I have overcome the world.

JOHN 16:33 NASB

You will I love, my Crown of gladness,
    You will I love, my God and Lord,
Amid the darkest depth of sadness;
    Not for the hope of high reward—
For your own sake, O Light Divine,
    So long as life is mine.

JOHANN SCHEFFLER

What is the secret of serenity? We all want to know it. Indeed, we
do know it already. There is no secret about it. St. Paul speaks it
out plainly enough. Everybody can see what it is: All things work
together for good to them that love God. We must love God, that is
the heart of it. Happiness, contentment, and right satisfaction, all
doubts answered, all dark places lighted up, heaven begun here [on
earth]—this is the reward of loving God. In this world, tribulation;
yes, but good cheer in spite of that, for the Son of God, whom we
love, has overcome the world.

GEORGE HODGES

Man's happiness consists in present peace, even in the midst of the
greatest trials, and in more than hope of a glorious future.

CHARLES G. GORDON

October 4

Bless the LORD, all his works in all places of his dominion:
bless the LORD, O my soul.

PSALM 103:22 KJV

O most high, almighty, good Lord God, to You belong praise, glory, honor, and all blessing.

Praised be my Lord God with all His creatures, and especially our brother the sun, who brings us the day; fair is he and shines with a very great splendor; O Lord, he signifies to us You. Praised be my Lord for our sister the moon, and for the stars, the which He has set clear and lovely in heaven.

Praised be my Lord for our sister water, who is very serviceable unto us, and humble and precious and clean. Praised be You, my Lord, for our brother fire; he is bright and pleasant and very mighty and strong. Praised be my Lord for our mother the earth, who doth sustain us and keep us, and brings forth diverse fruits and flowers of many colors, and grass.

Praised be my Lord for all those who pardon one another for His love's sake, and who endure weakness and tribulation. Praised be You, my Lord, for...the death of the body, from which no man escapes.

Praise you and bless you the Lord, and give thanks unto Him and serve Him with great humility.

FRANCIS OF ASSISI

October 5

It is good to give thanks to the LORD,
And to sing praises to Your name, O Most High;
To declare Your lovingkindness in the morning,
And Your faithfulness every night.

PSALM 92:1–2 NKJV

Praise to the Holiest in the height,
    And in the depth be praise;
In all His words most wonderful,
    Most sure in all His ways.

JOHN HENRY NEWMAN

If our hearts were tuned to praise, we should see causes
unnumbered, which we had never seen before, for thanking God.
Thanksgiving is spoken of as a "sacrifice well pleasing unto God."
It is a far higher offering than prayer. When we pray we ask for
things which we want; or we pour out our sorrows. We pray, in
order to bring down blessing upon ourselves; we praise, because
our hearts overflow with love to God, and we must speak it out to
Him. It flows out of pure love, and then the love goes back to our
hearts, and warms them anew, and revives and quickens them.

PRISCILLA MAURICE

Learn the lesson of thanksgiving. It is due to God, it is due to
ourselves. Thanksgiving for the past makes us trustful in the
present and hopeful for the future. What He has done is the pledge
of what He will do.

A. C. A. HALL

October 6

Rest in the Lord, and wait patiently for him.

Psalm 37:7 kjv

Is it the Lord that shuts me in?
　　Then I can bear to wait!
No place so dark, no place so poor,
So strong and fast no prisoning door,
　　Though walled by grievous fate,
But out of it goes fair and broad
An unseen pathway, straight to God,
　　By which I mount to Thee.

Susan Coolidge

We cannot be useless while we are doing and suffering God's will, whatever it may be found to be. And we can always do that. If we are bringing forth the fruits of the Spirit, we are not useless. And we can always do that. If we are increasing in the knowledge of God's will in all wisdom and spiritual understanding, we are not useless. And we can always do that. While we pray we cannot be useless. And we can always do that. God will always find us a work to do, a niche to fill, a place to serve, no, even a soul to save, when it is His will, and not ours, that we desire to do; and if it should please Him that we should sit still for the rest of our lives, doing nothing else but waiting on Him, and waiting for Him, why should we complain? *Here is the patience of the saints.*

Anthony W. Thorold

October 7

The share of the man who stayed with the supplies is to be the same as that of him who went down to the battle. All will share alike.

1 SAMUEL 30:24 NIV

Worship of service—which? Ah, that is best
To which He calls us, be it toil or rest—
To labor for Him in life's busy stir,
Or seek His feet, a silent worshiper.

CAROLINE A. MASON

Let us no more yearn for present employment when God's providence bids us "be still," than we would think it good to yearn after cessation while God bids us work. Shall we not miss a blessing if we call rest a weariness and a discontent, no less than if we called God's work a thankless labor? If we would be holy in body and spirit, shall we not keep smooth brow, light heart, whether He bids us serve His table, or wait our summons?

EDWARD WHITE BENSON

He who acts with a view to please God alone wishes to have that only which it pleases God that he should have, and at the time and in the way which may be most agreeable to Him; and, whether he have it or not, he is equally tranquil and contented, because in either case he obtains his wish, and fulfills his intention, which was no other than purely to please God.

LORENZO SCUPOLI

October 8

Don't be afraid of what you are about to suffer.

REVELATION 2:10 NLT

Let Your tender mercies come to me, that I may live;
for Your law is my delight.

PSALM 119:77 NKJV

O blessed life! The heart at rest
    When all without tumultuous seems;
    That trusts a higher Will, and deems
That higher Will, not mine, the best.

WILLIAM TIDD MATSON

Nothing is so trying to nature as suspense between a faint hope and a mighty fear; but we must have faith as to the extent of our trials, as in all else. Our sensitiveness makes us often disposed to suppose that we are tried beyond our strength; but we really know neither our strength to endure nor the nature of God's trials. Only He who knows both these, and every turn of the hearts which He has made knows how to deal out a due proportion. Let us leave it all to Him, and be content to bear in silence.

FRANÇOIS DE FÉNELON

It is not the sunny side of Christ that we must look to, and we must not forsake Him for want of that. Oh, how sweet a thing were it for us to learn to make our burdens light, by framing our hearts to the burden, and making our Lord's will a law!

SAMUEL RUTHERFORD

October 9

So is the man who stores up treasure for himself, and is not rich toward God.

LUKE 12:21 NASB

Just to leave in His dear hand
     Little things;
All we cannot understand,
     All that stings.
Just to let Him take the care
     Sorely pressing,
Finding all we let Him bear
     Changed to blessing.

FRANCES RIDLEY HAVERGAL

It seems as if God gathered into His storehouse, from each of our lives, fruit in which He delights. And the daily cross-bearings of self-denial, the bright word spoken when head and heart are weary, the meek endurance of misunderstanding, the steady going on in one unbroken round with a patient cheerfulness that knows nothing of "moods"—all these are garnered there, and add to our riches towards Him.

H. BOWMAN

It is a great matter to learn to look upon troubles and trials not as simply evils. How can that be evil which God sends? And those who can repress complaints, murmurs, and peevish bemoaning— better still, the vexed feelings which beset us when those around inflict petty annoyances and slights on us—will really find that their little daily worries are turning into blessings.

H. L. SIDNEY LEAR

October 10

For our heart shall rejoice in him, because we have trusted in his holy name.

PSALM 33:21 KJV

Take anxious care for nought,
 To God your wants make known;
And soar on wings of heavenly thought
 Toward His eternal throne;
So, though our path is steep,
 And many a tempest lowers,
Shall His own peace our spirits keep,
 And Christ's dear love be ours.

JOHN MOULTRIE

Cherish thankfulness with prayer. St. Paul gives us in two words this secret of peace. "In everything," (he excepts nothing, so do not yourself) "by prayer and supplication with *thanksgiving* let your requests be made known unto God. And the peace of God which passeth all understanding *shall* keep your hearts and minds through Christ Jesus." He does not say it as a benediction only: he tells us, it "*shall* keep your hearts and minds." Do the one and God will do the other. Ask what you will, be thankful; and not peace only, but peace which passes all which our poor minds can think shall keep these poor breaking, restless hearts—these ever wearying, worrying minds of ours—in Christ Jesus.

EDWARD B. PUSEY

October 11

Shall I not drink the cup which My Father has given Me?

JOHN 18:11 NKJV

Do not be conformed to this world, but be transformed by the renewing of your mind, so that you may prove what the will of God is, that which is good and acceptable and perfect.

ROMANS 12:2 NASB

We are often greatly hindered in the fulfillment of our duties by an unconscious clinging to self, which holds us back from God, and which leads us to seek our rest in something other than the simple fulfillment of His most holy will. If we honestly sought nothing save His will, we should always be in a state of perfect peace, let what may happen. But, very often, even when we ask that God's will may be done, we still wish it to be done after our fashion.

PERE HYACINTHE BESSON

When we are fully delivered from the influence of selfish considerations, and have become conformed to the desires and purposes of the Infinite Mind, we shall drink the cup, and drink it cheerfully, whatever it may be. In a word, we shall necessarily be submissive and happy in all trials, and in every change and diversity of situation. Not because we are seeking happiness, or thinking of happiness, as a distinct object, but because [of what] the glorious will of Him whom our soul loves supremely is accomplished in us.

THOMAS C. UPHAM

October 12

You say, "It's too hard to serve the LORD."

MALACHI 1:13 NLT

My soul clings to the dust; revive me according to Your word.

PSALM 119:25 NKJV

Awake, sleeper, and arise from the dead, and Christ will shine on you.

EPHESIANS 5:14 NASB

There are some who give up their prayers because they have so little feeling in their prayers—so little warmth of feeling. But who told us that feeling was to be a test of prayer? The work of prayer is a far too noble and necessary work to be laid aside for any lack of feeling. Press on, you who are dry and cold in your prayers, press on as a work and as a duty, and the Holy Spirit will, in His good time, refresh your prayers Himself.

ARTHUR F. WINNINGTON INGRAM

You do not feel in the spirit of prayer; you have no spiritual uplift; you are simply indifferent. Give that unhappy mood no heed.... You ought to present yourself before God; you ought to say your prayers. Do that, and the devout attitude, the bended knees, the folded hands, the quiet and the silence, the lips busied with holy words will induce the consciousness of the divine presence, and help you to pray in spirit and truth.

GEORGE HODGES

October 13

We have known and believed the love that God hath to us.

1 JOHN 4:16 KJV

Not what I am, O Lord, but what You art!
    That, that alone can be my soul's true rest;
Your love, not mine, bids fear and doubt depart,
    And stills the tempest of my tossing breast.

HORATIUS BONAR

When you go to prayer, your first thought must be: The Father is in secret, the Father waits me there. Just because your heart is cold and prayerless, get into the presence of the loving Father. As a father pities his children, so the Lord pities you. Do not be thinking of how little you have to bring God, but of how much He wants to give you. Just place yourself before Him, and look up into His face; think of His love, His wonderful, tender, pitying love. Tell Him how sinful and cold and dark all is; it is the Father's loving heart that will give light and warmth to yours.

ANDREW MURRAY

God is not found in multiplicity, but in simplicity of thoughts and words. If one word suffice for your prayer, keep to that word, and to whatever short sentence will unite your heart with God.

MARGARET MARY HALLAHAN

October 14

*My soul melts from heaviness; strengthen me according
to Your word.*

PSALM 119:28 NKJV

When I am with You as You are with me,
    Life will be self-forgetting power;
Love, ever conscious, buoyant, clear, and free
    Will flame in darkest hour.

GEORGE MACDONALD

Everything becomes possible to those who love. The commands
of the Lord are no longer grievous, for the soul that loves is gifted
by that love with fresh energies; it discovers in itself unsuspected
possibilities, and is supplied with ever-flowing currents of new
vigor. We shall be enabled to do so much if only we love. We live
by loving, and the more we love the more we live; and therefore,
when life feels dull and the spirits are low, turn and love God,
love your neighbor, and you will be healed of your wound. Love
Christ, the dear Master; look at His face, listen to His words, and
love will waken, and you will do all things through Christ who
strengthens you.

HENRY SCOTT HOLLAND

The noble love of Jesus impels a man to do great things,
and stirs him up to be always longing for what is more perfect.

THOMAS À KEMPIS

October 15

He has given us this command: Those who love God must also love their Christian brothers and sisters.

1 John 4:21 nlt

He who loves God all else above,
    His own shall also clasp
In circles ampler far of love
    Than weaker arms can grasp;
And farther down through space and time
His sympathies descend and climb.

Sir Aubrey de Vere

The true proficiency of the soul consists not so much in deep thinking, or eloquent speaking, or beautiful writing, as in much and warm loving. Now, if you ask me in what way this much and warm love may be acquired, I answer—by resolving to do the will of God, and by watching to do His will as often as occasion offers. Those who truly love God love all good wherever they find it. They seek all good to all men. They commend all good, they always acknowledge and defend all good. They have no quarrels. They hold no envy. O Lord, give me more and more of this blessed love! It will be a magnificent comfort in the hour of death to know that we are on our way to be judged by Him whom we have loved above all things. We are not going to a strange country, since it is His country whom we love and who loves us.

Teresa of Avila

October 16

*Let all bitterness, and wrath, and anger, and clamour,
and evil speaking, be put away from you, with all malice.*

EPHESIANS 4:31 KJV

The wider vision of the mind;
    The spirit bright with sun;
The temper like a fragrant wind,
    Chilling and grieving none;
The quickened heart to know God's will,
    And on His errands run.

SUSAN COOLIDGE

It is of the very greatest moment to know the occasions of our sin,
and the way in which it shows itself. To know the occasions puts us
on our guard; to know how our sin shows itself gives us the means
of stopping it. Thus, as to these occasions one is made angry if he
is found fault with roughly, or even at all, or slighted, or spoken
slightly of, or laughed at, or kept waiting, or treated rudely, or hurt
even unintentionally, or if his will is crossed, or he is contradicted,
or interrupted, or not attended to, or another be preferred to him,
or if he cannot succeed in what he has to do. These sound little
things when we speak of them in the presence of God, and in the
sight of eternity. But these and such like little things make up our
daily trials, our habits of mind, our life, our likeness or unlikeness
to God, who made us in His own image.

EDWARD B. PUSEY

October 17

Behold, I give unto you power to tread on serpents and scorpions, and over all the power of the enemy: and nothing shall by any means hurt you.

LUKE 10:19 KJV

Shed down on me Thy mighty power,
    To strengthen for each coming hour;
And then, through flood, through fire and sword,
    I'll follow Thee, my Lord, my Lord!

JOHANN RAMBACK

Why do we grow so little in grace? It is because we do not use our intellect to meditate upon the forces of the unseen world amidst which we live, or our will to draw upon them. We know that we are weak, and sin and Satan are strong, and we know the truth. But there is a third power stronger than either our weakness or the forces of evil, which we commonly forget, and which will never disclose itself except in our using of it. We must stir up the gift within us. Within us we have the Spirit of power, the Spirit of Jesus, the life of Jesus. It remains to us to appeal to it; in constant acts of faith to draw upon it and to use it. Thus it will become to each of us as much a truth of experience as it was to St. Paul, and no vague language of metaphor, that "it is no longer merely I that live, but Christ that lives in me."

CHARLES GORE

October 18

For our light and momentary troubles are achieving for us an eternal glory that far outweighs them all.

2 CORINTHIANS 4:17 NIV

Only be still, and wait His leisure
    In cheerful hope, with heart content
To take whate'er thy Father's pleasure,
    And all-discerning love has sent;
Nor doubt our inmost wants are known
To Him who chose us for His own.

GEORG NEUMARK

Oh, how is the face of life altered, as soon as a man has in earnest made his first object to do his Father's will! Oh, how do, what before seemed grievous burdens, bodily sickness, domestic trial, hardships, losses, bereavement, the world's scorn, man's ingratitude, or whatever grief his Father may put upon him, how do these things change! To those whose hope is in heaven, everything becomes a means of discipline, and instrument of strengthening their cheerful acceptance of their Father's will. Their irksome tasks, hardships, sickness, heaviness of heart, unkindness of others, and all the sorrows which their Father allots them in this world, are so many means of conforming them to their Savior's image. Then does everything which God does with them seem to them "very good," even because He does it.

EDWARD B. PUSEY

October 19

O my Father, if this cup may not pass away from me except I drink it, thy will be done.

MATTHEW 26:42 KJV

To do or not to do—to have,
　　Or not to have I leave to Thee;
To be or not to be, I leave—
　　Thy only will be done to me:
All my requests are lost in one,
Father, Thy only will be done!

CHARLES WESLEY

Offer yourself as a sacrifice to God in peace and quietness of spirit. And to better proceed in this journey, and support yourself without weariness and disquiet, dispose your soul at every step, by widening out your will to meet the will of God. The more you do widen it, the more will you receive. Your will must be disposed as follows: to will everything and to will nothing, if God wills it or wills it not.

LORENZO SCUPOLI

You must make, at least once every week, a special act of love to God's will above all else, and that not only in things supportable, but also in things insupportable.

FRANCIS DE SALES

October 20

My soul waits for the Lord more than the watchmen for the morning; indeed, more than the watchmen for the morning.

PSALM 130:6 NASB

The LORD my God will enlighten my darkness.

PSALM 18:28 KJV

A soul that is patient waits with calm endurance for light before acting, and in virtue of this calm and patient endurance suffers no pain or anxiety, because the soul possesses herself and waits for light; and when the mind waits patiently for light, sooner or later it is sure to come. Trials of mind affect us more deeply than pains of body, and if we give way to anxiety such trials become troubles, and are immensely increased. But this cannot happen to those patient souls, who feel that they are in the hands of God, and are encircled with His fatherly providence, and that all things are at His disposal. When we see not our way through some trial or difficulty, we have only to look to God, and to wait in patience, and in due time His light will come and guide us. This very attitude of waiting, this very patience of expecting, will dispose the mind to receive, and the will to rightly use, the needful light. Whenever you are perplexed as to what course you should take, if you go blindly into action you will be sure to repent it. Wait for light, wait with patience, and light will not fail you.

WILLIAM BERNARD ULLATHORNE

October 21

When you tell them all this, they will not listen to you.

JEREMIAH 7:27 NIV

His eyes were bright with intelligence and trained powers of observation; and they were beautiful with kindliness, and with the well-bred habit of giving complete attention to other people and their affairs when he talked with them.

JULIANA H. EWING

There is a grace of kind listening, as well as a grace of kind speaking. Some men listen with an abstract air, which shows that their thoughts are elsewhere. Or they seem to listen, but by wide answers and irrelevant questions show that they have been occupied with their own thoughts, as being more interesting, at least in their own estimation, than what you have been saying. Some interrupt, and will not hear you to the end. Some hear you to the end, and then forthwith begin to talk to you about a similar experience which has befallen themselves, making your case only an illustration of their own. Some, meaning to be kind, listen with such a determined, lively, violent attention, that you are at once made uncomfortable, and the charm of conversation is at an end. Many persons, whose manners will stand the test of speaking, break down under the trial of listening. But all these things should be brought under the sweet influences of religion.

FREDERICK W. FABER

October 22

You did not choose Me, but I chose you.

JOHN 15:16 NKJV

We have not chosen Thee,
    But us Thou deign'st to choose—
Not servants, but Thy friends to be,
    Whom Thou wilt never lose:
For never wilt Thou change—
    Who art all change above:
Nor life nor death shall us estrange
    From Thy most perfect love.

GEORGE B. BUBIER

We offer Christ the submission of our hearts, and the obedience
of our lives; and He offers us His abiding presence. We take Him
as our Master, and He takes us as His friends. Our Lord takes us
up into a relationship of love with Himself, and we go out into life
inspired with His Spirit to work His work. It begins with the self-
surrender of love; and love, not fear or favor, becomes the motive.
To feel thus the touch of God on our lives changes the world. Its
fruits are joy and peace, and confidence that all the events of life
are suffused, not only with meaning, but with a meaning of love.
The soul that is bound by this personal attachment to Jesus has
a life in the eternal, which transfigures the life in time with a
great joy.

HUGH BLACK

October 23

Now thanks be unto God, which always causeth us to triumph in Christ.

2 Corinthians 2:14 kjv

>Fight the good fight
>With all thy might;
>Christ is thy Strength, and Christ thy Right;
>Lay hold on life,
>And it shall be
>Thy joy and crown eternally.

J. S. B. Monsell

Let the first act on waking be to place yourself, your heart, mind, faculties, your whole being, in God's hands. Ask Him to take entire possession of you, to be the Guide of your soul, your Life, your Wisdom, your Strength. He wills that we seek Him in all our needs, that we may both know Him truly, and draw closer and closer to Him; and in prayer we gain an invisible force which will triumph over seemingly hopeless difficulties.

H. L. Sidney Lear

However matters go, it is our happiness to win new ground daily in Christ's love, and to purchase a new piece of it daily, and to add conquest to conquest.

Samuel Rutherford

October 24

Your life is hid with Christ in God.

COLOSSIANS 3:3 KJV

*Put on tender mercies, kindness, humility, meekness,
longsuffering; bearing with one another, and forgiving one another,
if anyone has a complaint against another; even as Christ forgave
you, so you also must do.*

COLOSSIANS 3:12–13 NKJV

It is not the deed we do,
    Though the deed be never so fair,
But the love that the dear Lord looks for,
    Hidden with holy care
    In the heart of the deed so fair.

HARRIET MCEWEN KIMBALL

These are duties which belong to us alike, whatever our outward
lot be, whether rich or poor, honored or despised, amid outward
joys or sorrows. For as our life is hidden in Christ, so have we all an
outward and inward, a hidden life. Outwardly, we seem busied for
the most part about common things, with trivial duties, worthless
tasks. Inwardly we are, or ought to be, studying how, in all, to
please God, walking in His sight, doing them in His presence,
seeking to know how He would have them done. So amid trivial
things we may be, no...are, in every station of life, pleasing to God,
that is, leading angels' lives, in that they are doing His will on
earth.... They are "servants of His, doing His pleasure."

EDWARD B. PUSEY

October 25

*My nourishment comes from doing the will of God, who sent me,
and from finishing his work.*

JOHN 4:34 NLT

They who treat the path of labor follow where My feet have trod;
They who work without complaining do the holy will of God.

HENRY VAN DYKE

From where does it come that we have so many complaints,
each saying that his occupation is a hindrance to him, while
notwithstanding his work is of God, who hinders no man? From
where does this inward reproof and sense of guilt come from
which torments and worries you? Dear children, know that it is
not your work which gives you this anxiety. No, it is your want of
order in fulfilling your work. If you performed your work in the
right method, with a sole aim to God, and not to yourselves...nor
sought your own gain or pleasure, but only God's glory in your
work, it would be impossible that it should grieve your conscience.
It is a shame for a man if he has not done his work properly...so
imperfectly that he has to be rebuked for it. For this is a sure sign
that his works are not done in God, with a view to His glory and
the good of his neighbor.

JOHN TAULER

October 26

I will give you the treasures of darkness and hidden riches of secret places, that you may know that I, the LORD, who call you by your name, am the God of Israel.

ISAIAH 45:3 NKJV

God! You are Love! I build my faith on that!
I know You, You have kept my path and made
Light for me in the darkness—tempering sorrow,
So that it reached me like a solemn joy:
It was too strange that I should doubt Your love.

ROBERT BROWNING

If I believe in God, in a Being who made me, and fashioned me, and knows my wants and capacities and necessities because He gave them to me, and who is perfectly good and loving, righteous, and perfectly wise and powerful—whatever my circumstances inward or outward may be, however thick the darkness which encompasses me—I yet can trust, yes, be assured, that all will be well, that He can draw light out of darkness, and make crooked things straight.

THOMAS ERSKINE

Though sorrows, heaviness, and faintness of heart ever so much increase, yet, if your faith increases also, it will bear you up in the midst of them. I would gladly have it go well with you.

ISAAC PENINGTON

October 27

Strengthened with all might, according to his glorious power, unto all patience and longsuffering with joyfulness.

COLOSSIANS 1:11 KJV

Rejoice in Christ always!
    When earth looks heavenly bright,
When joy makes glad the livelong day,
    And peace shuts in the night.
Rejoice, when care and woe
    The fainting soul oppress,
When tears at wakeful midnight flow,
    And morn brings heaviness.

JOHN MOULTRIE

A great point is gained when we have learned not to struggle against the circumstances God has appointed for us.

H. L. SIDNEY LEAR

All mental discomfort comes from our minds being in divergence from God's; when the two are agreed no warfare occurs, for they work together, and man's mind accepts God's rule, but reason tells us that disagreement must bring conflicts. He will have His way, and would have us accept all events with the knowledge that He is love…however contradictory those events may be to our comprehension of Him.

CHARLES GEORGE GORDON

October 28

Who then is willing to consecrate his service this day unto the Lord?

1 Chronicles 29:5 kjv

My blessed task from day to day
Is humbly, gladly, to obey.

Harriet McEwen Kimball

The only way to restore a weakened will is by exercising itself in details of duty. It may be in smallest acts of obedience, regularly done, "here a little, and there a little," content to grow by slow degrees into the use of lost powers through repeated acts of observance, however trivial or unobserved. Faithfulness to every smallest call of obedience, as it comes, is the means of gaining gradual accessions of strength, and thus tending more and more to higher degrees of conformity to the will of God. Only by such simple practical dutifulness can habits be formed.

T. T. Carter

Break off some one evil, seek to uproot some one sin, cut off some one self-indulgence, deny yourself some one vanity; do it as an offering to God, for the love of God, in hope once to see God; and some gleam of faith, and life, and love will stream down upon your soul from the everlasting Fount of love. Follow on, and you shall never lose that track of light.

Edward B. Pusey

October 29

I will walk in freedom, for I have devoted myself to your commandments.

PSALM 119:45 NLT

To be made with Thee one spirit,
  Is the boon that I lingering ask,
To have no bar 'twixt my soul and Thine;
My thoughts to echo Thy will divine,
  Myself Thy servant for any task.

LUCY LARCOM

There is more effort, more steadfastness, involved in diligent attention to little duties than appears at first sight, and that because of their continual recurrence. Such heed to little things implies a ceaseless listening to the whispers of grace, a strict watchfulness against every thought, wish, word, or act which can offend God ever so little, a constant effort to do everything as perfectly as possible. All this, however, must be done with a free, childlike spirit, without restlessness and anxiety. He does not ask a fretted, shrinking service. Give yourself to Him, trust Him, fix your eye upon Him, listen to His voice, and then go on bravely and cheerfully, never doubting for an instant that His grace will lead you in small things as well as great, and will keep you from offending His law of love.

JEAN NICOLAS GROU

October 30

In quietness and in confidence shall be your strength.

Isaiah 30:15 kjv

Be still, my soul—for just as you are still,
Can God reveal Himself to you; until
     Through you His love, and light, and life can freely flow.
In stillness God can work through you and reach
The souls around you. He then through you can teach
     His lessons—and His power in weakness show.

Bessie Porter

We are always wanting to be doing, to be giving, to be planning
for the future, to be mapping out all our life, instead of resting
and receiving day by day, leaving the morrow to our God, and
rejoicing in Jesus Christ amidst all our falls and failures. Instead of
going on rejoicing in Jesus, we are tempted to despair, and to go on
despairing, after every failure, negligence, and sin.

George H. Wilkinson

We seek God afar off, in projects perhaps altogether unattainable,
and we do not consider that we possess Him now in the midst of
confusion, by the exercise of simple faith, provided we bear humbly
and bravely the annoyances which come from others, and our
own imperfections.

François de Fénelon

October 31

You shall remember all the way which the LORD your God has led you.

DEUTERONOMY 8:2 NASB

Not mindless of the growing years
    Of care and loss and pain,
My eyes are wet with thankful tears
    For blessings that remain.

JOHN GREENLEAF WHITTIER

The years of available and happy life which have been already enjoyed ought to be the cause of thankfulness, even if "the days of darkness" were many. "The sorrow's crown of sorrow is remembering happier things," says Tennyson. Surely, in the sphere of faith, at least, there is some mistake here. "For what we *have* received the Lord makes us truly thankful."

JAMES SMETHAM

A bright, happy soul, rejoicing in all God's gifts, seeing cause for thankfulness and gladness in everything, counting up mercies rather than trials, looking at the bright side, even of sickness, bereavement, and death—what a very fountain of goodness and love of Christ such a one is! I remember one who, worn with sickness and sleepless nights, answered to the question if the nights did not seem interminable: "Oh no, I lie still, and count up my blessings!"

H. L. SIDNEY LEAR

NOVEMBER

Rejoice in the Lord your God,

for he has given you the autumn rains

because he is faithful.

He sends you abundant showers,

JOEL 2:23 NIV

November 1

That in the dispensation of the fullness of times he might gather together in one all things in Christ, both which are in heaven, and which are on earth.

Ephesians 1:10 kjv

For all the saints who from their labors rest,
Who Thee by faith before the world confessed,
Thy name, O Jesu, be forever blessed.
  Alleluia!
Oh! Blest communion! Fellowship divine!
We feebly struggle, they in glory shine;
Yet all are one in Thee, for all are Thine.
  Alleluia!

William Walsham How

In the glorious company of the apostles, the goodly fellowship of the prophets, the noble army of martyrs, the holy church throughout all the world is one. Therefore year by year let us reverently commemorate their names, remembering what they were, but steadfastly gazing at what they are. Their very words are still ringing in our ears: of some the beloved image too is full before us. Let us live as they would bid us, could they still speak; let us fulfill their known behests, following in their steps, filling up the works that they began, carrying on their hallowed offices.... Let us be like them in deadness to sin, and unceasing homage to our unseen Lord. As we grow holier, we grow nearer to them; to be like them is to be with them; even now they are not far from us, we know not how near.

Henry Edward Manning

November 2

He has enabled you to share in the inheritance that belongs to his people, who live in the light.

COLOSSIANS 1:12 NLT

Not their own, ah! Not from earth was flowing
    That high strain to which their souls were tuned;
Year by year we saw them inner growing
    More like Him with whom their hearts communed.
Then to Him they passed; but still unbroken,
    Age to age, lasts on that goodly line,
Whose pure lives are, more than all words spoken,
    Earth's best witness to the life divine.

JOHN CAMPBELL

Only to remember that such have been, that we walked for a season with them, is a restraining, a purifying, yes, and however much we may miss and mourn them, a gladdening thought.

RICHARD CHENEVIX TRENCH

The beatitude of the saints is the matured result of the long course of patient strivings, which may have passed wholly unobserved because of their minuteness. One step has followed another in the mysterious progress of daily, hourly acts, each seeming to pass away, as footprints on the sand are obliterated by the advancing tide; but the end is the vision of God, and the payback is the perfection of a nature made one with the mind of God.

T. T. CARTER

November 3

I have refined you, though not as silver; I have tested you in the furnace of affliction.

ISAIAH **48:10** NIV

I will not let Thee go; Thou Help in time of need!
    Heap ill on ill,
    I trust Thee still,
E'en when it seems that Thou wouldst slay indeed!
    Do as Thou wilt with me,
    I yet will cling to Thee;
Hide Thou Thy face, yet, Help in time of need,
    I will not let Thee go.

WOLFGANG C. DESSLER

Your afflictions are not eternal, time will end them, and so shall you at length see the Lord's salvation; His love sleeps not, is still working for you; His salvation will not tarry nor linger; and suffering for Him is the noblest cross out of heaven. Your Lord has the choice of ten thousand other crosses, beside this, to advance you further; but His wisdom and His love chose this for you, out of them all; and take it as a choice one, and make use of it. Let the Lord absolutely have the ordering of your evils and troubles, and put them off you, by recommending your cross and your furnace to Him, who has skill to melt His own metal, and knows well what to do with His furnace.

SAMUEL RUTHERFORD

November 4

As slaves of Christ, do the will of God with all your heart.

EPHESIANS 6:6 NLT

Lord Jesus, turn us from the noise
Of endless strivings and empty joys,
To find forever Your one true peace,
Rest from sorrow, from sin release!

HARRIET MCEWEN KIMBALL

Can He not enable you to do that will from your heart, in your
surroundings? Are you sorely tried by those surroundings?
Are they, in themselves, humiliating to you, or exasperating to
you? Are they full of acute heart-pangs, or heavy with a chronic
heartache? Not one of these things is forgotten before your Lord.
Your slightest pain finds response in His sympathy. But let
that thought be but the stepping-stone to this, that for you as
for the slave-saint of Ephesus there lies open in that same Lord
the blessed secret of a life which shall move amidst these same
unwelcome surroundings as a life free, and at leisure, and at peace,
full of love and rest, blessed and blessing; a life hid with Christ in
God; a life in which *everything*, from your rising up to your lying
down, the smallest cross and the largest, is seen in the light of the
holy, the beloved, will of God, and so is met not with a sigh, or a
murmur, but "from the soul."

HANDLEY C. G. MOULE

November 5

Love never fails.

1 CORINTHIANS 13:8 NASB

Your heart shall live for ever.

PSALM 22:26 KJV

Death has no bidding to divide
    The souls that dwell in Thee;
Yes, all who in the Lord abide
    Are of one family.

THOMAS H. GILL

Will not our own lamented and beloved be there, in the array of happy spirits? Will they not hail our coming with delight? Do they not remember us now, even in the sight of God? For to see His face does not extinguish but perfect all holy loves. God's love gathers up and perfects all pure love like His own, all love that is for His sake. When we meet our beloved in Him, we shall both know and love them so as we have neither loved or known before.

HENRY EDWARD MANNING

She is not sent away, but only sent before, like unto a star, which, going out of our sight does not die and vanish, but shines in another hemisphere: you see her not, yet she does shine in another country.

SAMUEL RUTHERFORD

Cast your cares on the LORD and he will sustain you; he will never let the righteous fall.

PSALM 55:22 NIV

To Thee I bring my care,
    The care I cannot flee;
Thou will not only share,
    But bear it all for me.
O loving Savior, now to Thee
I bring the load that wearies me.

FRANCES RIDLEY HAVERGAL

"Cast your burden upon the Lord, and He will sustain you"—
burden and all. "You" are the greatest burden that you have! All
other burdens are but slight, but this is a crushing burden. When
we come to the Lord with our burden, He just lifts up His child,
burden and all, and bears us all the way home.

CHARLES A. FOX

He lays his affairs and himself on God, and so has no pressing care;
no care but the care of love, how to please, how to honor his Lord.
And in this, too, he depends on Him, both for skill and strength;
and, touching the success of things, he understands that as none
of his cares are to be burdened with, casts them on God; and since
He cares for them, they need not both care, His care is sufficient.
Hence springs peace, inconceivable peace.

ROBERT LEIGHTON

November 7

As we have therefore opportunity, let us do good unto all men.

GALATIANS 6:10 KJV

She has done what she could.

MARK 14:8 NASB

Very consoling words, if we can be sure they apply to us. Very pungent condemnation if they apply not, and we allow opportunities to go by. The rule demands no impossibilities, but it does demand that every sphere, however humble, shall be filled with divine endeavors. You have not done what you could if you have not made it the problem of every day: how many burdens can I make lighter? how much heart sunshine can I shed about me? how much can I increase the sum of human blessing in the circle where my lines have fallen? How easily we slide into the delusion that we should do a great deal more good if we had the means, overlooking the means that lie close about us!

EDMUND H. SEARS

There is no act too trifling to be made by God the first link in a chain of blessing; whether some trifling incident is allowed on our part to drop unobserved, or is taken up and placed in its intended position, often depends on the entertainment we have given to some previously suggested idea of duty.

SARAH W. STEPHEN

November 8

Anyone who breaks one of the least of these commandments and teaches others to do the same will be called least in the kingdom of heaven.

MATTHEW 5:19 NIV

The great sterling duties, the exact truth of word, the resolute refusal to countenance wrong, the command of temper, the mastery of indolence, the unstained purity—these, and such as these, form the character, and fashion our souls into instruments in God's hands for high and heavenly purposes in His providence. But the carefulness over details, the watchfulness against faults which we know to be faults, but which, notwithstanding, seem excusable, the devout regularity and attention in our private prayers, the invariable good-humor of our manners, the seeking for occasions of kindness and unselfishness, the avoidance of little temptations, the care not to cause little annoyances and little troubles—to attend to all this for the sake of Christ our Master is the natural and fitting expression of a loving heart.

FREDERICK TEMPLE

The sins by which God's Spirit is ordinarily grieved are the sins of small things—laxness in holding our temper, slight neglects of duty, sharpness of dealing with others.

HORACE BUSHNELL

November 9

Continuing steadfastly in prayer.

ROMANS 12:12 NKJV

Prayer is a preparation for danger, it is the armor for battle. Go not into the dangerous world without it. You kneel down at night to pray and drowsiness weighs down your eyelids. A hard day's work is a kind of excuse, and you shorten your prayer, and resign yourself softly to repose. The morning breaks, and it may be you rise late, and so your early devotions are not done, or done with irregular haste. It is no marvel if that day in which your drowsiness interferes with prayer is a day on which you betray Him by cowardice and soft shrinking from duty.

FREDERICK W. ROBERTSON

Prayer to God regular and earnest, never intermittent for any reason, never hurried over for any weariness or for any coldness, this is one chief means of keeping our spiritual growth healthy and alive. If we would live in any degree by that ideal which our better selves sometimes set before us, we must steadily maintain the habit of regular prayer. For whether or not we are conscious of it at the time, there is a calm and unceasing strength which can then be grafted onto our souls, and only then.

FREDERICK TEMPLE

November 10

"Therefore, be patient," says the LORD.

ZEPHANIAH 3:8 NIV

That you may be filled up to all the fullness of God.

EPHESIANS 3:19 NASB

What is our work when God a blessing would impart?
To bring the empty vessel of a needy heart.

RICHARD CHENEVIX TRENCH

In praying, we are often occupied with ourselves, with our own needs, and our own efforts in the presentation of them. In waiting upon God, the first thought is of *the God upon whom we wait*; God longs to reveal Himself, to fill us with Himself. Waiting on God gives Him time in His own way and divine power to come to us. Before you pray, bow quietly before God, to remember and realize who He is, how near He is, how certainly He can and will help. Be still before Him, and allow His Holy Sprit to waken and stir up in your soul the child-like disposition of absolute dependence and confident expectation. Wait on God till you know you have met Him; prayer will then become so different. And when you are praying, let there be intervals of silence, reverent stillness of soul, in which you yield yourself to God, in case He may have anything He wishes to teach you or to work in you.

ANDREW MURRAY

November 11

I have learned, in whatsoever state I am, therewith to be content.

PHILIPPIANS 4:11 KJV

Forgive us, Lord, our little faith;
And help us all, from morn till e'en,
Still to believe that lot the best
Which is—not that which might have been.

GEORGE ZABRISKIE GRAY

You give within and without precisely what the soul needs for its advancement in a life of faith and self-renunciation. I have then only to receive this bread, and to accept, in the spirit of self-sacrifice, whatever You shall ordain, of distress in my external circumstances, or within my heart. For whatever happens to me each day is my daily bread, provided I do not refuse to take it from Your hand, and to feed upon it.

FRANÇOIS DE FÉNELON

Judge that only necessary which God, in His eternal wisdom and love, proportions out unto us. And when you come to this place, you will come to your rest; and as you abide here, you will abide in your soul's true rest, and know the preciousness of that lesson, and of whom you are to learn it, *even in every state to be content.*

ISAAC PENINGTON

November 12

Rejoice in the Lord always: and again I say, Rejoice.

PHILIPPIANS 4:4 KJV

Rejoice in hope and fear;
    Rejoice in life and death
Rejoice when threatening storms are near,
    And comfort languisheth:
When should not they rejoice
    Whom Christ His brethren calls—
Who hear and know His guiding voice
    When on their hearts it falls?

JOHN MOULTRIE

To "give thanks to Him for all things" is, indeed, a very difficult duty, for it includes giving thanks for trials of all kinds: for suffering and pain; for languor and weariness; for the crossing of our wills; for contradiction; for reproaches; for loneliness; for hardships. Yet they who have learned submission will not find it a hard duty, for they will so entirely love all that God wills and appoints, that they will see it is the very best thing for them. Hereafter they will see all the links of the chain, and how wonderfully even those have fitted, which at the time seemed to have no adaptation or agreement. This belief enables them to praise Him, and give thanks *now* for each thing, assured that as it has been, so it will be—that the God of love will do all things well.

PRISCILLA MAURICE

November 13

Not as though I had already attained, either were already perfect; but I follow after, if that I may apprehend that for which also I am apprehended of Christ Jesus.

PHILIPPIANS 3:12 KJV

Let no man think that sudden in a minute
 All is accomplished and the work is done—
Though with your earliest dawn you should begin it,
 Scarce were it ended in your setting sun.

FREDERICK W. H. MYERS

Nothing so purifies the thoughts, heightens the acts, shuts out self, admits God, as, in all things, little or great, to look to Jesus. Look to Him, when you can, as you begin to act, to converse, or labor; and then desire to speak or be silent, as He would have you; to say this word, or leave that unsaid; to do this, or leave that undone; to shape your words, as if He were present, and He *will* be present, not in body, but in spirit, not by your side, but in your soul. Faint not, any who would love Jesus, if you find yourselves yet far short of what He Himself who is Love said of the love of Him. Perfect love is heaven. When you are perfected in love, your work on earth is done. There is no short road to heaven or to love. Do what in you lies by the grace of God, and He will lead you from strength to strength, and grace to grace, and love to love.

EDWARD B. PUSEY

November 14

*I do not pray that You should take them out of the world,
but that You should keep them from the evil one.*

JOHN 17:15 NKJV

In the hour of trial,
    Jesu, plead for me;
Lest by base denial
    I depart from Thee.

JAMES MONTGOMERY

Our Lord would have His people to be in the world, and yet to
be separate from it. He would have them be separated, not by
living in isolation from it, but by living loyally under Him as
their King, where His claims are denied and His rule is rejected;
by courageously living in obedience to righteousness where desire
is too generally the impelling and formative power. To live in the
world as Christ's soldiers and servants; to witness for Him by word
and deed as we live in obedience to His will—this is the separation
which Christ teaches, this is the separation that gives glory to God.
Woe be to us if we fail in expressing by loyal obedience here, our
loyalty to Christ as our King! To fail here is to bear stamped on
us the brand of a traitor's moral cowardice, and a brand of greater
shame than it no mortal brow can bear.

GEORGE BODY

November 15

As pressure and stress bear down on me, I find joy in your commands.

PSALM 119:143 NLT

When black despair beats down my wings,
    And heavenly visions fade away—
Lord, let me bend to common things,
    The task of every day;

As when th'aurora is denied,
    And blinding blizzards round him beat,
The Samoyed bends, and takes for guide
    The moss beneath his feet.

WILLIAM CANTON

Whatever bad times may come, or whatever perplexity, there is almost always close at hand, waiting for one, some plain thing to be done. It may be a mere matter of routine, an item in the day's regular business; it may be the exercise of some consideration for another; it may be only silent patience; but it is always *something*. And always one has the choice to do it or decline it. One can go through his work well or shirk it. One can consider his neighbor or neglect him. One can repress the fever-fit of impatience or give it wild way. And the perpetual presence of such a choice leaves no hour without guidance.

GEORGE S. MERRIAM

November 16

The will of the Lord be done.

Acts 21:14 KJV

But if in parallel to Thine
    My will doth meekly run,
All things in heaven and earth are mine,
    My will is crossed by none;
        Thou art in me,
        And I in Thee—
Thy will—and mine—are done!

W. M. L. Jay

Sufferings arising from anxiety, in which the soul adds, to the cross imposed by the hand of God, an agitated resistance, and a sort of unwillingness to suffer—such troubles arise only because we live to ourselves. A cross wholly inflicted by God, and fully accepted without any uneasy hesitation, is full of peace as well as of pain. On the contrary, a cross not fully and simply accepted, but resisted by the love of self, even slightly, is a double cross; it is even more of cross, owing to this useless resistance, than through the pain it necessarily entails.

François de Fénelon

The basis of all peace of mind, and what must be obtained before we get the peace, is a cessation of the conflict of two wills— His and ours.

Charles G. Gordon

November 17

For whatever is born of God overcomes the world. And this is the victory that has overcome the world—our faith.

1 John 5:4 nkjv

What is victory over the world? It is to cut off as far as we may, every hold which everything not of God has over us; to study wherein we are weak, and there seek in His strength to be made strong. If your temptation is of the love of pleasure, it is to forego it; if of food, to restrain [from] it; if of praise, to put forward others rather than yourself; if of being right in the sight of men, be content to be misjudged, and to keep silence; if of self-indulgence, use hardness; if of display, cut off the occasions and give to the poor; if of having your own will, practice the submission of it to the wills of others.

Edward B. Pusey

If we aspire to walk in the power of the new life, we must cast away all hindrances, and it must cost something we really value.

Charles G. Gordon

The faith presses upon man his noblest desires as obligations, and makes their attainment possible by the gift of the Spirit.

Brooke Foss Westcott

November 18

*So be careful to do what the LORD your God has commanded you;
do not turn aside to the right or to the left.*

DEUTERONOMY 5:32 NIV

No duty, however hard and perilous, should be feared one-half
so much as failure in the duty. People sometimes shrink from
responsibility, saying they dare not accept it because it is so great.
But in shrinking from duty they are really encountering a far more
serious condition than that which they evade. It is a great deal
easier to do that which God gives us to do, no matter how hard it
is, than to face the responsibility of not doing it. We have abundant
assurance that we shall receive all the strength we need to perform
any duty of obedience; and refusing to do anything which we
ought to do, we find ourselves at once out of harmony with God's
law and God's providence, and cannot escape the consequences of
our failure.

J. R. MILLER

Knowledge is a call to action; an insight into the way of perfection
is a call to perfection.

JOHN HENRY NEWMAN

November 19

He knows what is in the darkness, and the light dwells with Him.

DANIEL 2:22 NASB

Take it on trust a little while;
Soon shall you read the mystery right
In the full sunshine of His smile.

JOHN KEBLE

God is too wise not to know all about us, and what is really best for us to be, and to have. And he is too good not to desire our highest good; and too powerful, desiring, not to effect it. If, then, what He has appointed for us does not seem to us the best, or even to be good, our true course is to remember that He sees further than we do, and that we shall understand Him in time, when His plans have unfolded themselves; meanwhile casting all our care upon Him, since He careth for us.

HENRY PARRY LIDDON

To be out of harmony with the things, acts, and events, which God in His providence has seen fit to array around us—that is to say, not to meet them in a humble, believing, and thankful spirit—is to turn from God. And, on the other hand, to see in them the development of God's presence, and of the divine will, and to accept that will, is to turn in the opposite direction, and to be in union with Him.

THOMAS C. UPHAM

November 20

The LORD will lighten my darkness.

2 SAMUEL 22:29 KJV

Doesn't his light shine on all the earth?

JOB 25:3 NLT

Hope, then, though woes be doubled,
    Hope, and be undismayed;
Let not your heart be troubled,
    Nor let it be afraid.
This prison where you art,
    Your God will break it soon,
And flood with light your heart
    In His own blessed noon.

PAUL GERHARDT

A Christian may for many days together see neither sun nor star, neither light in God's countenance, nor light in his own heart, though even at that time God darts some beams through those clouds upon the soul; the soul again by a spirit of faith sees some light through those thickest clouds, enough to keep it from utter despair, though not settle it in peace. In this dark condition, if they do as St. Paul and his company did, cast anchor even in the dark night of temptation, and pray still for day; God will appear, and all shall clear up; we shall see light without and light within; the day-star will arise in their hearts.

RICHARD SIBBES

November 21

Lord, what do You want me to do?

ACTS 9:6 NKJV

Every task, however simple, sets the soul that does it free;
Every deed of love and mercy done to man is done to Me.

HENRY VAN DYKE

For each one of us, whether on a bed of pain, in feebleness
and uncertainty of purpose such as comes with ill-health or
overstrained nerves, or whatever else may be our immediate
condition, nothing is more urgent, nothing more behooves us than
to ask, "What would You have me to do?" For, whatever our state,
however helpless and incapable, however little service to God or to
our neighbor seems within our power, there is no doubt at all as to
His willing us to do *something.* Not necessarily any great thing; it
may be only some little message of sympathy and comfort to carry
to one even more lonely than we are; it may be some tiny pleasure
to a little child, or a kindly word or glance to one whose own fault
has cut him off from general kindness and pity; it may be even
only in humble patience to stand and wait till He makes His will
plain, abstaining the while from murmur and fretfulness; but, in
some shape or other, be certain that your Master and Lord hears
and will answer your question, "What would You have me to do?"

H. L. SIDNEY LEAR

November 22

Therefore, brethren, we were comforted over you in all our affliction and distress by your faith.

1 THESSALONIANS 3:7 KJV

Just as God leads I am content:
    I rest me calmly in His hands;
That which He has decreed and sent—
    That which His will for me commands—
        I would that He should all fulfill;
        That I should do His gracious will
In living or in dying.

LAMPERTUS GEDICKE

Divine providence means the arrangement of all our life, not only of its bright side, but also of its dark. It may mean sickness as well as health; death as well as life; loss as well as gain; peril as well as safety; shipwreck by sea and accident by land; disease to our flocks; sickness in our homes.

ANTHONY W. THOROLD

How is it your faith sees but the black side of providence? Yet it has a better side, and God shall let you see it. We know that all things work together for good to them that love God; hence I infer that losses, disappointments, ill tongues, loss of friends, houses, or country, are God's workmen, set to work out good to you, out of everything that befalls you. When the Lord's blessed will blows cross your desires, it is best, in humility, to strike sail to Him, and to be willing to be led any way our Lord pleases.

SAMUEL RUTHERFORD

November 23

The LORD your God may bless you in all the work of your hand which you do.

DEUTERONOMY 14:29 NASB

Firm against every doubt of Thee
    For all my future way—
To walk in heaven's eternal light
    Throughout the changing day.
Ah! Such a day as Thou shall own
    When suns have ceased to shine!
A day of burdens borne by Thee,
    And work that all was Thine.

ANNA L. WARING

Let us give ourselves to God without any reserve, and let us fear nothing. He will love us, and we shall love Him. His love, increasing every day, will take the place of everything else to us. He will fill our whole hearts; He will deprive us only of those things that make us unhappy. He will cause us to do in general what we have been doing already. But which we have done in an unsatisfactory manner; whereas, hereafter, we shall do them well, because they will be done for His sake. Even the smallest actions of a simple and common life will be turned to consolation and compensation. We shall meet the approach of death in peace; it will be changed for us into the beginning of the immortal life.

FRANÇOIS DE FÉNELON

November 24

We command and exhort through our Lord Jesus Christ that they work in quietness.

2 Thessalonians 3:12 NKJV

Drop your still dews of quietness
Till all our strivings cease;
Take from our souls the strain and stress,
And let our ordered lives confess
The beauty of Your peace.

John Greenleaf Whittier

The enemy of that grand central habit of interior patience is haste: haste of thought, haste of judgment, haste of manner, haste of speech. Even natural powers of every kind become true strength when they work submissively and harmoniously under the direction of divine light and the movement of divine grace; and this disciplined subjection at every point under the dominion of Christ our Lord, ruling us by His grace, makes the soul the serene organ of the Holy Spirit, for the animating, controlling, and guiding of our souls.

William Bernard Ullathorne

We are conformed to Him in proportion as our lives grow in quietness, His peace spreading within our own souls. Even amid all that outwardly disturbs us we have, if we have Him, the same peace, because He is our peace, sustaining our whole being.

T. T. Carter

November 25

Joy and gladness will be found in her, thanksgiving and the sound of singing.

Isaiah 51:3 NIV

If you are living a righteous and a useful life, doing your duty orderly and cheerfully where God has put you, then you are making a sweeter melody in the ears of the Lord Jesus Christ than if you had the throat of a nightingale; for then you in your humble place are copying the everlasting harmony and melody which is in heaven.

Charles Kingsley

As the perfect obedience of the life of Christ comes, through humility and prayer and thought, to be the constant aim of all our efforts; in proportion as we try, God helping us, to think and speak and act as He did, and through all the means of grace to sanctify Him in our hearts, we shall, with growing hope and with a wonder that is ever lost in gratitude, know that even our lives are not without the earnest of their rest in an eternal harmony; that through them there is sounding more and more the echo of a faultless music: and that He who loves that concord, He who alone can ever make us what He bids us be, will silence in us every harsh, jarring note; that our service too may blend with the consenting praise of all His saints and angels.

Francis Paget

November 26

Be on the alert, stand firm in the faith, act like men, be strong.

1 Corinthians 16:13 NASB

Stand then in His great might,
    With all His strength endued;
But take, to arm you for the fight,
    The panoply of God.
Leave no unguarded place,
    No weakness of the soul;
Take every virtue, every grace,
    And fortify the whole.

Charles Wesley

Let every one consider what his weak point is; in that is his trial.
His trial is not in those things which are easy to him, but in that
one thing, in those several things, whatever they are, in which to
do his duty is against his nature. Never think yourself safe because
you do your duty in ninety-nine points; it is the hundredth which
is to be the ground of your self-denial. It is with reference to this
you must watch and pray; pray continually for God's grace to
help you, and watch with fear and trembling lest you fall. Oh that
you may (as it were) sweep the house diligently to discover what
you lack of the full measure of obedience! For, to be quite sure,
this apparently small defect will influence your whole spirit and
judgment in all things.

John Henry Newman

November 27

God is faithful, by whom ye were called unto the fellowship of his Son Jesus Christ our Lord.

1 CORINTHIANS 1:9 KJV

Give me a new, a perfect heart,
From doubt, and fear, and sorrow free;
The mind which was in Christ impart,
And let my spirit cleave to Thee.

CHARLES WESLEY

Since I attained to a clear consciousness, by inward experience, that there is no way of satisfying the needs of the soul, or tranquilizing the heart's longings, but by the inner life in Christ, I am aware of an increase of power for the work of my calling, whatever it be, and of joy and spirit in performing it.

CHRISTIAN K. J. BUNSEN

In my daily life I am to ask, "How would Christ have acted in my circumstances: How would He have me act? How would *Christ* fulfill my duties, do my work, fill my place, meet my difficulties, turn to account all my capacities and opportunities?" This is to be the law and inspiration of my whole life; not only of my outward acts, but of all my inward thoughts and desires. There is to be a manifestation of the Divine Nature in *me*.

A. C. A. HALL

November 28

Whoever keeps His word, truly the love of God is perfected in him. By this we know that we are in Him.

1 John 2:5 nkjv

I have called you friends.

John 15:15 kjv

The hands that tend the sick tend Christ; the willing feet that go on errands of love, work for Christ; the words of comfort to the sorrowful, and of sympathy to the mourner, are spoken in the name of Christ—Christ comforts the world through His friends. How much have you done for Him? What sort of a friend have you been to Him? God is working through His people; Christ is comforting through His friends—it is the vacancies in the ranks of His friends where the mischief lies: come and fill one gap.

Arthur F. Winnington Ingram

It is true that love cannot be forced, that it cannot be made to order, that we cannot love because we ought, or even because we want. But we can bring ourselves into the presence of the lovable. We can enter into friendship through the door of discipleship; we can learn love through service; and the day will come to us also, when the Master's word will be true, "I call you no longer servant, but friend."

Hugh Black

Through His will, loved and done, lies the path to His love.

Andrew Murray

November 29

Thank God! He gives us victory over sin and death through our Lord Jesus Christ.

1 Corinthians 15:57 NLT

Keep close to Christ, if conflict sore betide;
Stand fast, remembering He is at your side
    To give you strength
In battle, and the victor's palm at length.

Frances E. Cox, translator

If we would endeavor, like men of courage, to stand in the battle, surely we should feel the favorable assistance of God from heaven. For He who gives us occasion to fight, to the end we may get the victory, is ready to succor those that fight manfully, and do trust in His grace.

Thomas à Kempis

He will give the victory into your hands, if only you will fight manfully by His side, trusting not in yourself, but in His power and goodness. And if the Lord delay awhile to give you the victory, be not disheartened, but believe assuredly (and this will also help you to fight resolutely) that He will turn all things which may befall you, those even which to you may seem farthest removed from, yes, most adverse to your success, if you will but bear yourself as a faithful and generous warrior.

Lorenzo Scupoli

November 30

He said to them, "Follow Me."... Immediately they left their nets and followed Him.

MATTHEW 4:19–20 NASB

Jesus calls us; o'er the tumult
    Of our life's wild, restless sea,
Day by day His sweet voice soundeth,
    Saying, "Christian, follow me."
As of old St. Andrew heard it
    By the Galilean lake,
Turned from home, and toil, and kindred,
    Leaving all for His dear sake.

CECIL F. ALEXANDER

The will of God will be done; but oh, the unspeakable loss for us if we have missed our opportunity of doing it!

BROOKE FOSS WESTCOTT

God, who calls us, Himself gives us the strength to obey His call. He who is with us now to call us, will be ever present with us, in all where He calls us. All in His purpose and love, every degree of grace and glory, lies wrapped up in His next call. All eternity of bliss and the love of God will, through His grace...lie in one strong, earnest, undivided giving of your whole self to God, to do in you, through you, with you, His gracious, loving will.

EDWARD B. PUSEY

DECEMBER

Whoever sees, 'neath winter's fields of snow,

The silent harvest of the future grow,

God's power must know.

December 1

Be strong and courageous, be not afraid nor dismayed...with us is the LORD our God to help us, and to fight our battles.

2 CHRONICLES 32:7–8 KJV

We fling aside the weight and sin,
Resolved the victory to win;
No shrinking from the desperate fight,
No thought of yielding or of flight;
With the brave heart and steady eye,
We onward march to victory.

HORATIUS BONAR

If you, your heart, your will, are enlisted on the good side, if you are wishing and trying that the good in you should conquer the bad, then you are on the side of God Himself, and God is on your side; and "if God be for us, who shall be against us?" Take courage, then. If you are fighting against your worst feelings, so is God. On your side is God who made all, and Christ who died for all, and the Holy Spirit who alone gives wisdom, purity, nobleness. How can you fail when He is on your side? On your side are all spirits of just men made perfect, all wise and good souls in earth and heaven, all good and wholesome influences, whether of nature or of grace, of matter or of mind. How can you fail if they are on your side?

CHARLES KINGSLEY

December 2

I have told you this so that my joy may be in you and that your joy may be complete.

JOHN 15:11 NIV

Thou bringest all again; with Thee
Is light, is space, is breadth and room
For each thing fair, beloved, and free,
To have its hour of life and bloom.
Each heart's deep instinct unconfessed;
Each lowly wish, each daring claim;
All, all that life has long repressed,
Unfolds, undreading blight or blame.

DORA GREENWELL

Let us offer up to Him each day, and all its occupations, yes, and all its relaxations—as it begins—and beg Him to let us somehow "see" Him throughout it. Let us trust Him with the hallowing of our ordinary "secular" interests, let us try to shape each day's life so as best to please Him. "Would our Lord like me to say this or to read that? Would He sanction this train of thought or of fancy? When I go with that companion, can I imagine His drawing near and walking beside us?" This habitual "looking up to Jesus," this repeated reference to His will and pleasure—does it seem to us likely to be oppressive, restrictive, burdensome? Let us only try it, and judge for ourselves: it will turn out to be a source of peace and comfort indescribable.

WILLIAM BRIGHT

December 3

You have been my help, and in the shadow of Your wings I sing for joy.

PSALM 63:7 NASB

On our way rejoicing gladly let us go;
Conquered has our Leader, vanquished is our foe!
Christ without, our safety! Christ within, our joy!
Who, if we be faithful, can our hope destroy?
On our way rejoicing as we homeward move,
Hearken to our praises, O You God of love!

J. S. B. MONSELL

I cannot understand why those who have given themselves up to God and His goodness are not always cheerful, for what possible happiness can be equal to that? No accidents or imperfections which may happen ought to have power to trouble them, or to hinder their looking upward.

FRANCIS DE SALES

Why should we go to heaven weeping, as if we were about to fall down through the earth for sorrow? If God were dead (if I may speak so, with reverence of Him who lives forever and ever), we might have cause to look like dead folks; but "the Lord lives, and blessed be the Rock of our salvation." None have right to joy but we; for joy is sown for us, and an ill summer or harvest will not spill the crop.

SAMUEL RUTHERFORD

December 4

That you may know what is the hope of His calling, what are the riches of the glory of His inheritance in the saints, and what is the exceeding greatness of His power toward us who believe.

EPHESIANS 1:18–19 NKJV

> Thou dost well,
> And my heaven is here and now,
>   Day-star of my soul, if Thou
> Wilt but deign in me to dwell.

WOLFGANG C. DESSLER

Throw open all the windows of your soul to the influence of Jesus. By prayer, thought, and action, let His divine power move in and through your life; and be sure that a mighty work is within His power and your possibility. Not that of lifting you into ordinary spiritual vitality, but of transforming you through and through with His Spirit.

WILLIAM LAWRENCE

The life which we are meant to lead under the dispensation of the Spirit who has been given for our guidance into truth, is one which does not take us out of the world, but keeps us from its evil, enabling us to live a heavenly existence on earth, and so to span over the chasm which divides us from heaven.

EDWARD THRING

December 5

I want to know Christ and the power of his resurrection and the fellowship of sharing in his sufferings, becoming like him in his death.

PHILIPPIANS 3:10 NIV

What within me and without
    Hourly on my spirit weighs,
Burdening heart and soul with doubt,
    Darkening all my weary days;
In it I behold Your will,
    God, who gives all rest and peace;
And my heart is calm and still,
    Waiting till You send release.

A.H. FRANCKE

Whatever your grief or trouble is, take every drop in your cup from the hand of almighty God. He with whom "the hairs of your head are all numbered," knows each drop of sweat from your brow, each hardly drawn breath, each shoot of pain, each beating of the fevered pulse, each sinking of the aching heart. Receive, then, what are trials to *you*, not in the main only, but one by one, from His all-loving hands; thank His love for each; unite each with the sufferings of the Redeemer; pray that He will use them to make you holy. You will not know now what He then will work in you; yet, day by day, shall you be imprinted with the likeness of the ever-blessed Son, and in you, too, while you know it not, God shall be glorified.

EDWARD B. PUSEY

December 6

Casting all your care upon Him, for He cares for you.

1 PETER 5:7 NKJV

How gentle God's commands! / How kind His precepts are!
Come, cast your burdens on the Lord, / And trust His
constant care.
His goodness stands approved / Down to the present day;
I'll drop my burden at His feet, / And bear a song away.

PHILIP DODDRIDGE

She was not accustomed in these days to meet troubles, small or
great, with the small stock of strength her mind or body could
afford. She had acquired, by long habit, the power of putting
them from her until she could take them into the presence of her
Lord and there, in secret, commune with Him of all that was in
her heart.

SARAH W. STEPHEN

The Lord calls for our burdens, [He] would not have us wrestle
with them ourselves, but roll them over on Him. Now, the desires
that are breathed forth in prayer are, as it were, the very unloading
of the heart; each request that goes forth carries out somewhat
of the burden with it, and lays it on God. Tell Him what are your
desires, and leave them there with Him, and so you are sure to be
rid of all further upsetting care of them.

ROBERT LEIGHTON

December 7

We have the mind of Christ.

1 CORINTHIANS 2:16 KJV

Never further than Your cross; / Never higher than Your feet;
Here earth's precious things seem dross; / Here earth's bitter
things grow sweet.

Here we learn to serve and give, / And rejoicing, self deny;
Here we gather love to live, / Here we gather faith to die.

ELIZABETH R. CHARLES

Are we assimilating His mind, His way of looking at things, His
judgments, His spirit? Is the Christ-conscience being developed
in us? Have we an increasing interest in the things which interest
Him, an increasing love of the things that He loves, and increasing
desire to serve the purposes He has at heart? "You are my friends,
if you do whatsoever I command you," is the test by which we can
try ourselves.

HUGH BLACK

This I saw, that when a soul loves God with a supreme love, God's
interests and the soul become one. It will not matter when nor
where nor how Christ should send me, nor what trials He should
put me through, if I am prepared for His work and will.

DAVID BRAINERD

December 8

Lord, You will establish peace for us, for You have also done all our works in us.

Isaiah 26:12 nkjv

With that deep hush subduing all
    Our words are works that drown
The tender whisper of Your call,
As noiseless let Your blessing fall
    As fell the manna down.

John Greenleaf Whittier

Pray to be calm and quiet and hushed, and that He will permit you the sense of His blessed Presence; that you may do all things beneath His eye; to sit...calmly at His feet and hear His voice, and then calmly rise and minister to Him

Edward B. Pusey

Try to live in the light of God's love so that it becomes a second nature to you, tolerate nothing adverse to it, be continually striving to please Him in all things, take all that He sends patiently. Resolve firmly never to commit the smallest deliberate fault, and if, unhappily, you are overtaken by any sin, humble yourself, and rise up speedily. You will not always be thinking of God consciously, but all your thoughts will be ruled by Him, His Presence will check useless or evil thoughts, and your heart will be perpetually fixed on Him, ready to do His holy will.

Jean Nicolas Grou

December 9

Your love for one another will prove to the world that you are my disciples.

JOHN 13:35 NLT

Do I find love so full in my nature, God's ultimate gift,
That I doubt His own love can compete with it? Here, the
parts shift?
Here, the creature surpass the Creator—the end, what began?
Would I fain in my impotent yearning do all for this man,
And dare doubt He alone shall not help him, who yet alone can?

ROBERT BROWNING

"Come unto me," says the holy Jesus, "all ye that labor and are
heavy laden, and I will refresh you." Beg of Him to be the light
and life of your soul; love the sound of His name; for Jesus is
the *love*, the *sweetness*, the *compassionate goodness* of the Deity
Himself; which became man, so that men might have the power to
become the sons of God. Love, pity, and wish well to every soul in
the world; dwell in love and then you dwell in God.

WILLIAM LAW

The Lord's love is the love of communicating all that He has to all
His creatures; for He desires the happiness *of* all; and a similar love
prevails in those who love Him, because the Lord is in them.

EMANUEL SWEDENBORG

December 10

That we...may grow up in all things into Him who is the head—Christ—from whom the whole body, joined and knit together by what every joint supplies, according to the effective working by which every part does its share, causes growth of the body for the edifying of itself in love.

EPHESIANS 4:14–16 NKJV

We become the living means to a great end; and all our inner salvation—our finding of Jesus—is seen, not to center in ourselves, in our own gain, our own rescue, our own peace; but to lead out beyond itself; to have been our qualification for us and office, without which we could not be taken up, as workers with God, into that eternal husbandry whereby He sets Himself to win over the stubborn and thorny field of the world. Our eyes are taken off ourselves; we are not absorbed in rehearsing our own experiences, however blessed. We are caught up into the counsels; we serve to widen the frontiers of the kingdom; through us, correlated as we are, by joints and bands, into the articulate body, the Spirit of Christ can get abroad, can take a fresh step forward. We have become its vantage-ground from which it can again advance. Oh, that we were more quick to His touch, more ready for His needs, more serviceable in His ministry!

HENRY SCOTT HOLLAND

December 11

Light is sown for the righteous, and gladness for the upright in heart.

PSALM 97:11 KJV

Sun of the soul, Thou light divine,
Around and in us brightly shine,
  To strength and gladness wake us.
Where Thou shinest, life from heaven
There is given; we before Thee
For that precious gift implore Thee.

MICHAEL SCHIRMER

That is what our sacrifice of ourselves should be—"full of life."
Not desponding, morbid, morose; not gloomy, chilly, forbidding;
not languid, indolent, inactive; but full of life, and warmth, and
energy; cheerful, and making others cheerful; happy, and making
others happy; contented, and making others contented; doing
good, and making others do good, by our lively vivid vitality—
filling every corner of the circle in which we move, with the fresh
life-blood of a warm, genial, kindly Christian heart. Doubtless
this requires a sacrifice; it requires us to give up our own comfort,
our own ease, our own firesides, our dear solitude, our own
favorite absorbing pursuits, our shyness, our reserve, our pride,
our selfishness.

ARTHUR P. STANLEY

December 12

God...richly provides us with everything for our enjoyment.

1 TIMOTHY 6:17 NIV

Give me, O Lord, a heart of grace,
A voice of joy, a shining face,
That I may show where'er I turn
Thy love within my soul does burn!

A tenderness for all that stray,
With strength to help them on the way;
A cheerfulness, a heavenly mirth,
Brightening my steps along the earth!

LADY GILBERT

Those who love God are encompassed with gladness on every side,
because in every passing moment they see and feel the Father's
love, and nothing of this world can take it away or lessen it.

H. L. SIDNEY LEAR

My life is so strangely free from trial and trouble that I cannot
doubt my own happiness is one of the talents entrusted to me to
"occupy" till the Master shall return, by doing something to make
other lives happy.

CHARLES L. DODGSON

December 13

*He will come like a rushing stream which the wind of the
Lord drives.*

Isaiah 59:19 nasb

Still more and more do Thou my soul redeem,
From every bondage set me wholly free;
Through evil oft the mightiest power may seem,
Still make me more than conqueror, Lord, in Thee.

C. J. P. Spitta

Wait on the Lord in humility of heart, that you may daily feel
the change which is wrought in the heart and conscience by the
holy, eternal, ever-living Power; and so you may witness, "that
which is born of the Spirit, is spirit." And then you will feel that
this birth of the Spirit cannot fulfill the lusts of the flesh, but will
be warring and fighting the good fight against them; and thus, in
faithfulness to the truth, and waiting upon the Lord, you shall
witness an overcoming, in His due time. Oh, the conquering faith,
the overcoming life and power of the Spirit! We cannot but speak
of those things; and call up the perfect gift, and the power of Him,
who is not only able to perfect His work in the heart, but delights
so to do; and even to tread down Satan under the feet of those that
wait in patience for the perfect conquest.

Isaac Penington

December 14

Perplexed, but not in despair; persecuted, but not forsaken; cast down, but not destroyed.

2 CORINTHIANS 4:8–9 KJV

Exhausted but still in pursuit.

JUDGES 8:4 NKJV

I, even I, am the one who wipes out your transgressions for My own sake, and I will not remember your sins.

ISAIAH 43:25 NASB

I don't think it is possible to overrate the hardness of the first close struggle with any natural passion, but indeed the easiness of after-steps is often quite beyond one's expectations. The free gift of grace with which God perfects our efforts may come in many ways, but I am convinced that it is the common experience of Christians that it does come. There *may* be some souls, whose brave and bitter lot it is to conquer comfortless. Perhaps some terrible inheritance of strong sin from the father is visited upon the son, and, only able to keep his purpose pure, he falls as fast as he struggles up, and still struggling falls again. Soft moments of peace with God and man may never come to him. He may feel himself viler than a thousand deceptive souls who could not have borne his trials for a day. For you and me is reserved no such cross and no such crown as theirs who falling still fight, and fighting fall, with their faces Zionwards, into the arms of the everlasting Father. "As one whom his mother comforts" shall be the healing of their wounds.

JULIANA H. EWING

December 15

This is my command: Love each other.

JOHN 15:17 NIV

Yet habits linger in the soul;
    More grace, O Lord! More grace!
More sweetness from Your loving heart,
    More sunshine from Your face!

FREDERICK W. FABER

If your disturbance of mind proceeds from a person who is so
disagreeable to you, that every little action of his annoys or
irritates you, the remedy is to force yourself to love him, and to
hold him dear; not only because he is a creature formed by the
same sovereign hand as you are, but also because he offers you an
opportunity (if you will accept it) of becoming like your Lord, who
is kind and loving unto all men.

LORENZO SCUPOLI

The habit of letting every foolish or uncharitable thought, as it
arises, find words, has a great deal to do with much evil in the
world. Control the habit of uttering the words, and gradually
you will find that you control the habit of thought too. A
resolution always to turn to some distinctly good thought when a
complaining or unkind one arises in the mind, is a great help—
as it is to turn every thought condemnatory of our neighbor into
a prayer for him. We never can long continue to dislike people for
whom we pray.

H. L. SIDNEY LEAR

December 16

God forbid that I should sin against the Lord in ceasing to pray for you.

1 SAMUEL 12:23 KJV

More things are wrought by prayer
Than this world dreams of. Wherefore, let thy voice
Rise like a fountain for me night and day.
For what are men better than sheep or goats
That nourish a blind life within the brain,
If, knowing God, they lift not hands of prayer
Both for themselves and those who call them friend?
For so the whole round earth is every way
Bound by gold chains about the feet of God.

ALFRED, LORD TENNYSON

Perhaps we do not think enough what an effective service prayer is, especially intercessory prayer. We do not believe as we should how it might help those we so willingly would serve, penetrating the hearts we cannot open, shielding those we cannot guard, teaching where we cannot speak, comforting where our words have no power to soothe; following the steps of our beloved through the toils and perplexities of the day, lifting off their burdens with an unseen hand at night. No ministry is so like that of an angel as this—silent, invisible, known, but to God.

ELIZABETH RUNDLE CHARLES

December 17

The Teacher has come and is calling for you.

JOHN 11:28 NKJV

Stir in us the might of faith,
    Light in us the fire of love!
Then will smile Your angel Death,
    Opener of the gate above;
Sweet Your summons then will come;
Gladsome then shall we go home.

THOMAS H. GILL

Beyond all secondary causes, deeper than disease of accident, lies
the loving will of Him who is the Lord of life and death. Death is
Christ's minister, "mighty and beauteous, though his face be dark,"
and he, too, stands amidst the ranks of the "ministering spirits
sent forth to minister to them that shall be heirs of salvation."

ALEXANDER MACLAREN

Until our Master summons us, not a hair of our head can perish,
not a moment of our life be snatched from us. When He sends for
us, it should seem by the message that the child is wanted at home.

ANTHONY W. THOROLD

December 18

O our God, we thank you and praise your glorious name!

1 Chronicles 29:13 NLT

Rejoice in the Lord, you who are righteous, and praise his holy name.

Psalm 97:12 NIV

And now the wants are told, that brought
    Thy children to Thy knee;
Here, lingering still, we ask for nought,
    But simply worship Thee.

The hope of heaven's eternal days
    Absorbs not all the heart
That gives Thee glory, love, and praise
    For being what Thou art.

William Bright

Let praise—I say not merely thanksgiving, but praise—always form an ingredient of your prayers. We thank God for what He is to us: for the benefits which He confers, and the blessings which He gives us. But we praise Him for what He is in Himself—for His glorious excellence and perfections, independently of their bearing on the welfare of the creature. And it shall often happen that when your heart is numb and cold, and yields not to the action of prayer, it shall begin to thaw, and at last bursts, like streams under the breath of spring, from their icy prison, with the warm and genial exercise of praise.

Edward M. Goulburn

December 19

Your ears will hear a word behind you, "This is the way, walk in it," whenever you turn to the right or to the left.

ISAIAH 30:21 NASB

The ways of the LORD are right, and the just shall walk in them.

HOSEA 14:9 KJV

Yet more and more this truth doth shine
    From failure and from loss,
The will that runs transverse to Thine
    Does thereby make it cross:
        Thine upright will
        Cuts straight and still
    Through pride and dream and dross.

W. M. L. JAY

Let us remember that it is not God who makes many of the crosses that we find in our way, such as we commonly call "crosses." Our heavenly Father makes "straight paths for our feet," and, if we would *go in His way*, if we would straighten our wills to His will, and lay them side by side, there would be no crosses. But when the path that God points out goes north and south, and our stubborn wills lead us east and west, the consequence is *"a cross"*—a cross of our own making, not that which our Master bids us "take up and carry after Him," and of which it has been well said, "He always carries the heaviest end Himself."

ANNIE WEBB-PEPLOE

December 20

I would like you to be free from concern.

1 Corinthians 7:32 NIV

He who trusts in the Lord, lovingkindness shall surround him.

Psalm 32:10 NASB

I have no cares, O blessed Will!
    For all my cares are Thine;
I live in triumph, Lord, for Thou
    Hast made Thy triumphs mine.

Frederick W. Faber

Let my soul roll itself on Him, and adventure there all its weight.
He bears greater matters, upholding the frame of heaven and
earth, and is not troubled or burdened with it.

Robert Leighton

What is needed for happy and effectual service is simply to put
your work into the Lord's hands, and leave it there. Do not take it
to Him in prayer, saying, "Lord, guide me, Lord, give me wisdom,
Lord, arrange for me," and then arise from your knees, and take
the burden all back, and try to guide and arrange for yourself.
Leave it with the Lord, and remember that what you trust to Him
you must not worry over nor feel anxious about. Trust and worry
cannot go together.

Hannah Whitall Smith

December 21

I am the way, the truth, and the life. No one comes to the Father except through Me.

JOHN 14:6 NKJV

Blessed are they that have not seen, and yet have believed.

JOHN 20:29 KJV

The Way, the Truth, the Life Thou art,
    This, this I know; to this I cleave;
The sweet new language of my heart,
    "Lord, I believe."
I have no doubts to bring to Thee;
My doubt has fled; my faith is free.

HARRIET MCEWEN KIMBALL

We have been placed upon the Way. We have been taught the Truth. We have been made partakers of the Life. The Way must be traversed; the Truth must be pursued; the Life must be realized. Then comes the end. Our pilgrimage, long as it may be or short, if we have walked in Christ, will leave us by the throne of God; our partial knowledge, if we have looked upon all things in Christ, will be lost in open sight; our little lives, perfected, purified, harmonized in Him whom we have trusted, will become, in due order, parts of the One Divine Life, when God is all in all.

BROOKE FOSS WESTCOTT

December 22

Those who live in the shelter of the Most High will find rest in the shadow of the Almighty.

PSALM 91:1 NLT

My soul and all its powers
 Thine, wholly Thine shall be;
All, all my happy hours
 I consecrate to Thee:
Me to Thine image now restore,
And I shall praise Thee evermore.

CHARLES WESLEY

If the wish is wakened in our soul to be ever in His presence, let us go to Him this moment, and ask Him what to do, and how to feel, believing that He is more ready to hear than we to pray. He will give us realization of His love, and convictions of duty. Let us follow those convictions implicitly; let us ask Him every day to teach us more, and help us more; and we shall soon say, with Paul, "Thanks be unto God, for His unspeakable gift!"

WILLIAM R. HUNTINGTON

The all-important thing is not to live apart from God, but as far as possible to be consciously with Him. Inevitably those who look much into His face will become like Him.

CHARLES H. BRENT

December 23

*Thus you shall do in the fear of the LORD, faithfully
and wholeheartedly.*

2 CHRONICLES 19:9 NASB

In little things of common life,
There lies the Christian's noblest strife,
     When he does conscience make
Of every thought and throb within;
And words and looks of self and sin
     Crushed for Jesus' sake.

J. S. B. MONSELL

Wherever we are, whatever we are doing, in all our work, in our
busy daily life, in all schemes and undertakings, in public trusts,
and in private retreats, He is with us, and all we do is spread before
Him. Do it, then, as to the Lord. Let the thought of His eye unseen
be the motive of your acts and words. Do nothing you would not
have Him see. Say nothing which you would not have said before
His visible presence. This is to do all in His name.

HENRY EDWARD MANNING

If one sign surer than any other is chosen to mark the progress of
the divine life, it is when sanctity prevails even in the minutest
points of character, and in ordinary ways. The least look, the
faintest expression, the casual act, may tell more of the secret
power of Jesus in the soul than world-famed acts of self-devotion.

T. T. CARTER

December 24

There was no room for them in the inn.

LUKE 2:7 KJV

God often would enrich, but finds not where to place His treasure—nor in hand nor heart a vacant space.

RICHARD CHENEVIX TRENCH

The soul, in its highest sense, has a vast capacity for God. It is like a curious chamber added on to our being, and somehow involving our being, a chamber with elastic and moveable walls, which can be expanded, with God as its guest, illimitably, but which without God shrinks and shrivels until every vestige of the divine is gone.

HENRY DRUMMOND

All that God desires is to give you His great love, so that it may dwell in you, and be the principle of your life and service; and all that withstands God's desire and His gift is the want of room for it, and for its free movement, when that room is taken up with yourselves and your little personal interests.

WILLIAM BERNARD ULLATHORNE

By rooting out our selfish desires, even when they appear to touch no one but ourselves, we are preparing a chamber of the soul where the Divine Presence may dwell.

ELLEN WATSON

December 25

I no longer live, but Christ lives in me.

GALATIANS 2:20 NIV

Christ in you, the hope of glory.

COLOSSIANS 1:27 KJV

Though Christ a thousand times in Bethlehem be born,
If He's not born in you, your soul is still forlorn.

JOHANN SCHEFFLER

The great mystery of the gospel does not lie in Christ without us
only (though we must know also what He has done for us), but the
very core and kernel of it consists in Christ inwardly formed in
our hearts.

RALPH CUDWORTH

When therefore the first spark of a desire after God arises in thy
soul, cherish it with all your care, give all your heart to it; it is
nothing less than a touch of the divine lodestone, that is to draw
you out of the vanity of time, into the riches of eternity. Get
up therefore, and follow it as gladly as the wise men of the east
followed the star from heaven that appeared to them. It will do for
you as the star did for them, it will lead you to the birth of Jesus,
not in a stable at Bethlehem in Judea, but to the birth of Jesus in
the dark center of your own soul.

WILLIAM LAW

December 26

Our Lord Jesus Christ, who died for us, that, whether we wake or sleep, we should live together with him.

1 THESSALONIANS 5:9–10 KJV

Be ours the faith that sees Thee stand
    Beside the throne of God on high,
To succor with Thy strong right hand
    Thy soldiers when to Thee they cry.

Be ours the love, divine and free,
    Which asks forgiveness for our foes;
Which draws, in life, its life from Thee,
    And, dying, find in Thee repose.

J. F. THRUPP

"If He has done so much for me, what can I do for Him?" is the question which a Christian life should answer. He may ask little or much. He may demand heroic sacrifices, or He may require only punctual attention to daily and prosaic duty. But He has a right to make any demands He will, and it should be a point of honor with every Christian to satisfy Him. It is this simple self-surrender, in a spirit of love for God and for the souls of men, which makes life strong and noble.... It is this self-surrender which makes death, whenever or wherever it may come, a "falling asleep in Christ."

HENRY PARRY LIDDON

December 27

They took note that these men had been with Jesus.

Acts 4:13 NIV

O hearts of love! O souls that turn
    Like sunflowers to the pure and best!
    To you the truth is manifest;
For they the mind of Christ discern
    Who lean like John upon His breast.

JOHN GREENLEAF WHITTIER

Will you with St. John rest on the loving heart of our Lord Jesus Christ, you must be transformed into the beauteous image of our Lord by a constant, earnest contemplation thereof, considering His holy meekness and humility, the deep, fiery love that He bore to His friends and His foes, and His mighty, obedient resignation which He manifested in all the paths wherein His Father called Him to tread. And now you must gaze much more closely and deeply into the glorious image of our Lord Jesus Christ than I can show you with my outward teaching, and maintain a continual, earnest effort and aspiration after it. Then look attentively at yourself, how unlike you are to this image, and behold your own littleness. Here will your Lord let you rest on Him. In the glorious likeness of Christ you will be made rich, and find all the solace and sweetness in the world.

JOHN TAULER

December 28

Truly I say to you, whoever does not receive the kingdom of God like a child will not enter it at all.

Luke 18:17 NASB

Dear soul, could you become a child
While yet on earth, meek, undefiled,
Then God Himself were ever near,
And Paradise around you here.

Gerhard Tersteegen

Childlikeness, in its Scripture sense, is a perfectness of trust, a resting in a Father's love, a being carried in its power, living in it—it means a simplicity which resolves all into the one idea of lowly submissiveness to One in whom it lives; a buoyancy of spirit, which is a fountain of joy in itself, always ready to spring forth afresh brightly and happily to meet the claims of the present hour, not looking lingeringly back to the past, nor making plans independently, as of oneself, for the future; a resting contented in one's lot, whatever that lot may be; a singleness of intention; a pliancy, a yielding of the will, a forgetfulness of self in another's claims. To be thus childlike in the pure sense of such an ideal is to be living in God, as one's Father, one's Preserver, one's Guide, felt to be a perpetual Presence and Providence.

T. T. Carter

December 29

With goodwill doing service, as to the Lord, and not to men.

EPHESIANS 6:7 NKJV

Yet take the tiny stones which I have wrought,
    Just one by one, as they were given by Thee,
Not knowing what came next in Thy wise thought.
Set each stone by Thy Master-hand of grace;
    From the mosaic as Thou wilt for me,
And in Thy temple pavement give it place.

FRANCES RIDLEY HAVERGAL

What God may hereafter require of you, you must not give yourself
the least trouble about. Everything He gives you to do, you must
do as well as ever you can, and that is the best possible preparation
of what He may want you to do next. If people would but do what
they have to do, they would always find themselves ready for what
came next.

GEORGE MACDONALD

Nothing can excuse the neglect of the duties of the position of life
which God has conferred upon us. All is delusive where these are
not attended to, and made much of.

FREDERICK W. FABER

If you would advance in true holiness, you must aim steadily at
perfection in little things.

ABBE GUILLORE

December 30

Whatever you do or say, do it as a representative of the Lord Jesus, giving thanks through him to God the Father.

Colossians 3:17 NLT

Yea, through life, death, through sorrow and through sinning,
    He shall suffice me, for He has sufficed;
Christ is the end, for Christ was the beginning;
    Christ the beginning for the end is Christ.

F. W. H. Myers

Let this be your whole endeavor, this your prayer, this your desire—that you may be stripped of all selfishness, and with entire simplicity follow Jesus only.

Thomas à Kempis

Do what is pleasing to Jesus Christ, and neglect nothing which pleases Him.

Lorenzo Scupoli

To "do all things in the name of Jesus" is the lesson of a life; do not be angry with yourselves, nor despair of ever learning it, because you are slow to learn the first few syllables. When you have learned to do all things to Jesus, it will shed pleasure over all dull things, softness over all hard things, peace over all trial and woe and suspense. Then will life be glad, when you live to Jesus; and how sweet death, to die in Jesus; with Him, and to Him, and in Him, to live for evermore.

Edward B. Pusey

December 31

We are labourers together with God.

1 Corinthians 3:9 KJV

Then bear a joy where joy is not,
    Go, speak a kindly word in love,
Less bitter make some loveless lot,
    Now earth is linked to heaven above.

Frederick G. Lee

Do what you can—give what you have. Only stop not with feelings; carry your charity into deeds; do and give what costs you something.

J. H. Thom

"Up and be *doing*," is the word that comes from God for each of us. Leave some "good work" behind you that shall not be wholly lost when you have passed away. *Do* something worth living for, worth dying for. Is there no want, no suffering, no sorrow that you can relieve? Is there no act of tardy justice, no deed of cheerful kindness, no long-forgotten duty that you can perform? Is there no reconciliation of some ancient quarrel, no payment of some long-outstanding debt, no courtesy, or love, or honor to be rendered to those to whom it has long been due; no charitable, humble, kind, useful deed by which you can promote the glory of God, or good will among men, or peace upon earth? If there is any such deed, in God's name, in Christ's name, go and do it.

Arthur P. Stanley